NEW HEMI
ENGINE SWAPS

How to Swap 5.7L, 6.1L, 6.4L, and Hellcat Engines into Almost Anything

Joseph Hinds

CarTech®

CarTech®

CarTech®, Inc.
6118 Main Street
North Branch, MN 55056
Phone: 651-277-1200 or 800-551-4754
Fax: 651-277-1203
www.cartechbooks.com

Edit by Bob Wilson
Layout by Connie DeFlorin

ISBN 978-1-61325-729-6
Item No. SA522

Library of Congress Cataloging-in-Publication Data Available

Written, edited, and designed in the U.S.A.
Printed in China
10 9 8 7 6 5 4 3 2

All photos are courtesy of Joseph Hinds unless otherwise noted.

DISTRIBUTION BY:

Europe
PGUK
63 Hatton Garden
London EC1N 8LE, England
Phone: 020 7061 1980 • Fax: 020 7242 3725
www.pguk.co.uk

Australia
Renniks Publications Ltd.
3/37-39 Green Street
Banksmeadow, NSW 2109, Australia
Phone: 2 9695 7055 • Fax: 2 9695 7355
www.renniks.com

Canada
Login Canada
300 Saulteaux Crescent
Winnipeg, MB, R3J 3T2 Canada
Phone: 800 665 1148 • Fax: 800 665 0103
www.lb.ca

CONTENTS

ACKNOWLEDGMENTS

This book has been a long time coming and very nearly did not exist at all. I first approached CarTech about writing it in late 2013, and the project began with Paul Johnson as editor. Paul's efforts made the completion of my first book project, *GM G-Body Performance Upgrades*, possible, and he provided the encouragement that I needed as the project fought for my time.

Running and working in my own shop made it a difficult balancing act, and the closing of my shop in 2017 was, in many ways, a blessing in disguise. I finished the manuscript in early 2018, and disagreement over the content and scope of the book led to it not being published. At the time, I was very upset, but in retrospect, it was good because the Gen III Hemi swap community and the products to support this swap have grown exponentially since then. Paul is pursuing other opportunities now, but Bob Wilson of CarTech was willing to take a chance on a second effort, and for that I will be eternally grateful. I addressed Paul's original concern that I did not have enough hands-on content and have done it without sacrificing any of the technical information required to properly plan and execute the swap. Thank you Paul and Bob (and everyone at CarTech) for everything. I tried to address every detail of the typical and atypical swap, and that has been a monumental task.

Many others deserve my thanks for their contributions to this project, including Anthony Coles (Super Shops), Greg Senser, Tom Kise, Harrison Alford, Ethan Moss, Zach Roloson, Shane Whitescarver, Jason Bruce, Ty Cobb, Matt Bell, Doug Marino, Bill Tichenor (Holley), Mike Copeland (Arrington Performance/ Diversified Creations), Joe O'Cone (OCP), Mike Staveski (RMR Dreamcars), David Weber (MMX/Modern Muscle), and many others who helped with photos, build details, and questions along the way. I'd also like to thank my wife, Nancy, since this project has consumed a great deal of my free time over the last several years and kept me from other projects.

ABOUT THE AUTHOR

Joe Hinds is a technical services team lead for Holley Performance Products. He has been a lifelong car guy and has over 37 years of experience repairing, restoring, and modifying cars. He began his professional automotive career working for Year One and Mustangs Unlimited, and he ran his own shop for many years. His shop time is now spent mostly on his own projects. This includes a '55 Chevy Bel Air that is getting a Hilborn EFI-equipped big-block Chevy engine as well as his son's wild Gen III Hemi–equipped 1972 Gremlin X that is being built to race in hill-climb, drift, land-speed events, and possibly some drag and drive events.

This is his second book for CarTech. His first book, *GM G-Body Performance Upgrades*, marked him as a GM guy, but he is a lifelong hot rodder with little brand loyalty and a great appreciation for anything mechanical.

INTRODUCTION TO GEN III HEMI ENGINES

The owner of this 1973 Duster wanted better power, fuel economy, and drivability, and he knew the 318 wasn't going to cut it. He originally planned to swap in a 360 Magnum from a 1990s full-size truck, but his power goals and the lack of potential with the factory EFI of that time called for something better.

While the looks of this Duster are fairly aggressive with the hood scoop, the tired 318 didn't match the exterior presence.

After the performance revival of the 1960s, the 1970s hit the muscle-car market hard. Increasing insurance rates due to high power levels (some of which were severely underestimated), an oil crisis, a poor economy with high interest rates, ever-tightening emissions standards, and poor build quality made this decade a very dark time for the Big Three manufacturers (General Motors, Ford, and Chrysler) as a whole. Chrysler nearly didn't survive, even with a government bailout, and Mopar performance enthusiasts could only look back to the good old days.

By the 1980s, cars may have looked like muscle cars with a V-8 engine, manual transmission, and lots of tape stripes and spoilers, but these vehicles lacked most attributes of a true performance car. Chrysler's only offerings were front-wheel drive, and while some were quick, such as the Omni GLHS, they were of no interest to the typical muscle car enthusiast.

Dodge released the Viper in January 1992, but it wasn't the everyman's car that the muscle-car era

Mike Copeland's Dodge Rampage

For a book such as this, a 1984 Dodge Rampage is probably the least-likely Mopar you'd expect to see. Based on the front-wheel-drive Dodge Omni, the Rampage was Mopar's version of the Australian "ute."

They weren't very popular even when new, but this creation by Mike Copeland of Arrington Performance/Diversified Creations is nothing like the original. Based on a cut-down Factory Five GTM chassis that was lengthened 3 inches and narrowed by 7 inches, this was a great start toward a mid-engined Rampage that Mike calls *Outrage*.

The GTM chassis uses C5/6/7 Corvette suspension components and normally a GM LSx engine ahead of the Mendiola transaxle. However, Mike adapted an Arrington 650-hp 392 Hemi with Borla stack injection that is run by a Holley Dominator electronic control unit (ECU). Even with air conditioning, a powerful sound system, and a full interior, this "truck" only weighs 2,900 pounds. While very well built, it was built to drive, and it's not unusual to see it at events, such as Hot Rod Power Tour or Holley's Moparty. ■

As suspected, the factory unibody is long gone, and it was replaced by a cut-down Factory 5 GTM Supercar chassis. Fender flares alone aren't enough to contain the Forgeline wheels and BFG Rival P315/30ZR18 tires. The huge Baer brakes with six-piston calipers hint of the power contained between the frame rails.

A Dodge Rampage, known for its uninspiring 2.2L front-wheel-drive drivetrain, seems out of place in this book. Its owner, Mike Copeland of Arrington Performance, isn't one to let the factory limitations get in the way.

offerings had been and was beyond the budget of the typical driver. Many of the Mopar faithful gave up and surrendered their allegiance to GM or Ford to get their late-model performance fix. The Ford Fox Body Mustang and the GM F-Body and G-Body were glad to claim this market, as Ford dominated most of the late 1980s and into the early 1990s.

By 1993, the newly-designed fourth-generation F-Body dominated until it too was gone after 2002. The Mustang survived but wasn't very impressive—other than the Terminator Cobras from 2003–2004. Unless you wanted a truck or a Viper, Mopar still had nothing for its faithful fan base. In 2003, the first real excitement in the Mopar camp came with the release of a new 5.7L V-8 that is now known as the Gen III Hemi.

The low-mileage 6.1L Hemi and 545RFE will really wake up the Duster.

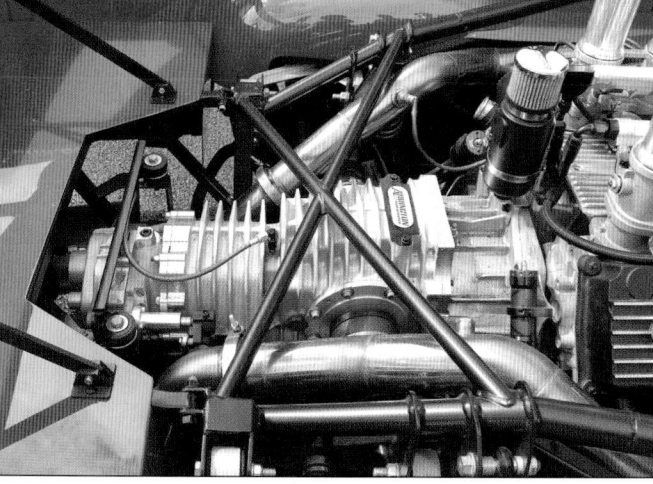

Power comes from an Arrington-built 392 Hemi with Borla stack injection, CNC-ported heads, and a large camshaft. Mike originally planned on Hellcat power for this truck, but engine placement and wheelbase limitations made it impossible without intruding into the cab.

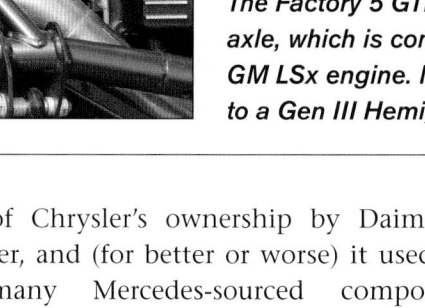

The Hemi's mid-engine placement improves grip, and an adjustable rear wing provides added downforce.

The Factory 5 GTM is designed to use a Mendiola transaxle, which is commonly found in Lamborghinis, behind a GM LSx engine. No bellhousings are available to mate this to a Gen III Hemi, so an adapter plate was used.

Initially, the Hemi was only available in trucks, and it wasn't universally accepted. Diehards said it wasn't a "real" Hemi due to the lack of a true hemispherical combustion chamber, and it didn't deserve the Hemi name. It really couldn't shine in a truck, and the Gen III Hemi wasn't offered in a passenger car until 2005.

For the 2005 model year, the Gen III Hemi was offered in the new LX platform. The LX, which included the Chrysler 300 sedan, Dodge Charger sedan, and Dodge Magnum station wagon, was a product of Chrysler's ownership by Daimler, and (for better or worse) it used many Mercedes-sourced components. These included the front and rear suspensions, transmission, and differential.

The Challenger, based on a shortened platform that was designated the LC, came out in 2008. While the car has been popular and offers good power and a smooth ride, it doesn't exactly feel like a muscle car. Challengers are heavy, have relatively narrow wheel and tire packages, and feel nothing like a current Mustang or Camaro. The NAG1 transmission, while reasonably strong, didn't have much of an aftermarket. The 6-speed manuals available in the Challenger starting in 2009 helped considerably, but the cars are still very large, heavy, and not conducive to major modifications, at least not on a budget. They do look enough like classic muscle cars, especially with the bright colors, retro badging, and other touches to make them more interesting, but it's hard to get past the fact the platform was designed as a plain sedan with mass appeal

Paul Terlosky of House of Mouse Racing built this 1978 D100 dually with a Hellcat drivetrain. It is one of many vehicles he has swapped. This is the first version of the truck. (Photo Courtesy Paul Terlosky)

Firewall clearance is tight with the Hellcat swap. Paul used the factory cooling manifold at the rear of the supercharger in this instance. Everything was done with a stock appearance. It's almost as if Dodge built it this way. (Photo Courtesy Paul Terlosky)

The second version of Paul's truck was unchanged mechanically but has a completely different look with the white paint, Viper Blue striping, and chrome wheels. (Photo Courtesy Paul Terlosky)

Paul's Hellcat swap uses many components from factory vehicles (Dodge trucks) for a clean look and easy serviceability. (Photo Courtesy Paul Terlosky)

and not just to the traditional performance enthusiast.

I, like many of the Mopar loyal, want to love these cars but don't. In all fairness, I don't like the Camaro, either, for many of the same reasons. I have no doubt the popularity of the Gen III Hemi would be greater if it wasn't saddled with such a large, overweight chassis whose only purpose seemed to help clean out Daimler's leftover parts inventory.

The introduction of the 6.4L Apache engine in trucks (and then in Chargers and Challengers) really woke things up and started to generate serious interest in spite of a heavy and outdated chassis. The Hellcat (and several iterations later, such as the Redeye, Demon, and Super Stock) ensured the Gen III Hemi's status as legendary all on its own. The Gen II 426 Hemi was impressive for its time, but now you can buy cars, SUVs, and trucks with more than 700 hp straight from the dealership, and racers are pushing the platform into the 2,000-hp range. No factory-based

Big Oak Garage 1965 Dart

Speaking of unusual, the Big Oak Garage's 1965 Dart SL is hardly typical, especially when you check out the fabrication that was done to build it.

Unless you're an expert on the bodystyle, you'll never find all 110 of the body modifications made or the dozens of one-off components. This car was a Great 8 Finalist at the 2015 Detroit Autorama—and rightfully so. The custom chassis features Ridetech components and is powered by a stroked 5.7L (392 ci) engine with a Magnuson supercharger and a Tremec 6-speed transmission. ∎

A custom shroud covers a huge radiator, dual fans, and the air-conditioning condenser and heat exchanger for the supercharger to ensure that everything stays cool. Unlike show vehicles of the past, today's show vehicles are built to be driven.

The 1965 Darts aren't common anymore and never had the popularity of some of the later models. Despite humble beginnings, the Dart SL built by Big Oak Garage is stunning. The list of modifications to the body is virtually endless, and it rides on a custom-built chassis and Schott 18-inch wheels.

The Dart SL's front end is built around the cooling components in a way that combines form and function. The bespoke grille assembly mimics later Dodge products without the cheesy plastic and funnels all the outside air through the radiator for a cool-running combination.

The Dart is powered by a 6.4L Hemi with a Magnuson supercharger and backed by a Tremec TR6060 6-speed manual transmission. Beautifully sculpted sheet metal surrounds the 614-hp Hemi to accent the flawless black finish. Custom-built panels around the air box and clutch/brake master cylinders allow for easy servicing when needed.

This Dodge stops in a hurry with its 14-inch Wilwood disc brakes and 6-piston calipers.

Jeff Keen's Mullis dragster used to have a Reher-Morrison big-block Chevy (BBC) engine, but he swapped in this 6.2L Hellcat, which uses a Holley Dominator EFI system. It is reliable and consistent, which is perfect for a bracket racer such as Jeff. Note the Meziere electric water pump. The BBC pattern is commonly used with motor plates in doorslammers and rails (like this one).

The radiator and fans are rear mounted. This used to be mostly seen in rails, but it is becoming more popular in other applications, such as drag racing, drifting, and road racing. Weight distribution is a factor, as is avoiding damage to cooling components and ease of service in tighter engine compartments.

Gen 2 Hemi comes close to that, and they can't compete with the drivability, reliability, and fuel economy that these engines can provide.

The idea for this book came about in the summer of 2013, and due to several setbacks on my part, it almost didn't happen. So much has changed since then as far as aftermarket parts solutions for these swaps that I am now glad things were delayed. At the time, there were few choices of parts, engines were less commonly available, and the more complex swaps just weren't feasible for most people unless you were a skilled fabricator.

Back then, Gen III Hemi swaps were relatively uncommon and were almost always performed on the traditional Mopar A-Body, B-Body, and E-Body cars. There was little support and interest in much of anything else. You could go online and find people on various forums who performed the swap on their own vehicle, but the problem was that every swap was different. Unless you planned the exact same combination as someone else, usually with the car's original transmission, there wasn't a lot of

The mid-plate supports a Powerglide with a Reid case, which is available with the Gen III/small Mopar bolt pattern.

This clean example of a 6.4L swap features aftermarket air conditioning and Hydroboost braking to allow more room for the Hemi.

information available.

The basics were easy. TTI and Schumacher have made engine mounts and headers for the classic A-Body, B-Body, and E-Body cars for several years, and Hotwire made harnesses as well, but the real issue was in all the details. How do I make this work with the donor transmission? Which PCM should be used? Who makes the parts I need? How do I make these accessories fit with my chassis? There was good information out there, but you had to search for it, and many of the pioneers of the swap were reluctant to share their knowledge. There was very little in the way of pre-engineered solutions. With that being said, there are combinations not addressed and details not explored due to the nearly endless choice of engines, transmissions, swap recipients, and aftermarket parts. For that reason, use the source guide at the end of this book to get the answers you need from the best people in the business.

Today, things are much different. Thanks to the contributions of people like David Weber of Modern Muscle Extreme, Mike Copeland of Diversified Creations and Arrington Performance, Joe O'Cone of OC Performance, and Randy Bouchillon of Bouchillon Performance Engineering, the Gen III Hemi swap community grew. Swaps

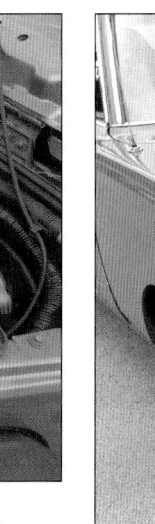

This clean swap in a late-model Jeep Wrangler looks factory other than the aftermarket air filter. However, swapping into a late-model vehicle can present its own challenges.

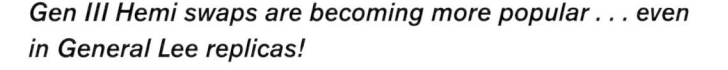

Gen III Hemi swaps are becoming more popular . . . even in General Lee replicas!

Squarebody Dodge trucks are very popular for Gen III Hemi swaps. This one is a 4WD model. It retains the stock engine position so as not to disturb the original transmission and transfer case, which eliminates the need for a lot of fabrication and driveshaft replacement.

A late-model truck 5.7L engine was used along with components from the donor truck and other similar years. This creates a swap that looks like it was done by the factory.

are now found in all sorts of vehicles and not just the A-Body, B-Body, and E-Body Mopars that originally popularized the swap. The mystique of a Hemi is something bigger than Mopar itself, and this is evident by the wide variety of vehicles that have

the engine today.

While these swaps are not as ubiquitous as the GM LSx swap, the Gen III Hemi swap community as a whole is knowledgeable, skilled, and willing to share what individuals have learned through their own

triumphs and mistakes. I have been a hands-on car guy for 38 years and a part of countless car clubs, email lists, online forums, and Facebook groups (particularly G3 Hemi Swap). I can honestly say everyone I have encountered while writing this book has been polite, respectful, and helpful.

One of the major drivers of interest in these swaps has come from Holley. When I first started this project, Holley had many items that were of interest to swappers, mostly on the EFI and fuel-system side. Since then, the company devoted a massive effort to the Gen III Hemi market by adding engine mounts, headers, exhaust systems (Hooker Blackheart), oil pans (Weiand and Holley), and many other problem-solving parts specific to these swaps in a number of different chassis. The people at Holley are true enthusiasts.

Swap engineers, such as Matt Bell and Doug Marino, have worked hard to solve a lot of problems so that the end user doesn't have to figure it out.

When trying to find radiator hoses, avoid the temptation to use flex hose. Solutions such as this factory hose that has been cut and spliced together with sections of tubing or couplers works well for odd hose routing.

Bill Olson's Duster has RMS AlterKtion front suspension with coilovers, rack-and-pinion steering, and a 6.1L engine with an NAG1 transmission. Bill was one of the pioneers of the NAG1 swap, which is now more common.

I was concerned the amount of attention given to Holley products in this book would seem like advertising, but my intention is only to showcase the available parts and give as much information as possible for the reader to make an informed decision.

I made the decision to use many Holley products on a Gremlin swap project many years ago, and that interest in its products eventually led to my full-time job as a technical sales team leader at Holley.

While many of the parts in this book were provided as part of my training at Holley, the information provided is based on my own opinion, experience, and preferences and not swayed by corporate interests. I am acting as an independent writer and not as a Holley employee. I have not been asked to present its product favorably over the competition, nor would I do so unfairly.

Keep in mind that even though these swaps are easier than they used to be, due to the parts availability, they are still a bit more difficult than the typical GM LSx swap. The engines are roughly 100 pounds heavier than an aluminum-block LSx but about the same as an iron one at about 585 pounds fully dressed. All production Gen III Hemis have iron blocks. This isn't really an issue in most cases, but a front spring change may be needed. Overall, they are fairly compact for a modern V-8 engine.

The only real obstacle is the width of the engine at 24 to 25 inches, which is about 3 inches wider

Bill's 6.1L engine was installed on the supplied Reilly Motorsports mounts with the recommended headers. There is plenty of clearance for the manual brakes. The wiper motor is close but does not touch the intake manifold. The open-element air filter has since been replaced with a fabricated tube that picks up cooler air.

The cooling system is based around a Champion radiator with dual electric fans and an overflow tank. This Duster was built to drive and went on the Hot Rod Power Tour several years ago.

The stock Hemi power-steering pump provided too much pressure for the Mustang-based rack, so Bill used a Heidt's adjustable valve to cut it down a suitable amount.

For years, trucks (such as this Dodge D100) were ignored, but today they are appreciated. This was one of my favorites from the Holley Moparty 2021. The color, stance, and detailing work together very well.

than an LS. However, the angle of the cylinder heads makes exhaust routing easier. Even compact cars with large shock towers, such as a Gremlin, leave enough clearance for long-tube headers. Brake booster, heater/AC boxes, and wiper motors on some models can be a problem so plan accordingly. Oil pans are available for front, mid, and rear sumps, so there is something for just about any combination. Note that Hellcat pans have a different bolt pattern at the timing cover area. Passenger-car and Jeep engines are typically easier to install in other passenger cars due to more compact accessories that use different timing covers. Either will work fine in most trucks.

All Gen III Hemis come with drive-by-wire (DBW) throttle bodies,

Under the D100's hood is a stock-appearing passenger-car 5.7L Hemi. Mounts were custom built because no manufacturers make them for this chassis. The stock D100 frame has been modified with a Ford Crown Victoria front suspension, which is a very popular upgrade for many trucks. A later-model master cylinder and brake booster were used.

Coolant hoses have been clamped with Gates Powergrip heat-shrink clamps. They aren't reusable, but they seal well and look clean. Note the stock exhaust manifold, which has been equipped with exhaust wrap to prevent heat damage to the inner fender paint and keep heat in the manifold. A Lokar flexible transmission dipstick was used to better clear the firewall.

This Duster has a nice restomod look to it with the drivability of a modern 6.4L Hemi.

The "392" that is incorporated into the graphics is a nice touch. Nitto drag radials on Rocket wheels with Wilwood brakes were used.

so you'll have to either switch to the appropriate DBW pedal assembly or convert to cable. To run the factory automatic transmission found behind these engines, you'll have to run factory PCMs (no aftermarket ECUs) or a standalone controller for the transmission.

The transmission can be a bit large, so tunnel modifications are necessary on most older vehicles. If your vehicle to receive the swap is anything other than a traditional Mopar A-Body, B-Body, E-Body, D100, Jeep, Dakota, or a 1973–1987 Chevrolet C10, you probably won't be able to buy engine mounts and headers for your specific application.

If none of that scares you away (and it shouldn't), this book provides the information you need to help solve the typical swap pitfalls and prepare you for some of the more extreme swaps as well.

In the last few years, something that has changed with G3 Hemi swaps is the number of high-powered builds being done. There have always been a few cars with aftermarket superchargers and custom turbo set-ups, but the proliferation of super-charged 6.2L Hemi Hellcat engines has really changed the hobby.

Innovators, such as Mike Staveski of Lexi J. Inc./RMR Dreamcars, have been building Hellcat-swapped cars for years with Holley Dominator engine management. Mike Copeland famously swapped David Freiburger's *General Mayhem* nearly seven

Dodge Dakotas have become popular for swaps. This is due to the large engine compartment that often came with the V-8 and the roomy interior that feels almost like a full-size truck. This one has an SRT8 6.4L Hemi.

years ago, which was arguably the first running swap to use the factory electronics, although it was recently swapped back to a motor home 440. At the 2021 Holley Moparty event in Bowling Green, Kentucky, Hellcat-based swaps were common. They are becoming more popular than the GM LSA/LT4/ZL1 swaps seen at the LS Fest due to Mopar's tendency to put a supercharged Hemi in anything that rolls (rather than leave it for a few low-production cars) and make crate engines and swap components readily available. Because of the popularity of these engines and forced induction in general, I felt it deserved its own chapter.

The 6.4L fits well, although the brake booster clearance is a little tight. This truck is equipped with a Holley Terminator X Max ECU, which is visible in the passenger-side fender well.

Larry Doehr's 1967 Satellite convertible is absolute stunning with many custom modifications. The lo stance is due to a Ridetech air system with a Mustar II–based front suspension and a 4-link rear. This c has hundreds of modifications and one-off par

David Kruk's 1970 Super Bee is a nicely built car that gets driven and raced in autocross. This is what pro touring is all about.

One of my favorite cars at Moparty 2021 was John Gaddy's 1969 Coronet 500 wagon. Woodgrain, red-line tires, and the A12 promotional-style wheel discs that were used in original advertising all hint at a restoration, but this one has a Hellcat 6.2L Hemi backed by a 4L80E with a Compushift controller. The rear is a Moser M60, its version of the stout Dana 60 found in many Mopar muscle cars.

Ringbrothers 1972 AMX *Defiant!*

The Ringbrothers 1972 Javelin AMX was built by Jim and Mike Ring for Prestone and is one of the duo's most extensively modified builds to date. The front suspension was moved forward 6.5 inches, and all new body panels were crafted from carbon fiber. The wheel wells were enlarged and moved upward to house the P285/30 front and P335/20 rear tires on 20x11 and 20x13 forged HRE wheels.

Virtually all exterior trim pieces and underhood hardware were custom CNC machined in-house by Ring. The hood is bulged twice in an unusual but striking manner, and while the overall effect is a car that is identifiable as Javelin, it has so many stylistic changes that others may not be sure of its origin. Most of the changes are positive ones in my opinion, and overall, it is a beautifully designed car.

The suspension is a hydroformed Detroit Speed subframe in the front that was originally intended for a Camaro with a custom-built 4-link in the rear. Ridetech splined sway bars and coilover shocks round out the suspension. Six piston Baer brakes bring it all to a halt.

The reason this amazing vehicle is featured is what lies under the hood. The engine is based on a Hellcat 6.2L but has been reworked by Wegner Motorsports to have 1,036 hp at the crank. This is largely due to the massive 4.5L Whipple supercharger that replaced the original unit. The engine is backed by a Bowler 4L80E transmission and a 12-bolt Chevrolet rear.

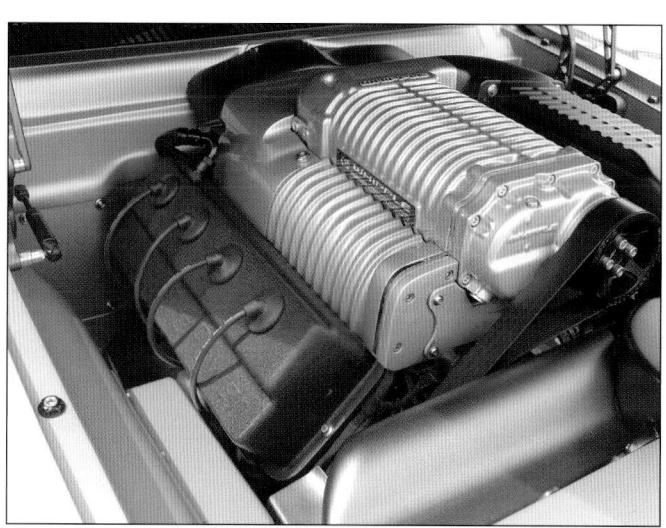

While the AMC faithful may not approve, the Wegner Motorsports 6.2L Hellcat engine with a blower swap by Whipple puts out more than 1,000 hp with the reliability of any new car. Numbers that were impossible in a drivable combination 20 years ago are now commonplace.

Jim and Mike Ring of Ringbrothers really outdid themselves on the Prestone 1972 Javelin AMX. This car features the detail and extensive modifications for which Ringbrothers cars are known. This is definitely in the category of automotive art, and it is very capable.

I'm not a huge fan of the air intake that dominates the driver's side of the engine compartment, but it illustrates that these swaps can lend themselves to whatever look you desire. As with all Ringbrothers builds, the workmanship is flawless.

The Hellcat badge in the grille indicates that this doesn't have the stock 440.

While the Gen III Hemi swap is never expected to be more popular than the now-ubiquitous GM LSx, the high number of engines produced over a 20-year run will ensure that more swappers will consider it due to its larger displacement than the typical GM engines. The 4.8L and 5.3L engines have proven their worth, but without forced induction, they leave a lot of torque on the table in comparison to the Hemi.

The Battery Man 1954 Studebaker

I met Steve Ashby, owner of this 1954 Studebaker truck, completely by accident. An employee of my old shop told me about a nearby battery dealer who specialized in refurbished absorbed glass mat (AGM) batteries, such as Optima and Odyssey.

I went by to check them out because I needed a battery for a customer's project and noticed the truck outside the building. It's not unusual for an automotive business to have an interesting shop truck, but this one caught my eye when I noticed the Hemi lettering on the rear roll pan. I made arrangements to come back with my camera and learn more about the truck from Steve himself.

The truck was built as a shop truck and wears flat-black tractor paint from the local farm supply store. This truck is driven extensively and has been as far as Las Vegas and back to Georgia for shows. The front suspension was removed and replaced with a Fatman Fabrications Mustang II–based clip that provided disc brakes, rack-and-pinion steering, and a lowered stance. The rear was lowered with blocks on the original springs.

The 5.7L Hemi engine is from a Dodge Ram, and the truck still uses the 545 RFE transmission that came with it. The shifting duties are carried out with the original 3-speed manual column shift. Engine management is factory Dodge with a tune and a Hotwire harness. ■

The early 5.7L Hemi still uses the stock Ram induction system and is backed by the 545RFE transmission. Everything is stock except for the Moroso valve covers and open-element air filter.

The only hint as to the Studebaker's powerplant is on the rear roll pan.

Not every builder realizes the engine's true potential, such as the weak early Gen III engine that was featured on an episode of *Engine Masters*, but the parts and information are available. I look forward to seeing more of these swaps in cars and trucks of all kinds.

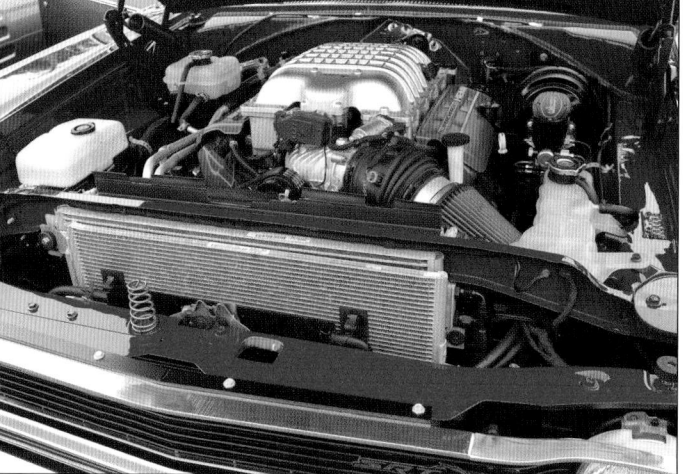

This car is a rotisserie restoration, and the engine compartment has an OEM-but-nicer feel to it. Much of what you see is late-model Mopar sourced from Hellcat donors. The engine came from a 2019 Challenger.

This clean 1954 Studebaker has a near-stock appearance but is powered by a 5.7L Hemi from a Ram and is backed by a 545RFE transmission.

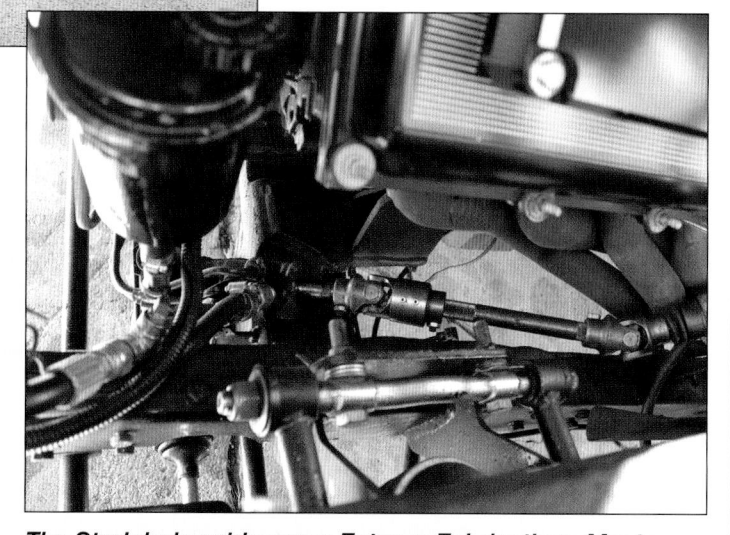

...e clutch pedal led me to believe this truck was a manual, but it isn't. The neutral safety switch was wired into the ...utch pedal. Additional senders were added to operate ...e original gauges that were converted to 12V.

The Studebaker rides on a Fatman Fabrications Mustang II–based clip. The factory column is still used and mated to the rack with U-joints and splined shafts.

ENGINE AND TRANSMISSION SELECTION

Now that you have a better understanding of the engines in the Gen III Hemi family, this is the question: "Which one is best for my swap?"

While this seems like a simple decision, the one with the most horsepower is not necessarily the correct answer. First, make an honest assessment of what you want out of your swap. Are you interested in daily-driver dependability and fuel economy, building a weekend car for shows and ice-cream runs, or trying to set a land speed record? This can be a confusing area for some. Without clear goals at the beginning of the project, there will undoubtedly be more delays and financial pain.

The early 5.7L engines have a lot going for them: they are plentiful in salvage yards and there are many running-and-driving donor vehicles with these engines that can often be inexpensively purchased. For $250 and an afternoon at Pull-A-Part, you can get a starting point that makes enough power for the milder applications or a great basis for a stroker or forced-induction build. These engines are found in the 2005–2008 LX-series cars (Chrysler 300C, Dodge Charger, Dodge Magnum), pre-2009

This engine was dressed up with a custom cold-air intake and paint detailing on the valve covers, but it is a 2005–2007 5.7L Hemi truck engine that was found in the Ram. It is similar to the Studebaker's engine in Chapter 1. These are plentiful and inexpensive, and they provide great power.

Rams, and some Jeep models. These engines are typically reliable. The main issue is that when severely overheated, the pressed-in valve seats can drop into a cylinder and destroy the piston. A machine shop can stake the seats to prevent this issue.

Want a little extra power? The 2009-and-newer Eagle heads bolt on, offer 330-cfm flow, and allow

the better-flowing later intakes to fit. Thicker head gaskets or a custom piston are required, but it is a worthwhile upgrade.

The wiring is fairly simple on the early engines. DIY Hemi, Hotwire, and other companies can assist with reworking or replacing the harness. They are all coil-on (or near) plug, depending on the year, and

This early Gen III 5.7L Hemi (2005–2008 based on the coils) is a passenger-car engine, as found in the Charger R/T, Magnum R/T, and Chrysler 300C. The main differences between the passenger-car and truck engines are the intake that has a forward-facing throttle body (rather than facing upward), and the lower accessory drive. These engines make 340 hp and 390 ft-lbs of torque.

controller for the transmission (available from Sound German Automotive) is required if you're using an aftermarket ECU or carburetor.

These engines have the multiple displacement system (MDS). You can keep it with a factory ECU, but most swappers delete it due to the cam and lifter issues for which this system is known. This can be as simple as unplugging the MDS solenoids, but the preferred method is to remove the MDS lifters, replace them with standard ones, and plug the hole. Mopar Performance, as well as other vendors, has a kit for this. If you're using an aftermarket cam, this is a must.

The passenger-car and Jeep engines have a forward-facing throttle body with a phenolic intake and lower-slung accessory drive to clear the intake plumbing. These can be swapped into pretty much anything with few changes. The truck 5.7L engines have a throttle body that points upward as well as taller front

use a 32-tooth crank reluctor. The passenger-car versions come with the NAG1 automatic transmission, and the trucks have a 545RFE. Either can be used for your swap, but a factory-type PCM or a stand-alone

This completely stock 5.7L Hemi is from a 2007 Jeep Commander. These use the passenger-car-style intake and accessory drive.

The SRT8 6.1L engines were rated at 425 hp and 420 ft-lbs of torque in stock form. In a typical swap with no catalytic convertors, headers, and a less-restrictive exhaust, they can make a bit more. The 6.1L engines are easily recognized by the aluminum intake manifold (this one has been chromed), which is opposed to the plastic ones used on other engines.

This 6.1L is more typical of a used engine. This one went in the Duster featured later in this book. The high-flow exhaust manifold at the top left is what these engines came with. They flow well but fit very few chassis.

The 6.1L engines are fairly rare in the used market. Production of the crate versions was discontinued, but some vendors, such as Indy Cylinder Head, still have a few.

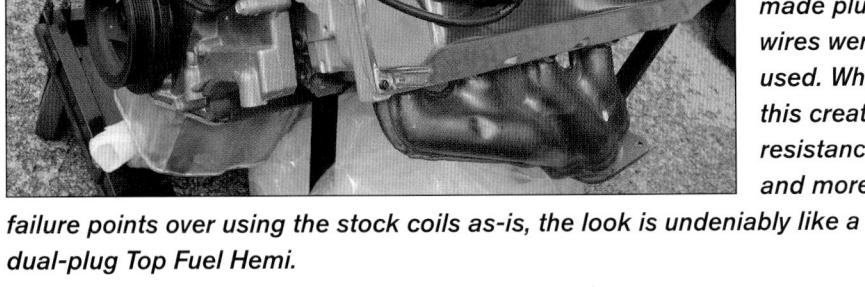

Do you notice anything odd about this 6.1L engine? Instead of having the coils mounted to the covers (as stock), the coils are hidden, and specially made plug wires were used. While this creates resistance and more failure points over using the stock coils as-is, the look is undeniably like a dual-plug Top Fuel Hemi.

accessories. In many cases, the existing truck accessories can be used on cars, but they are better suited for taller engine compartments. The passenger-car accessories and timing cover will fit on a truck engine and require no intake changes. However, the passenger-car intake will not work on an engine with truck accessories.

The 6.1L Hemi was used in 2005–2010 SRT8 models and featured many improvements over the 5.7L engine. Those improvements included higher-flowing cylinder heads (around 320 cfm) and exhaust manifolds, a less-restrictive aluminum intake manifold, a strengthened block, a forged crankshaft, improved rods, and flat-top pistons with oil squirters that took compression up to 10.3:1 from the 5.7L engine's 9.6:1. This resulted in 425 hp and 420 ft-lbs of torque. Unlike the 5.7L engines, these engines didn't have MDS. These engines are highly sought after and command a premium over a comparable 5.7L.

Newer Options

The 2009-and-newer 5.7L engines came with several changes, including the revised cylinder heads previously mentioned that are similar in flow but better than the 6.1L castings. These engines are known as Eagle engines and offer a few upgrades over the earlier engines. The blocks and crankshafts are stronger, and the compression is higher at 10.5:1. The crank reluctor on these engines is a 58-tooth version for higher resolution, which is needed for the variable valve timing (VVT) and short runner valve intake (SRV). Manual-transmission applications and heavy-duty truck applications forgo the MDS, but it is still present

This 5.7L Hemi is a 2009-and-newer passenger-car version, so it has the improved Eagle cylinder heads. These engines produce 368 hp and 395 ft-lbs of torque in stock form.

The 6.4L Hemi, as found in this Challenger put together by Holley, makes an astounding 485 hp and 475 ft-lbs of torque because of the extra displacement and high-flowing Apache cylinder heads. The VVT and SRV provide a flatter torque curve than the previous 6.1L engines. The Terminator X Max ECU on the fender well is capable of controlling both of these systems.

This 6.4L swap is nicely done and shows how clean and orderly even a virtually stock engine can be with a little effort.

on all other 5.7L engines. All have VVT, although Dodge calls it variable cam timing (VCT). VVT engines use a specific timing cover so that they are a little easier to spot.

Rams and Durangos have an active intake with the short runner valve (SRV), which is closed at lower RPM to enhance torque and opened at higher RPM for enhanced horsepower. These engines were rated as high as 390 hp, depending mostly on camshaft design and exhaust for the difference. There are five different profiles. Often, the first thought of a swapper is to disable some of these systems, but the VVT and SRV work very well and result in more horsepower and torque with the systems than without.

The 6.4L, or 392 Hemi, was first debuted in 2011 as a replacement for the 6.1L engine. Known as the Apache, the 6.4L is used in passenger cars, trucks, and Jeeps, and has been rated as high as 485 hp. The heads flow a whopping 340 cfm in stock form. They are VVT and SRV equipped, and the truck versions have a top-mounted throttle body like the 5.7Ls. Because the truck engines are built to maximize torque, they give up some horsepower but do have a stronger block that is cast either "BG" or "BGE" for "big gas engine."

Unless you're building for solely racing, retaining the SRV and VVT is worthwhile. The 5.7Ls and 6.1Ls are great engines, but the extra cubic inches and torque along with the block strength make the 6.4L a great choice, especially if you want to make a lot of power. These engines are coming down in price, though low-mileage examples still command a premium. Note that BGE blocks are the same as the Hellcat block. The only difference is the

Jim Cain's 1966 Charger was one of the first 6.4L swaps I ever saw and is one of my favorites. Jim equipped his Charger with a Reilly Motorsports AlterKtion front suspension and the RMS Street-Lynx 4-link in the rear. The Charger has an elaborate center console from the factory, and altering the tunnel too much was not an option, so Jim used a 727 TorqueFlite transmission with a Gear Vendors overdrive unit to keep RPM down.

Mopar Performance was quick to release crate versions of the 6.2L Hellcat engine. They are among the most powerful crate engines available today. The first engines were rated at 707 hp and 650 ft-lbs of torque. (Photo Courtesy Chrysler Corp)

While slightly taller and more complex to swap than a naturally aspirated engine, these still fit about anywhere the other engines fit, and they make more than enough power to be worth the extra installation headaches.

No power ratings were listed for this Scoggin-Dickey Performance Center Hellcrate engine, but the company will tailor a package to your specific needs. It offers the standard Hellcrate as well as the Hellcrate Redeye, which makes 807 hp and 717 ft-lbs of torque. The Redeye is just shy of $20,000 as of this writing (not including tax or shipping). You'd be hard pressed to duplicate that level of performance with a warranty any other way.

Speedtech's AAR 'Cuda is Hellcat powered and is backed by a Quick Time bellhousing and Tremec T56 Magnum. This car is a work of art and has the performance to match the looks.

This immaculate Monte Carlo SS by Schwartz Performance is Hellcat powered and naturally rides on a Schwartz chassis. I would have never imagined Dodge engines being swapped into G-Bodies when I wrote my last book, GM G-Body Performance Upgrades, *but I love it! (Photo Courtesy Schwartz Performance)*

The Boosted Motorsports Dakota has a very clean Hellcat swap. The fitment is tight, but it looks like a factory installation.

color of the block. BGE is black and Hellcat Hemi is orange. These blocks are very popular for big-inch strokers, such as the 411, and 426 kits are available from MMX, Arrington Performance, and others.

If you're looking for the most power you can get but still want a streetable swap, the 6.2L Hellcat engine and its variants are a great place to start. Impressive as they are in the Challengers and Chargers in which they originally came, these engines really come to life in a lighter-weight vehicle. Starting at 707 hp, they more than live up to the Hemi name and offer a combination of power, reliability, and daily-driver street manners that are unmatched. Stellantis put them in the Jeep Trackhawk and the RAM TRX, so the engines aren't as uncommon as one would think. The supercharger and ancillary components that are needed to support it (intercooler pumps, hoses, and reservoirs) add some weight, bulk, and complexity, but that is a small price to pay for what these engines offer. It's no wonder they are showing up in all types of vehicles.

Once you decide what engine is best for your needs, where will you source the engine? This is where your budget, skill level, and degree of risk aversion comes in. Used engines can be a gamble, but careful inspection can save thousands of dollars. Be very careful when dealing with online sellers. There are many types of scams, and the risk of buying stolen merchandise is high.

I only buy used engines online from reputable salvage dealers. In-person deals are far better when possible. To avoid those issues, purchase new crate engines directly from your local dealer or specialists, such as Modern Muscle, Arrington, and Bouchillon Performance. They can also assist you with custom engine projects to suit your specific requirements and help with the parts needed for installation.

Automatic Transmission Selection

The transmission selection needs to be carefully considered to best match the engine choice and body-style of your swap recipient. Some swaps are easier than others, and hopefully the following will help you decide what is best for your swap.

If you are dead set on retaining the original look of the traditional Mopar muscle car and don't want to modify the transmission tunnel, console, and shifter, you can most likely keep what you have. The Gen III Hemi bellhousing flange is the same as an LA series or Magnum small-block Mopar (273/318 [non-poly]/340/360), so those who prefer a small-block are in luck. For a big-block (B or RB) pattern transmission, you'll need to either swap the case or the bellhousing. It's easy with a manual, and for automatics, use something like the JW UltraBell.

The 727 and 904 TorqueFlites can be used as is with the proper flexplate for the Gen III Hemi engine, such as Hays 40-518, which also fits A500 and A518 (46RH/46RE) transmissions. The overdrive 46RE transmissions are popular swaps in older cars and anything with a smaller tunnel since they are TorqueFlite derivatives. They are often retained in Dakota applications since they are relatively compact for an OD and can be built to hold considerable power.

All of the auto transmission engines come with a pressed-in pilot for the torque convertor that has to be removed for this conversion. Since all of these transmissions have a throttle valve (TV) cable and not a conventional kickdown, and the Gen III Hemi only comes with a DBW throttle body in stock form, you'll

You can use a TorqueFlite or any other Mopar transmission behind your Gen III Hemi if the transmission in question has a small Mopar bellhousing pattern. (Photo Courtesy Holley)

need a way to actuate the TV cable. The 2003 Dodge Rams with the 5.7L Hemi had a special pedal and servo assembly to accommodate the 46RE (a similar assembly was used in similar year Mercedes applications).

This can be used with any of the earlier-mentioned transmissions to handle the TV functions. As you can imagine, this assembly is getting a little difficult to find, and Bouchillon Performance offers its own kit to serve the same purpose. In the case of the 46RE, you'll also need a way to control the electronic functions, which is currently either an OEM ECU, or Holley Terminator X Max. This will be covered in detail later.

Manual transmissions, whether passenger-car or later truck versions, can also be retained. For older 4-speed manuals, such as the A-833, use an original factory bellhousing, an aftermarket bell like the older Lakewoods (no longer available), or one of the newer Quick Time bellhousings (part number RM-6072 fits the A-833; it is listed as SBM but will work). These retain the factory clutch Z-bar mounting as long as you install the engine in the same location as stock.

Lakewood also has a new alu-

To swap any of the TorqueFlite-based automatic transmissions, such as the A727, A904, or A518 (46RE/RH), a flexplate like this from Hays (part number 40-518) is needed. It is SFI certified and works with any Gen III Hemi. Be sure to remove the pressed-in pilot bushing present on NAG1- and 5454RFE-equipped vehicles so that the convertor will seat properly. (Photo Courtesy Holley)

minum bellhousing that accepts original 3- and 4-speeds, as well as Ford-style Tremec TKX and TKO 5-speeds. If you have a non-Mopar 4-speed, such as a Muncie, T10/Super T10, or Jericho, Quick Time has a bell for that also: RM-6083. With any of these, you'll need to run an appropriate flywheel, such as McLeod part number 464400. It works with most factory bellhousings, has 130 teeth, and accepts a 10.5-inch clutch. Factory manual flywheels can also be

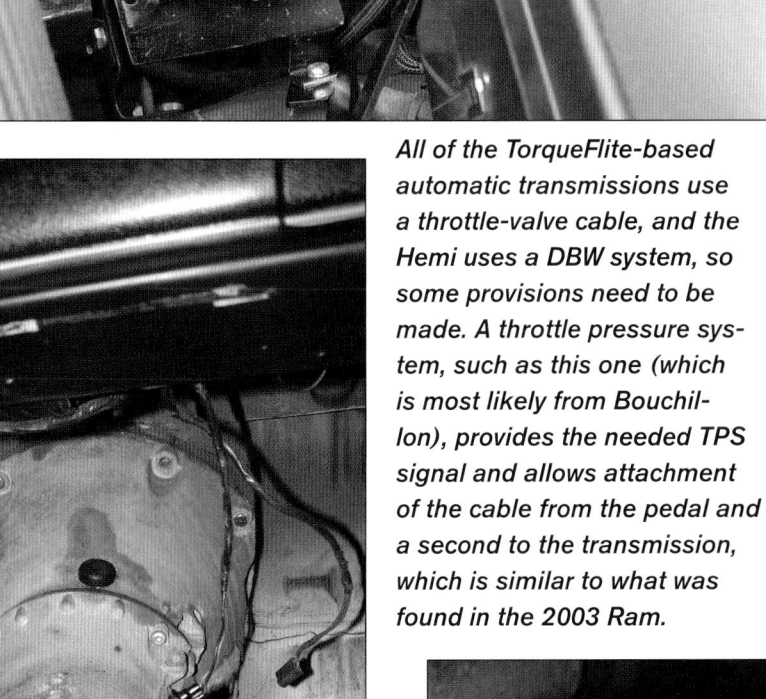

used. Early truck applications are recommended by Lakewood. Aftermarket hydraulic-clutch actuation can be used if you don't want to stay with mechanical linkage.

While the Gen III Hemi engine is a great upgrade for about any vehicle, a modern transmission to go with it will allow you to reach the combination's full potential. For earlier engines (mostly automatics with the exception of some Challengers), you'll have either an NAG1 (LX-platform passenger cars) or a 545 RFE (trucks, the Chrysler Aspen, and Jeeps). The later engines came with the 8HP70/90 transmissions.

All of these transmissions are rather large and require some cutting of the floor pan and tunnel area for most swaps, so be aware of this. Additionally, if your swap project has torsion bars, the torsion bar crossmember will likely have to be cut out and rebuilt for clearance. This is best done with the bars out to avoid tweaking the mounting points at the rear.

All of the TorqueFlite-based automatic transmissions use a throttle-valve cable, and the Hemi uses a DBW system, so some provisions need to be made. A throttle pressure system, such as this one (which is most likely from Bouchillon), provides the needed TPS signal and allows attachment of the cable from the pedal and a second to the transmission, which is similar to what was found in the 2003 Ram.

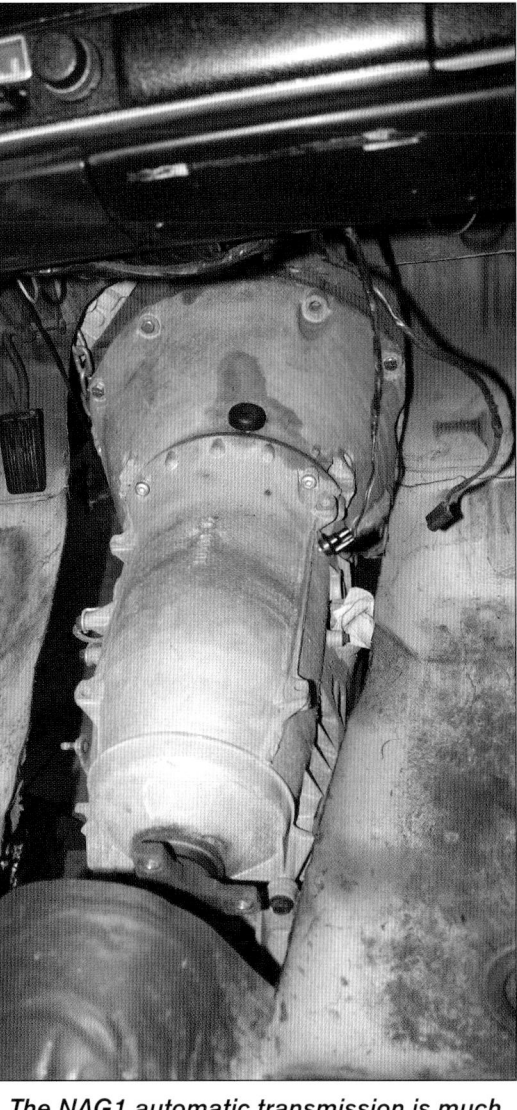

The NAG1 automatic transmission is much shorter than a TorqueFlite but has a larger case, so floor-pan surgery is needed (as is seen in this A-Body).

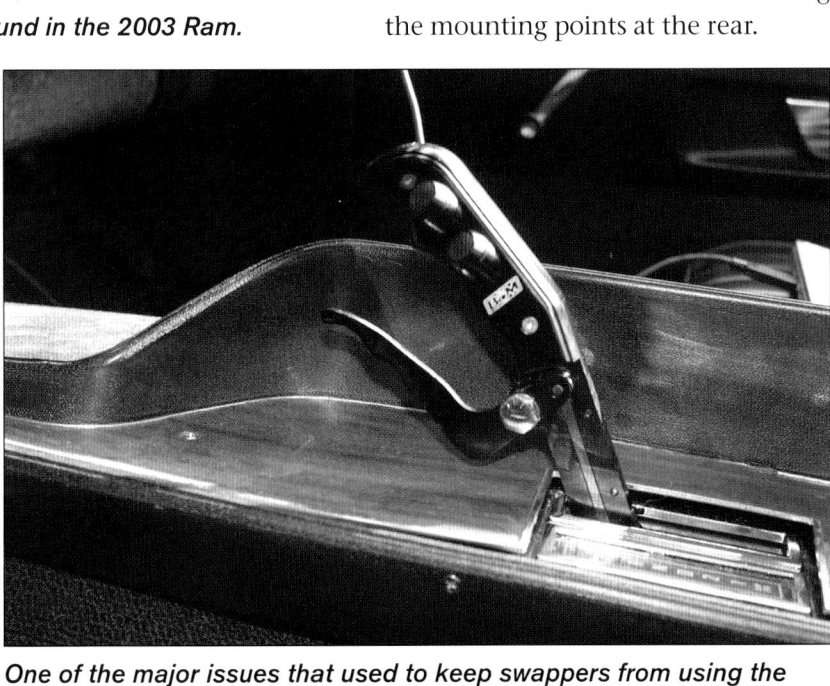

One of the major issues that used to keep swappers from using the NAG1 is that the electronic shifter had to be used, although some have modified it to look more appropriate in an older vehicle. B&M solved this problem with part number 8188.

The GM 4L80E has become very popular for Gen III Hemi swaps, especially high-powered swaps, such as this Hellcat engine in a Coronet. Any GM automatic transmission swaps in the same manner with a bolt-on bell or adapter plate. For strength reasons, most are a 4L80E or GM Powerglide for drag racing. The availability of a controller for the 8HP70/90 series of transmissions likely makes these less common than in the past.

The 545RFE isn't quite as thick at the front but is still very large and long. This means more fabrication.

Of the transmissions mentioned, the 545RFE requires the least to adapt to another car on the electronics side, but the amount of floor modification required is substantial due to the large bellhousing area. It also is weaker than the other options. The NAG1 fits a bit better, as does the 8HP-series transmissions, but both need to see inputs from vehicle speed sensors to work properly. This was once more of an obstacle than it is today thanks to companies like Hotwire and Sound German Automotive. The NAG1 requires a factory-style shifter or the new B&M part number 8188 Magnum Grip Pro Stick. The 8HP can be actuated via paddle shifters or the factory shifter. No conventional aftermarket shifters are currently available. More specifics on these swaps are covered in the next chapter.

For drag racing, the GM Powerglide has been a popular choice for

TCI offers its 6X 6-speed automatic transmission (based on the 4L80E) with a Reid SFI bellhousing for use behind the Gen III Hemi.

If you are using an original mechanical speedometer and have a modern transmission with a VSS output, you can use a signal converter, such as this one from Dakota Digital.

many years, and it is possible to retrofit one to your Gen III Hemi. JW and Reid both offer aftermarket bellhousings to perform this swap, and ATI makes a Supercase with bell and flexplate for this swap. Being fairly light and compact, this is an easy swap in just about any vehicle. Aftermarket support for this transmission is near endless.

It is possible to retrofit other GM transmissions in the same manner by using aftermarket adapter plates or bellhousings. Many require machining to install as they bolt to the front pump assembly. The TH400s are popular, as are the 4L80E 4-speed overdrive automatics. Many early Hellcat engine swappers chose the 4L80E for their builds, and they remain popular due to the reliability, parts support, and a more common knowledge of these transmissions than their Mopar counterparts. Bowler offers complete packages with new transmissions built on custom cases with aftermarket bellhousings and all the accessories needed to make the swap. These transmissions are a bit easier to swap in that they are relatively compact and don't require as many inputs as the NAG1 and 8HP. There are also more options for controlling them.

Manual Transmission Selection

If the donor engine had a manual transmission behind it, it most likely is a Tremec TR6060. Derived from the older BorgWarner T56, which was first used in Vipers and fourth-generation GM F-Bodies, the TR6060 is a great transmission and has been used by all the Big 3 manufacturers at one time or another: GM in the Cadillac CTS-V and Chevrolet Camaro, and Ford in the S197

Hays offers an SFI-certified flexplate for passenger-car applications that include the NAG1, 8HP70, and 8HP90. The part number is 40-510. (Photo Courtesy Holley)

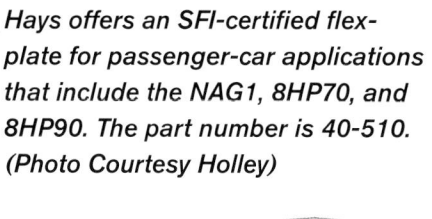

Aftermarket manual transmissions require a new bellhousing. This is Quick Time part number RM-8077. It is SFI approved, steel, and fits Viper or GM LS-style T56s, including the T56 Magnum. (Photo Courtesy Holley)

If you don't plan to race and want a factory appearance, Lakewood offers cast-aluminum bellhousings for popular transmissions. Part number LK7000X works with any of the original Mopar 3- and 4-speeds, as well as Ford pattern TKX and TKO transmissions. (Photo Courtesy Holley)

The Tremec TKO 500 and 600 have been available for years as a heavy-duty replacement for the BorgWarner T5 in Mustang applications. While strong, the toploader gear design makes fitment difficult in some tunnels, and some people complain about shift quality. It is still a great transmission, although it is being replaced by the TKX.

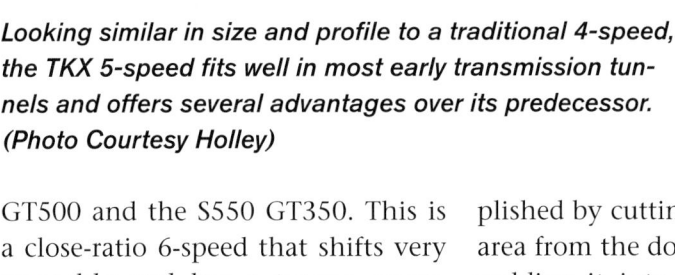

Looking similar in size and profile to a traditional 4-speed, the TKX 5-speed fits well in most early transmission tunnels and offers several advantages over its predecessor. (Photo Courtesy Holley)

This T56 Magnum is now in the Gremlin. I wanted a steel bellhousing for safety since this car will be raced, and the Quick Time unit provides it.

GT500 and the S550 GT350. This is a close-ratio 6-speed that shifts very smoothly and has a torque capacity of 650 ft-lbs. It has a built-in gerotor-style fluid pump for cooling. The shifter is remotely mounted behind the tailshaft, which can cause issues in some installations.

As with the NAG1 and 8HP transmissions, it has a solid flange for the driveshaft rather than a slip yoke, which isn't needed with an independent rear. If the position of the remote-mount shifter isn't a problem, it can be used, but be sure the shifter is bolted to the floor pan like the original. This is best accom-plished by cutting out the mounting area from the donor car's tunnel and welding it into your tunnel. Alter-natively, the entire remote assembly can be removed and replaced with an aftermarket shifter. I did this once using a shifter from Silver Sport. Note the Mopar shifter mechanism goes to a rear shifter location that is not present on GM transmissions. The GM version uses the forward position located on the main case. I have yet to see a Mopar TR6060 that had the shaft machined for a shifter at the front location, though with some parts from a GM transmission, it can easily be done.

The lack of a slip yoke was over-come by having a custom drive-shaft made that had a slip compo-nent built in, like a 4WD application, with a puck-style coupler. Alter-natively, adapters are available to bolt on a 1350 Spicer–style U-joint, though the slip is still needed. BRP Musclerods makes a spacer so the TR6060 mount can be used on a T56 Magnum crossmember.

Since the T56 Magnum is based on the TR6060, another option is to use a T56 Magnum tail housing assembly. These are available from several sources, and they consist of a new tail housing with a rear-position

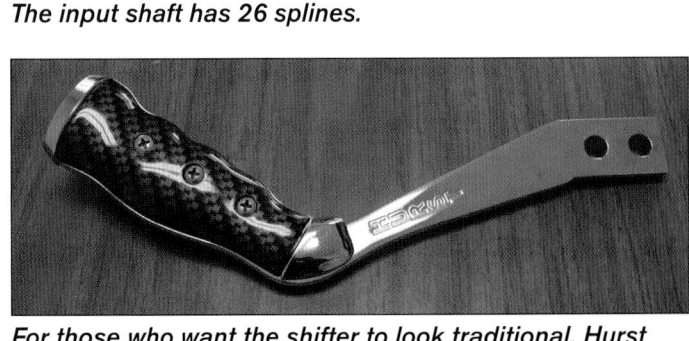

The bell is deeper than it looks and easily accommodates the twin-disc McLeod clutch. The input shaft has 26 splines.

For those who want the shifter to look traditional, Hurst offers a pistol grip–style stick. The two-bolt attachment allows dozens of shifter handle possibilities.

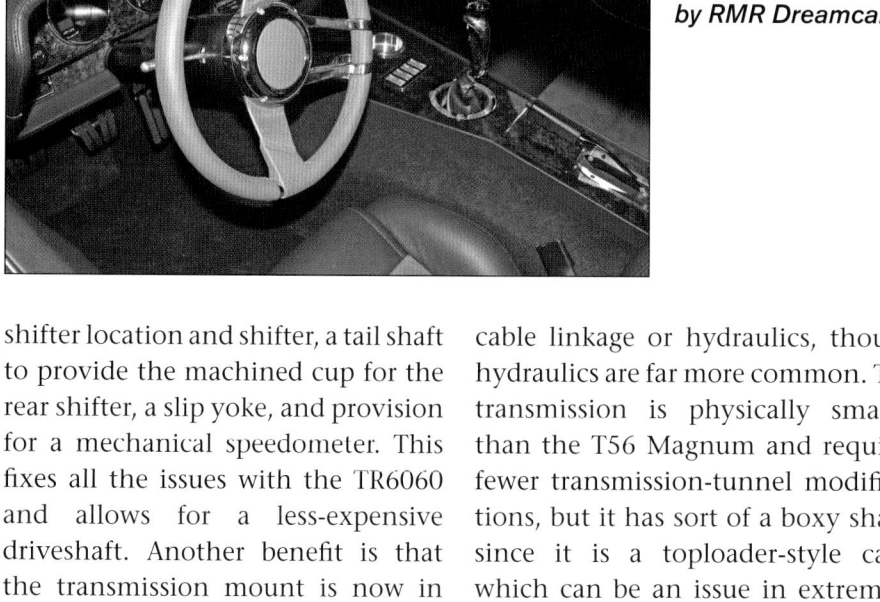

The Hurst pistol grip–shifter handle is installed on a build by RMR Dreamcars.

shifter location and shifter, a tail shaft to provide the machined cup for the rear shifter, a slip yoke, and provision for a mechanical speedometer. This fixes all the issues with the TR6060 and allows for a less-expensive driveshaft. Another benefit is that the transmission mount is now in a lower position and can be used with the T56 Magnum crossmembers available from several sources.

Aftermarket manual transmissions are more popular than ever with plenty of choices out there. Tremec offers a variety of 5- and 6-speed transmissions, but I'll concentrate on the ones most likely to be used by Gen III Hemi swappers. These include the TKO 500/600, the new TKX, and the T56 Magnum.

Tremec has offered the 5-speed TKO 500 and 600 for many years in various configurations for Ford and GM applications. This transmission is a toploader design and was originally intended as a heavy-duty replacement for the lighter-duty T-5 World Class (WC) transmission used in Fox Body Mustangs. They have since become very popular for retrofits. All the Tremec dealers offer packages to use it behind just about anything, including the Gen III Hemi.

Adapters are available to fit most original 4-speed bellhousings. These can be used with either mechanical/

cable linkage or hydraulics, though hydraulics are far more common. The transmission is physically smaller than the T56 Magnum and requires fewer transmission-tunnel modifications, but it has sort of a boxy shape since it is a toploader-style case, which can be an issue in extremely tight tunnels. Most vendors mill the cases to shed unnecessary protrusions to help the installation. The transmission has four shifter locations, so chances of it working well with any combination is likely. Some complain of a notchy feeling when shifting this transmission, but that is mainly from fighting the spring-loaded shifter gate. Like the Magnum, mechanical and vehicle speed sensor (VSS)-style speedometers are accommodated.

Tremec's latest offering is the TKX. While it is similar to the TKO series, it has a narrower case that is easier to fit in tight tunnels, but it still has 600 ft-lbs of torque capacity. It is very similar in size to most traditional 4-speeds but has the advantage of an overdrive fifth gear. The case is streamlined with no need for additional machining operations to better fit it in early car tunnels. It has three shifter locations.

TKO shifters are not interchangeable, but the aftermarket is stepping up with more options for this trans-

mission as it becomes more popular. The transmission mount is in the same location as on TKO 500/600 transmissions, so existing swap crossmembers for the older series of transmission can be used with the TKX.

The T56 Magnum is by far the most common choice because it holds up to 700 ft-lbs of torque in stock form and offers three different shifter positions. The two rear-most positions are covered by the stock shifter plate, which places the shifter in the rear in stock form. By unbolting the shifter and turning it around, it can pick up the middle position (the shaft is machined for it) to provide extra clearance for bench seats, consoles, etc. if needed. The front position, which is covered by a square plate, can be removed and fitted with a special shifter (it only fits one way) and the rear positions blocked off. This is very handy and allows the T56 magnum to fit just about anything.

Hurst, Silver Sport Transmission, American Powertrain, and others offer shifters and interchangeable sticks to easily accommodate most vehicles. This transmission is large, and many stock transmission tunnels require some modification for fitment. However, its double overdrive and resulting ability to run lower rear-end gears while maintaining reasonable RPM and fuel economy on the highway make it a worthwhile swap. You can run either mechanical or electronic speedometers with this unit. Bellhousings are available through Quick Time, Lakewood, Silver Sport, and others. This transmission is equipped with a slip yoke, so no special driveshaft is needed. The T56 Magnum is set up for hydraulic clutch actuation. Several choices of gear ratios are available.

ENGINE AND TRANSMISSION MANAGEMENT

It may seem counterintuitive, but when discussing engine management, I am starting with the simplest engine management system for an internal combustion engine: the carburetor. In spite of the many advantages of EFI, there are some people who just want a carburetor. Whether for looks, nostalgia, or a comfort level with the ease of tuning and

modification, there are many reasons one might be tempted to use a carburetor on a Gen III Hemi application.

Carbureted Gen III Hemis

Some may argue it is cheaper than EFI, but much like the same argument from the GM LSx crowd, it really isn't cheaper. Every Gen III Hemi engine

comes with a well-engineered EFI manifold, DBW throttle body, and multi-port injection, so much of the cost of EFI is already addressed with your typical donor engine.

In most cases, you still need an electric fuel pump with a fuel-pressure regulator and appropriate plumbing, although this can usually be done less expensively in a carbureted

This 6.1L engine could be mistaken for an older powerplant at first glance. The dual plug wires hint at a distributor, but it is powered by stock coils under the Mod Man dual-quad intake. I didn't see a control box, but it is likely an MSD 6-Hemi controller. The carburetors are 500-cfm Edelbrock part number 1404 units. Both the intake and valve covers are from Indy Cylinder Head.

A simple dial-type fuel-pressure regulator is used with an electric pump that is mounted at the rear of the vehicle. Edelbrock carburetors don't like high fuel pressure.

application. The real cost, however, has always come in the engine management. In the early days of the swap, if you weren't an electrical engineer, you were forced to spend $2,000 or more on an aftermarket harness, PCM, aftermarket tuner, and custom program to run a stock engine. If you wanted to really modify things, you had to spend even more. Many weren't willing to do that but ended up spending more on a carbureted setup to get away from the ugly EFI intakes and calibration hassles. Of course, if you already own an appropriate carburetor and an electric fuel-pump system to support it, staying carbureted is a great option.

Ignition Options

To perform a carb swap on a Gen III Hemi, you'll need to address the ignition system. There is no provision on a stock Gen III Hemi for a distributor, so you'll need a way to drive the existing ignition coils. There was a kit from Mopar Performance (P5155929, 2009-and-newer 5.7L Hemi and all 6.4L; P5155930, pre-2009 5.7L and 6.1L Hemi) that included a machined front timing cover, cam timing gear, and fuel pump pushrod and bolt kit, and allowed for the use of an AMC-style distributor, but unfortunately it is no longer available. This timing cover is also the only way to use a mechanical fuel pump on a Gen III Hemi, so keep that in mind.

Unless you really want the look of a distributor or run in a racing class that requires it, there is no advantage to a distributor over coil-on-plug

The vast majority use the factory coils, even with a carburetor, and the MSD 6-Hemi controller is the most popular way to accomplish that. Timing can be programmed, as well as retarded for nitrous or boost. These are also popular for use with TBI conversions, such as the FAST EZ-EFI or Holley Sniper. (Photo Courtesy Holley)

The early 5.7L Hemi has already had a cam swap, and the MDS lifters were replaced with factory 6.1L Hemi lifters and new trays.

Block-off plugs were installed in the valley in place of the MDS solenoids.

ignition. There are many disadvantages, such as greater potential for spark scatter and more moving parts, such as distributor drive gears, to wear and cause issues.

The most common option to drive the coils separate of an EFI system is the MSD 6-Hemi controller (part number 6013). Harnesses were available for 2003–2005 5.7L engines (part number 88863) and 2006–2008 5.7L/6.1L engines (part number 88864) only, but the early harness has been discontinued.

You can switch a 2003–2005 engine to the later-style coils, which are more desirable anyway, and use the part number 88864 harness. The unit plugs into the coil connectors, and the cam, crank, and manifold absolute pressure (MAP) sensors can be used with both EFI and carbureted applications. Software can be downloaded from Holley's website that allows the programming of a standard naturally aspirated (NA) timing curve and accommodates nitrous and forced induction, respectively, through a nitrous retard and boost/timing control.

Another option for coil control is the stand-alone XIM ignition control module from Fuel Air Spark Technology (FAST). This is available for several applications including 5.7L, 6.1L, and 6.4L engines. Unlike the MSD unit, it isn't adjusted by software but rather by adjustment dial pots. This system can be used with a carburetor or any engine-management system that doesn't control timing independently. It has fewer features than the MSD unit and is more expensive, so it isn't seen quite as often.

An option that is rarely seen outside of the drag racing world but may be a viable option for some is to use an aftermarket ECU (such as the Holley Terminator X, HP, or Dominator) to control the ignition functions while retaining a carburetor for fuel delivery only. This can offer advantages, such as the built-in data-logging capability, boost and nitrous controls, and staging aides, such as transmission brakes and bump boxes that can be commanded by the ECU.

Fuel Systems

As mentioned previously, most of you will need to build a new fuel system with an electric fuel pump. The typical carbureted fuel system consists of an electric fuel pump; a fuel-pressure regulator that can be set up as a dead-head system or with a return line; appropriately sized (in this case, 3/8 inch or -6 AN at a minimum) lines, hoses, and fittings; filters; and the carburetor.

When selecting a fuel pump, be sure that the pump will support the choice of engine. This is based on the horsepower that the engine produces and the amount of fuel it requires to produce that power. (This is discussed more in later chapters because it applies to both carbureted and EFI applications.)

Most street-driven vehicles do best with a vacuum-secondary carburetor. With a vacuum secondary, the engine is given only what it needs, so if the carburetor is a little larger than the ideal, it will still perform well with proper tuning. Mechanical secondary carburetors are best left for more serious street/strip cars that are lightweight, have low rear-end gears, and have either a manual transmission or an automatic with a high-stall torque convertor. This type of carburetor on a heavier car with milder gearing usually results in fouled plugs, tuning headaches that aren't easily resolved, and poor mileage and performance.

Finally, an intake manifold is needed for this particular application. When it comes to intakes for these engines, there are very few choices. Mopar Performance offers single-plane, single 4-barrel intakes for the 5.7L engines under part number P4510581AB. OC Performance (OCP) offers a dual-plane intake manifold for all of the Gen III Hemis. Mopar Performance and Edelbrock both offer cast dual-quad intakes for the early 5.7Ls.

For more race-oriented engines, Indy Cylinder Head offers its Mod Man intake for early 5.7L and 6.1L engines that can be set up for single or dual 4-barrel carburetors,

Surprisingly, none of the big companies make a dual-plane intake for the Gen III Hemi, so Joe O'Cone took it upon himself to design and produce one. It is a nice piece and can be ordered with drilled injector bungs and an adapter to run a DBW throttle body.

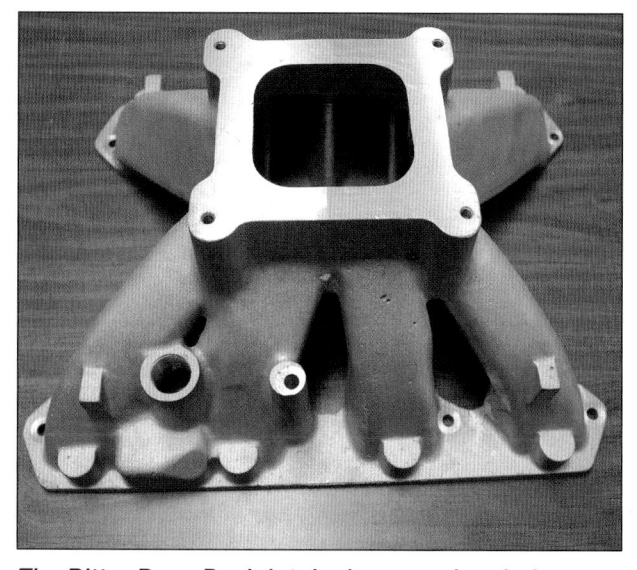

The OCP intake installs easily and comes with all of the required hardware. The carburetor is a 750 Holley.

The Ritter Drag Pack intake is a popular choice, especially for high-compression and high-RPM race builds. This is the short version with a 4150 flange.

This Mod Man intake uses a throttle-body-injection unit that appears to be an early FAST EZ-EFI. At first glance, it looks carbureted, especially with the air cleaner obscuring most of the unit.

This wild truck has a Quick Fuel carburetor on a Mod Man intake that is fed by a TorqStorm centrifugal supercharger.

three 2-barrel carburetors, and even a 6-71 supercharger. Ritter Racing offers a Drag Pack intake with two height options and either a conventional 4150/4160 flange or a 4500 Dominator-style flange.

Transmission Controls

The Gen III Hemi shares the same bellhousing pattern as the traditional LA and Magnum small-block V-8s, so any of the older non-computer-controlled transmissions will bolt up with the right flexplate and torque convertor. Transmissions, such as the 727 and 904 TorqueFlites, which you may already have in your vehicle, are quite common in these swaps since they don't require any tunnel modifications to install and can be built to handle most power levels.

If you have a computer-controlled automatic you want to use, such as the NAG1, 545RFE, or 8HP70/90, you can do so with a stand-alone controller from Sound German Automotive. As an alternative, adapter plates and bellhousings are available to facilitate the use of popular GM automatic transmissions, such as the 4L60E and 4L80E and their derivatives. Aftermarket stand-alone controllers are available for these from a variety of sources, such as TCI, B&M, and many others.

Keep in mind that a throttle-position sensor (TPS) needs to be added to your carburetor for any of these electronic transmission options. Several are available from the aftermarket that will work with the most popular carburetors, such as Holley, Edelbrock, and Demon. Another factor to consider is that some transmission parts suppliers offer full-manual valve bodies for these transmissions. While they do forgo the convenience of automatic operation, they do not require the addition of a controller or a TPS sensor. That may not be an option for everyone. (Specifics on the nuts and bolts of all these automatic transmission installations are covered in more detail in Chapter 2.)

Throttle-Body Injection

Dating back to the 1980s, there have been aftermarket throttle-body EFI systems designed to easily convert a carbureted vehicle to fuel injection. These systems are great for those who don't want to go to the added expense of converting to a multi-port system, since they typically bolt on like a carburetor and house the injectors in the throttle body, so no drilling or welding of the manifold to install injectors is needed. For an older engine with a 4-barrel intake, this is a relatively inexpensive and easy way to get EFI. No Gen III Hemis came with a carburetor or an intake manifold that will accept one, but this approach is still an option. Using a carburetor-style intake and an MSD 6-Hemi ignition controller, any of the popular 4-barrel-style TBI units can be installed on a Gen III Hemi. The most popular units are from Holley, FiTech, MSD, and FAST.

I have installed many of these throttle-body injection (TBI) units over the years and am pleased with the results. When properly installed, these systems can be virtually trouble free. A few years ago, if you didn't want to go with a factory EFI setup and weren't willing to spend a considerable amount of money on an aftermarket multi-port system, these were a great alternative that offered better looks and most of the performance of a multi-port setup.

The main selling point is they are self-tuning, so you don't have to hire a professional tuner. I'd like to see those words stricken from every ad, website listing, and installation video. They can generate what I call a start-up tune close enough to get your engine running. In some cases, that start-up tune may be close to what is needed. They do have a self-learning capability that will help smooth out any rough spots in the tune if there are no other issues, such as RMI interference, poor rotor phasing, incorrect oxygen-sensor and fuel-pump placement, or vehicle electrical problems. Typically, they require a professional tune to reach their full potential even in a perfect installation.

I had considered a TBI conversion for our Gremlin's 5.7L Hemi in early 2016. I had an engine with no intake manifold. At the time, Gen III Hemis weren't often seen in self-service-type salvage yards. Buying a new intake, injectors, and all the components needed was going to make this a very expensive proposition. I also had to purchase a new harness, the proper ECU, and custom programming. I figured that it would cost a minimum of $3,000, even with a used intake setup.

Around that time, Joe O'Cone came out with his dual-plane OCP intake in a 4150 Holley pattern. I decided to go that route and add MSD Atomic EFI and the MSD 6 Hemi box to run the coils. Overall, this wasn't a lot less expensive. At today's prices, it's about $2,600 for everything needed. If you already had a usable intake, staying with a factory multi-port system would be cheaper, even with the cost of the aftermarket harness and basic tuning thrown in. Now, you can buy an aftermarket ECU and harness system for a little more than half of that, so my biggest question for anyone contemplating using TBI on a Hemi is, "Why?" The cost of multi-port EFI is now so low that even carburetors are difficult to justify.

I suspect there are a lot of people who have been building a project in stages, gradually making improvements to it as they drive, who may have already installed TBI on an older engine in their project car and want to reuse it on the Hemi. Others may have a carbureted Gen III Hemi swap and want to keep the overall look but gain the advantages of aftermarket EFI. For those folks, I will give a brief overview of the most popular systems.

FAST EZ-EFI

The first of these types of systems I installed, and one of the first modern systems on the market, was the FAST EZ-EFI. It did very well on the mild big-block it was used on and should do just as well on a Gen III Hemi. The base version will handle applications up to 650 hp (4 injectors) and has the typical Holley 4150 bolt pattern.

It comes with a touchscreen handheld device and harness and only controls fuel in its base version. Fuel system kits are available with external or in-tank pumps. The EZ-EFI 2.0 has 8 injectors and is good for 1,200 hp. It has timing-control options using FAST distributors or crank triggers. Nitrous control is standard, and the units are com-

patible with E85. These units use a separate ECU and do not offer transmission control.

MSD Atomic

MSD's Atomic EFI is a unit I have a lot of experience with since I've installed several of them in my own shop with good results in a wide variety of applications. The MSD Atomic has the ECU and many of the sensors built into the throttle body (MAP, TPS, IAT, and fuel pressure) for an easy installation. No laptop is needed, nor is any connection provided to use one. All programming is done through a handheld monitor.

The system includes a wideband oxygen sensor and a power module that is the communication hub for the system and provides the fuel-pump circuit and other inputs and outputs (I/Os) for optional features. Atomic can control timing through the use of a locked-out MSD Billet distributor and CD box. A rev limiter is built in. It can be run as a return or returnless system. No transmission control is

supported, although MSD has controllers for GM electronic overdrive transmissions.

FiTech

FiTech offers a wide variety of TBI systems, including 2-barrel, Tri-Power (three 2-barrel), and 4-barrel systems. The 4-barrel systems have a dual bolt pattern. Their systems are available in 400-, 550-, 600-, 650-, 800-, and 1,200-hp versions and feature an ECU that is mounted on the throttle body. All have a one-bar MAP except the 1,200-hp version. No transmission control is offered.

Holley Sniper

Holley's basic Sniper 4-barrel system supports up to 650 hp and has versions, such as the Super Sniper and X-Flow, that can handle up to 1,250 hp. It is available in 1-, 2-, and 4-barrel versions, and even a 2x4 version for tunnel rams or superchargers. It probably has the most options to suit just about any build.

These systems can be set up

The original MSD Atomic has been around for a long time and works well. I originally planned to use one on an OCP intake until the plans for our Gremlin changed substantially.

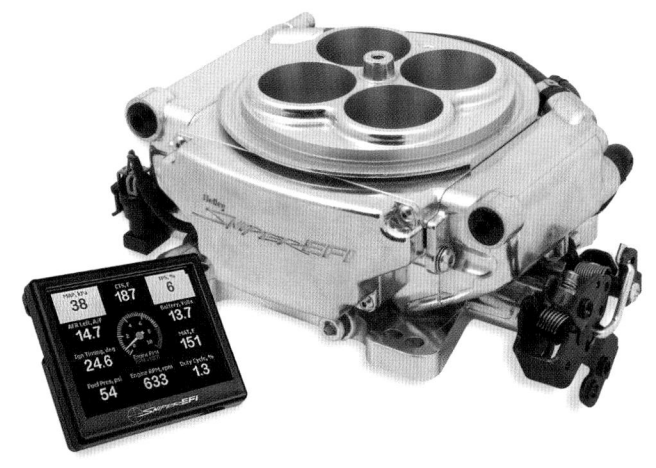

The Sniper is Holley's entry-level unit and was intended to compete with the lower-priced FiTech units. It is one of the easier units to install with no external ECUs or boxes, but it is susceptible to radio frequency interference (RFI), especially with front-mounted distributors, due to the ECU location. (Photo Courtesy Holley)

with a handheld touchscreen or with a laptop. Most use an internal fuel-pressure regulator that is pre-set. The Stealth versions look like a traditional Holley 4150 carburetor and are functionally similar to the other Sniper units other than they require an external fuel-pressure regulator.

The basic system includes the throttle body with built-in ECU and main harness; an oxygen sensor with installation hardware; coolant temp sensor; a 3.5-inch touchscreen for setup and basic tuning; a power harness that also powers the fuel pump; an auxiliary harness for fans, AC kick, and other functions; and a coil driver module. K-kits with a complete external fuel system are available, as are many options for in-tank/in-cell fuel pumps.

MSD Atomic 2

While the MSD Atomic 2 looks much like the original version, it could have been marketed as an upgraded Sniper unit. It uses the same internal ECU as the Sniper and eliminates the original MSD

Atomic's external power module, but it is located in the side to minimize RFI issues with front-mounted distributors.

It uses the same 3.5-inch touchscreen as a Sniper and has similar software and firmware. Additional features include roller-bearing throttle shafts for smoother transitions and a built-in fuel-pressure transducer so fuel pressure can be observed inside the vehicle, which is great for tuning and troubleshooting.

Terminator X/X Max Stealth

Holley's Terminator X series offers a TBI version (with or without transmission control) that eliminates some of the headaches of the Sniper. It is fully upgradable to port EFI with proper hardware and harness changes. The features are similar to those found in the multi-port systems and have the same ECU.

Terminator Stealth

The Holley Terminator was the original Holley EFI throttle-body system that used an HP or Dominator ECU, depending on the need for transmission control. It has been discontinued, but the Stealth version is still available. While expensive, it is the best of Holley's TBI systems.

Which is the best choice? That part is completely up to you and based on your needs and budget. If you already have a good carburetor or throttle body EFI unit, by all means, use it if you are comfortable with it and it meets your criteria. I hesitate to recommend aftermarket TBI to non-EFI savvy individuals a certain degree of knowledge and troubleshooting ability is needed.

Unless you are dealing with a long-block with no intake or intake hardware, such as injectors, rails, sensors, throttle body, etc., your cheapest alternative is an aftermarket port fuel-injection system that can use the stock hardware. Most builds are going to need new fuel lines, filters, and an electric fuel pump and regulator.

The Terminator X/X Max Stealth provides the looks of a 4150 carburetor with all the advantages of EFI. This system uses a separate ECU and is not affected by RFI (like the Sniper units can be). I prefer a system with an ECU that can be mounted away from the engine rather than on top of it. (Photo Courtesy Holley)

MSD's Atomic II is a mix of Atomic and Sniper. It uses a Sniper ECU and touchscreen with the addition of built-in fuel-pressure monitoring. (Photo Courtesy Holley)

Holley's Terminator system is no longer made, but the Stealth version shown here is available. If you want the best TBI system on the market with nearly infinite upgradability for future combinations, this is it. (Photo Courtesy Holley)

The EFI stuff isn't much more expensive than those for carburetors. For stock engines, keeping a stock ECU and appropriate harness (home modified, custom built, or a crate engine harness) ensures ease of use and reliability. With even mild modifications, the aftermarket systems start to look more attractive because they are typically easier to use and tune than a factory-based system.

Factory-Based Systems

The most common method of engine and transmission management with these swaps is using the factory controllers with either a modified stock or stock-based aftermarket harness. If you are planning to modify a stock harness yourself, be aware that lots of patience, wiring skill, and some specialized tools for crimping, de-pinning connectors, etc. will be required.

If you are planning to modify a factory harness yourself, there is a lot of information available through the DIYHemi.com website and YouTube page. The videos explain what components need to be removed from a donor vehicle (such as ECMs, TCMs, and pedal modules for the earlier applications) and how to modify them for your application. This allows the use of the stock engine harness.

In addition to information available through DIY Hemi, get wiring diagrams and pinouts for your particular year and model engine. These can be sourced from a factory service manual or through sources such as All-Data and Mitchell. DIY Hemi also has plenty of harness-related parts available, including connectors, OBD-II ports, power distribution modules, manuals on modifying your harness, and getting your Gen III Hemi running on a budget. They also offer a Quick Hemi harness that can be used with your existing engine harness to simplify your swap. This eliminates a lot of the hassle for a reasonable cost. Keep in mind these components and swaps are for applications with non-computer-controlled transmissions or ones that are using stand-alone controllers.

What do you do if you want to run the factory harness from your donor vehicle and keep most of the modern functions and comforts found with the vehicle? This type of swap is pushed by some of the late model salvage yards that offer engine and transmission pullouts that can be run on the pallet they come on.

However, when installing them into an older or non-similar vehicle, many problems will surface. If you want to run the donor dash, steering column, ABS module, fuel tank (won't fit anything well except the car it came in), differential (even the gearing can be a problem, especially with Hellcat swaps), and the taillights, you can probably make it work. But short of that? It isn't worth it. Some have done this with a degree of success, but there are easier ways to do these swaps, in many cases, for less money, extraneous wiring, control boxes, and clutter.

An easier solution, especially if you have a low-mileage stock engine or crate engine, is to use one of the Mopar Performance Hemi crate engine kits. It offers two EC kits for 5.7L/345-ci and 6.4L/392-ci

The Duster project's 545 RFE transmission required a PCM change, custom tune, and harness from Hotwires to make it communicate properly.

All Gen III Hemis come with a DBW throttle body. If you want a cable-type throttle body, aftermarket EFI is preferable.

The original 6.1L engine's PCM was incompatible with the 545RFE, so I used a 2005 Dodge Ram PCM. This was a programming issue that has likely been rectified by HP Tuners.

The Diablo tuner pictured was used to recalibrate the PCM using a custom tune from David Weber at Modern Muscle/MMX.

engines to install an engine into an emissions-controlled 1976–1995 vehicle that includes needed parts, such as catalytic convertors, additional oxygen sensors, an evaporative emissions control system (EVAP), purge solenoid, charcoal canister, and air-filter assembly.

For older vehicles used on public highways and off-road vehicles not used on public highways, four different kits are available to cover 345-ci, 392-ci, 6.2L supercharged, and 426-ci supercharged engines. These kits include the accelerator pedal, ground jumper, engine wiring harness, oxygen sensors, chassis harness, PCM, power distribution center, and a charge air-temperature sensor. The supercharged versions also include a fuel pump control module. For what you get, these kits are reasonably priced: $1,795 to $2,265 for the non-emissions kits and $3,295 for the EC kits. If you are modifying the engines in any way, additional tuning is required, so these setups are best for stock engines. The major downfall of these kits, in my opinion, is no transmission control. A

transmission controller from Sound German Automotive can always be added if you wish to stick with your OEM automatic.

Another option for using factory-style engine management is a harness from Hotwire of Mena, Arkansas. I used one of their harnesses on a 1973 Duster many years ago to swap a 6.1L SRT8 engine and 545RFE

transmission, and it worked well. Hotwire's harnesses are well made and feature factory-style connectors, so everything is plug-and-play with only a minimum of power and ground connections needed.

For this swap, a 2005 Ram PCM was needed. Modern Muscle provided a Diablo tuner with a preloaded custom tune that eliminated

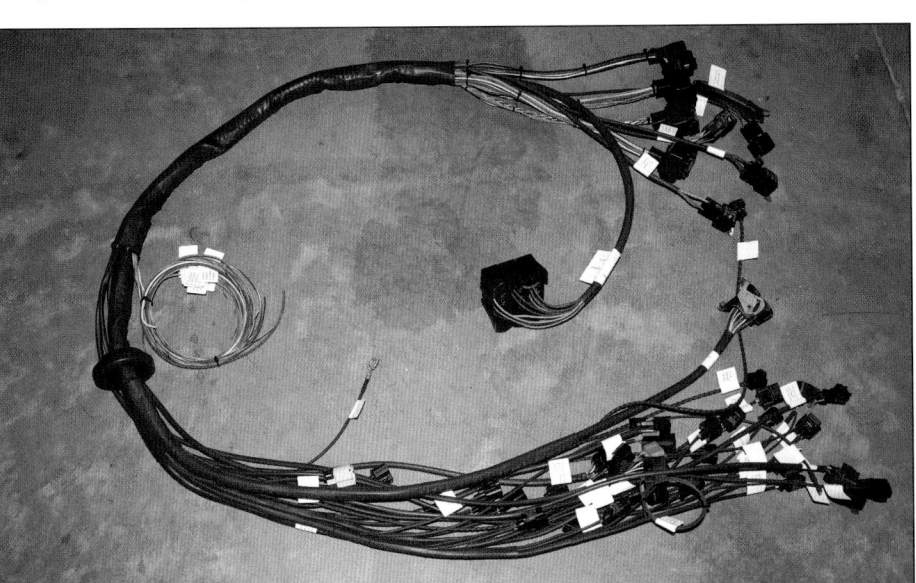

It looks a bit intimidating, but all the connections on the Hotwire harness are clearly labeled. In most cases, it is impossible to plug it in incorrectly. Take your time and route it well to avoid abrasions or high-heat areas.

Some say the factory-style wiring is ugly, but it's all about how it is routed and presented. This Dodge truck is likely using Hotwire or a Mopar controller. The wiring that is visible looks very clean.

This Road Runner uses a factory-type harness (likely Hotwire) and looks very sanitary.

the factory Sentry Key Immobilizer Module (SKIM) security function and allowed for running the engine and transmission. Hotwire currently produces harnesses for 5.7L, 6.1L, and 6.4L engines using the 545RFE truck transmission, NAG1/A580, or manual transmissions. No support is currently offered for the 8HP70/90 or 46RE. This may change by the time this publication reaches your hands, so check the company's website if your combination isn't covered.

Swap Specialties also offers its own harness for 5.7L, 6.1L, and 6.4L Hemis. It offers DBW and VVT control, and control for the 545RFE transmission. NAG1 and 8HP70/90 are supported through Sound German Automotive and can be ordered directly through Swap Specialties. They can provide a tuned PCM or tune yours if you are willing to customize the harness to suit your application.

Multipoint Aftermarket EFI

What if you want to retain all the great engineering built into your Gen III Hemi's EFI system but without the cumbersome tuning and compatibility hassles of the factory controllers? There are many choices in that area.

Holley EFI has by far the most

choices in this market with three different systems (Terminator X/X Max, HP, and Dominator) to fit applications from mild to wild with specific harnesses available for a plug-and-play installation.

FAST has its 2.0 Crate/Transplant Engine Management kits for 5.7L and 6.1L/6.4L applications.

EFI Source, known for its MS3 Gold Box, has systems for both early and late Gen III Hemis and builds harnesses to suit based on customer needs.

BigStuff3 offers its GEN III PRO SEFI System for the 6.1L Hemi.

Recently, Edelbrock entered this market with its Pro-Flo 4+ system for both early and late 5.7Ls, as well as 6.1L and 6.4L engines. While there are other systems that could be configured to work with the Gen III Hemi platform, these are the only ones as of this writing that are specifically tailored for it with premade harnesses.

When selecting an aftermarket

EFI system, many questions need to be asked. Some of the most important ones are the following:

- Will it control my engine of choice?
- Does the ECU support any factory functions you'd like to retain, such as drive-by-wire (DBW) throttle bodies, VVT, SRV, and transmission control?
- What injector types are supported?
- Are premade harnesses available, or do I have to build them?
- Is the system upgradable?
- Is it affordable?
- Is technical support available if I have a problem?
- Is there anyone near me who can tune this system for me?
- Can I use the system with E85 fuel?
- Are power adder applications supported?
- Can I monitor and data log non-engine functions with this system?

These are just a handful of items to consider when selecting the right system.

Holley Terminator X and Terminator X Max

Holley's current entry-level multipoint EFI is the Terminator X/Terminator X Max series. This system is currently available for 2003–2006 and 2007–2022 models. There are many similarities between these two ECUs, but the differences are simple. Terminator X only controls the engine and is set up for cable-driven throttle bodies. Terminator X Max adds either DBW throttle-body control, electronic transmission control, or both.

All Gen III Hemi engines come with DBW throttle bodies, but many swap to a cable-driven unit, typically a GM LS type, so the use of the Max isn't mandatory. Keep in mind that you can use a Max ECU and not use the DBW or transmission control functions. Separate pigtails are provided to run the TPS and IAC of a non-DBW throttle body. This is a good plan, especially if there is a chance that you may upgrade the engine or transmission in the future or use the ECU in another project later on.

Holley doesn't mention it in the website description, but the Max ECU can control the electronic functions of the 46RH transmission, Ford 4R70W, and GM 4L60E and 4L80E. While it isn't likely that anyone is going to install a 4R70W behind a Gen III Hemi, the use of the GM overdrive is fairly common. Hopefully, this unit will be able to control the NAG1, 545RFE, and 8HP70/90 transmissions in future revisions. As of now, there is no aftermarket EFI system that can. When considering the Terminator X/X Max, another important consideration is what type of injectors you plan to run.

This Terminator X Max kit (part number 550-1425) is equipped with DBW throttle-body control and EV6 injector connectors for 2013–newer Gen III Hemis. This system can also control VVT and SRV, and the electronic functions of the 46RE/RH or GM 4L60E and 4L80E. Additional harnesses are sold separately. (Photo Courtesy Holley)

For 46RE transmission control, use part number 558-473. (Photo Courtesy Holley)

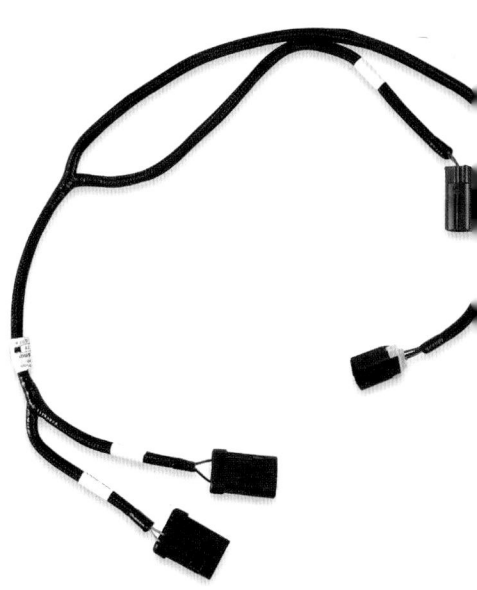

The VVT/SRV harness for the Terminator X Max is part number 558-132. (Photo Courtesy Holley)

Port Fuel Injectors

Modern EFI port fuel injectors fall into two categories: high impedance (also known as saturated injectors) and low impedance (also known as peak-and-hold injectors).

High-impedance injectors are typically used by manufacturers mainly because they are more reliable. This increased reliability comes from the fact they don't require as much amperage to operate. High-impedance injectors are opened with relatively low amperage compared to a low-impedance injector (11.5 amps compared to 56 amps).

The low-impedance injectors have two distinctive signals: the initial high amperage that opens the injector and a lower secondary amperage that is sufficient to keep the injector open. The lower secondary current allows the injector to close more rapidly since there is less time required for the weaker electric field to collapse. This drastic difference in amperage and heat requires a more robust and expensive driver. It is noteworthy that in the early days of EFI, all higher-flow injectors were the low impedance/peak and hold type due to the higher flow and greater reliability that was possible with the limited technology of the time.

Ask most racers or EFI enthusiasts, and you'll generally be told that for the highest performance applications, you need low-impedance injectors because there aren't as many large injectors in the high-impedance range. Look at the listings on Holley's website, and you will find that is no longer the case. Holley offers them in 31 various sizes (note that some are of different types, such as EV1, EV6, or Multec),

ranging from 15 pounds per hour up to a whopping 220 pounds per hour.

Low-impedance injectors start at 65 pounds per hour and go up to 220 pounds per hour with eight sizes in between. The majority of applications they are designed for are high horsepower. So, typically, low-impedance injectors are only in larger sizes. Since only the higher-end ECUs, such as HP and Dominator, can run them, are they better? No. Just as in every other area of our lives, technology has moved forward. The same high flow rates that used to be solely the domain of a low-impedance injector are possible with a high-impedance version. Faster response time and more consistent pulse widths in the lower duty cycles are of great benefit, but the removal of the heat generated by higher amperage is the greatest benefit.

What is the downside of a high-impedance injector? Other than slightly higher cost and less availability in all the sizes needed, there really aren't any. They can be used with any EFI system, generate less heat, are more precise, and don't require the same heavy-duty drivers as a low-impedance injector. Sizing is really the only reason you wouldn't use a high-impedance injector. Many boosted applications, particularly those on E85 or methanol fuel, need large injectors, but they don't necessarily need 205-pound-per-hour injectors. That is enough for 2,600 hp on gasoline!

While other manufacturers offer more high-impedance injector sizes, they aren't as easily obtainable as low-impedance versions. For that reason, low-impedance injectors will be with us for a long time. ■

Most naturally aspirated and mildly boosted engines use high-impedance injectors, just like a factory ECU. If you are running higher boost levels or E85 fuel that requires a much larger injector, then Terminator X/X Max may not be the best choice. Determine your injector needs before choosing your system.

The Terminator X and X Max systems support the VVT and SRV systems found on the newer Gen III Hemis and do not support MDS, which no one really wants anyway. The lifters are problematic even in stock form, and most tuners recommend removing the special lifters, replacing them with standard ones, and plugging the holes in the valley. SRV is found in the 6.4L intakes and allows the ECU to vary the length of the intake runners internally to maximize torque.

This table is pre-populated but can be tweaked if desired. Most tuners report the Holley settings are spot-on for this system. The units feature a built-in 1-bar MAP sensor (others can be configured in the software for simplicity with naturally aspirated engines and have four programmable inputs and outputs. Base maps for common Hemi engine combinations are preloaded and accessible with the 3.5-inch touchscreen or through software downloaded from Holley's website.

Terminator X and X Max are plug-and-play for the Gen III Hemi engines. The kits come with the necessary harnesses and coil drivers needed to drive the "dumb" coils found in these applications to hook up to your stock coils and sensors. A MAP sensor connector is included if you want to run an external MAP sensor, such as for a boosted application. The ECU has a built-in 1-bar MAP that is recommended for non-boosted applications. To use it, route the blue hose at the bottom of the ECU to a good manifold vacuum source using the supplied vacuum-hose adapters.

The software is preconfigured for this sensor, so you only have to change the software if you are using a different one. The system uses a single Bosch LSU 4.9 wideband oxygen sensor that is commonly available. Nitrous, boost controls, and safeties are built in to allow many options, so add-on devices are not needed to handle these functions. This unit is plug-and-play compatible with most Holley EFI accessories, such as shift lights, analog CAN gauges, and Pro Dashes.

Terminator X and X Max come with four inputs and outputs. Three of the outputs are preconfigured and cannot be changed. The electric fans number-1 and -2 and a wide-open throttle (WOT) shutdown for AC are all ground outputs. One of the inputs, AC kick (ground), is also preconfigured, which leaves one available output and three inputs for customization. Is this not enough for your application? It used to be a problem that was only solved by adding a digital dash or upgrading to a Dominator ECU, but now, a CAN input/output module kit is available (part number 554-166) that allows the addition of eight inputs and outputs.

For programming and tuning, the unit comes with a 3.5-inch touchscreen with a calibration wizard to quickly build base tunes to suit your parameters. Using an available cable and splitter from Holley, a laptop can also be used. Free software is available for download on Holley's website.

Built-in diagnostic lights help with troubleshooting any installation or sensor issues. The unit also has a built-in data logger. It does not have a system log to check sensor function.

Holley HP

Holley's HP ECU has been around for many years and is still a great option for any swap. Unlike the Terminator X, it currently is not offered in kit form for the Gen III Hemi engines, although that could change in the future. However, there is interchangeability of harnesses between Holley's Terminator X/X Max, HP, and Dominator, so a complete package to suit nearly any application can be easily configured. The HP is a high-powered, premium-quality ECU with an aluminum case and fully potted electronics for increased durability. It uses different software than the Terminator X/X Max. This software is shared with the Dominator system and is Holley's premier EFI software.

The HP has a lot of similarities to the Terminator X as far as capabilities, but many things are added. It can run up to 16 low- or high-impedance injectors with multiple-stage injector strategies. It can run the Davis Technologies traction control, which can reduce power under wheelspin conditions via timing, nitrous percentage, or boost.

The HP is also capable of directly driving smart coils and can use either NTK or Bosch LSU4 wideband oxygen sensors. These sensors are hand-calibrated for Holley EFI systems, so don't use generic replacements because they are not the same. There is an option for a volumetric efficiency (VE)-based fueling strategy in addition to speed density and

The Holley HP ECU (part number 554-113) is great for installations that are fairly simple and don't need DBW, VVT, SRV, or electronic transmission control. It does use the more powerful HEFI software, so it is still very capable. (Photo Courtesy Holley)

Alpha-N. A four-stage progressive nitrous controller and integrated water/methanol injection control eliminate the need for add-on devices.

Like the Terminator X, the HP has four inputs and four outputs, but they are all user-configurable. If that isn't enough for your setup, but a Dominator isn't in the budget or is overkill for what you are trying to do, you may want to look closely at the Holley CAN input/output module kit. HP does have a system log capability, which can be handy when diagnosing sensor issues.

Since it is an older ECU, there are two things you won't find in an HP: it cannot control an electronic transmission and it does not support DBW throttle bodies.

Holley Dominator

Holley's Dominator has been around for several years, but its potential has not yet been fully realized. This ECU can be found anywhere from hot street cars to Pro Mods and is very adaptable to about any situation. It uses the same software and harnesses as the HP (all Holley harnesses are interchangeable between Terminator X/X Max, HP, and Dominator), so if you are upgrading from an HP no changes are needed other than for the additional features and I/Os.

Like the HP, it is a fully potted unit in a sturdy aluminum case for extra durability and uses sealed automotive and marine-grade connectors. The Dominator accommodates electronic transmission control and a variety of DBW throttle bodies (can control two throttle bodies if desired) and can utilize dual wideband oxygen sensors, either NTK or Bosch LSU4. It will work on 4- through 10-cylinder engines and has 12-channel DIS outputs to directly drive smart coils or Holley DIS coils.

To run the Gen III Hemi's two-wire coils, you'll need the eight-channel coil driver kit (part number 554-122). Dominator is equipped with 12 sequentially driven 8:2 peak-and-hold injector drivers that can handle up to 24 low- or high-impedance injectors with a variety of injector strategies. Your tuner can choose from speed density, Alpha-N, Alpha-N combination, or VE fueling strategies. Fuel and spark control can be done on an individual cylinder basis. The system has a 1-to-7 bar MAP-sensor capability. The ECU does have a self-tuning function, but tuning is recommended for best performance.

EFI Inputs and Outputs

As a technical sales team lead for Holley, I often encounter customers who could meet most of their EFI needs with Terminator X/X Max or HP except for one issue: the number of available inputs and outputs.

This is especially true with Terminator X/X Max. Although it has the same number of inputs and outputs as HP, many are preconfigured and may not be set up for the features the customer wishes to add. If they plan to run one of Holley's digital-dash options, this may not be a problem since they add up to 13 user-configurable inputs and 4 ground-switched outputs. But what if you want to go a different route, either for cost or personal preference? Some people still prefer a conventional analog gauge. Until recently, their only choice was to jump up to the Dominator ECU at a much higher cost.

Fortunately, Holley came up with a solution to this dilemma: the EFI CAN input/output module kit, part number 554-165. This module adds eight inputs and eight ground/PWM outputs to any of the Holley ECUs. Monitoring the data streams and controlling the additional functions can be done through the ECU.

The inputs can be individually configured as switched high (H) for 12V switched inputs; switched low (G) for ground switched inputs; 5V analog (5) for any transducers or sensors with a 0–5 volt input; 20 analog (2) when reading a signal from 0–20 volts; thermistor (T) for 2-wire temperature sensors; or frequency (F) used for Hall-effect (three-wire) speed sensors. The outputs can be configured as switched low (G) or switched low PWM (P).

For Terminator X and X Max, you'll need V2 software Build

If you need additional inputs and outputs over what the Terminator X/X Max or HP offer, add the CAN input/output module for eight inputs and outputs each. It is sold under part number 554-165

51 or higher. HP and Dominator require the V6 software.

Wiring the unit is fairly simple with a 34-pin I/O module connector that plugs into the unit. The 4-pin CAN connector plugs directly into the main harness, and the 3.5-inch screen (if present) is plugged into the I/O module CAN wiring. The bundled four-wire ground is connected to the negative battery terminal (preferred) or a good chassis ground. Wiring the I/Os themselves and setting them up in the software is very straightforward, just as with setting up the original ones in the ECU. Holley includes all the connectors, pins, and wiring needed for the swap.

This unit can be added to any of the Holley EFI systems, including the Dominator, but it is highly unlikely that many will need the extra I/Os with a Dominator ECU. ■

The Dominator has dedicated fuel- and oil-pressure inputs and a wide array of user-configurable inputs and outputs. How wide? There are 13 multi-inputs that can be configured for 0 to 5V sensors, 0 to 20V sensors, thermistor (temp) inputs, or high- and low-voltage inputs. There are 30 0 to 5V sensor inputs, 4-speed inputs that can be configured as digital (square wave) or inductive inputs, 20 12V PWM outputs that can be configured as PWM or switched ground outputs, and 16 ground PWM inputs that can be configured as PWM or switched ground outputs. These are all programmed using a pin-mapping strategy that allows inputs and outputs to be pinned as needed by the user rather than wasted on unneeded options by designating them for certain functions. The user programmable caution and warning outputs for all sensors are a nice touch.

The internal data logger had 4GB of memory, and you can view real-time data. There is a fully configurable gauge panel that is built in and can be viewed on a laptop screen if you don't have a digital dash. Do you have a Racepak? There is a module available to cleanly integrate it into the system.

If you are running nitrous, you can run wet or dry with up to eight stages without any additional electronics. This saves space, money, and wiring complexity. The progressive control can be based on time, RPM, or boost (high-current solenoid driver number 554-111 is required).

Are you running turbos? The boost controller is built in and can control boost based on time, gear, speed, and manual inputs. The boost builder feature can assist in building boost on the starting line and can be used as an anti-lag function. Water/methanol control is built in as well.

Because of the large number of outputs, just about anything in your street or race car can be controlled through the ECU. Transmission brakes, scramble buttons, wastegate or nitrous solenoids, interior and exterior lighting, and almost anything that can be controlled by a switch can be run through the Dominator. It is limited only by your imagination. This can greatly simplify your electrical system and eliminate the clutter under your dash.

FAST XFI 2.0

FAST offers its XFI 2.0 for the 5.7L, 6.1L, and 6.4L engines. The XFI system comes with the XFI 2.0 ECU, XIM ignition controller, NTK wideband oxygen sensor, all harnesses that are needed, air temperature sensor, Big Mouth 92-mm cable-driven throttle body, and chrome XFI emblem. Part number 301012 is listed for 5.7L applications, and part number 301013 is listed for 6.1L and 6.4L applications. These systems do not support DBW throttle bodies, transmission control, MDS, VVT, or SRV, so that needs to be considered when planning your swap. The ECU and ignition controller are both cased in the traditional FAST red anodized aluminum for durability and corrosion resistance.

FAST's system boasts its "advanced forced induction, power adder, and race controls," which includes two programmable sequential rev limiters for staging or boost building and has six options for activation, four priority assignments, and a user-selectable sequential or random mode rev limiter. It features a time-based boost controller, selectable fixed VE and/or fixed timing for boost building and staging, and several nitrous options for wet or dry systems. There are separate tables for solenoid control and fuel control for dry nitrous tuning, adjustable solenoid pulse frequency, a choice of fixed or standard air/fuel tables for correction, and a fuel delay for correcting rich spikes on activation.

The self-learning auto-tuning VE table allows quick and easy fuel mapping, but this feature can be turned off for manual tuning. The self-learning mode can be used to populate a base tune and then deactivated for fine tuning or custom control by the user.

The C-Com XFI software, like most other EFI software, is Windows-based and can be flashed with software updates via email or the FAST website. The Qwik Tune technology allows ECU programming without a laptop. Up to four different maps can be programmed and selected via an in-car switch. The system also has on-board diagnostics, EZ test indicator lights, 5-bar MAP sensing, and controls for power adders and torque convertors.

An upgrade to the XFI 2.0 ECU is available, which adds internal data logging, intelligent traction control, and an injector driver upgrade that allows the operation of up to 16 injectors.

EFI Source MegaSquirt III Gold Box

The MS3 Gold Box ECU is available with a custom-built harness for both 2006–2008 and 2009–up Gen III Hemis. Interestingly, these harnesses can be built to accommodate Mopar or GM throttle bodies (DBW or cable) and retain functions like VVT and SRV that most people with newer engines, especially crate engines, want to keep. Harnesses that use GM 4L60E or 4L80E transmissions are available

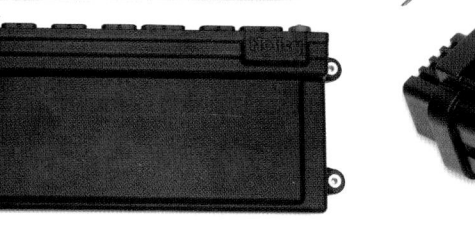

Holley's Dominator is its most capable ECU, although it currently doesn't support VVT or SRV. This is due to it being a more race-oriented system. Hopefully, these features will be added along with support for Mopar transmissions, such as the NAG1 and 8HP70/90. (Photo Courtesy Holley)

but require an additional MicroSquirt transmission control unit. No other transmissions are covered at this time.

The Gold Box ECU is very versatile and is designed to be easily used on a variety of engines. It features USB, RS232, and CAN communication and can be tuned using VE, speed density, Alpha-N, or MAF using Tuner Studio tuning software. It also has a self-tuning feature. Ten high-impedance injector drivers are provided, but no low-impedance injectors are available. It has an onboard SD card for data logging and is Racepak compatible.

It supports more than 50 OEM and aftermarket ignition systems, including the Gen III Hemi coils, without any additional hardware needed. Fans, fuel pumps, transmission brakes, boost, alternator, and water/methanol outputs are preconfigured with additional inputs provided (three general purpose, one analog, four VR inputs). The system

also has two wideband sensor inputs. Boost control, a three-step rev limiter, and traction control are built in.

BigStuff3

BigStuff3 is the product of John Meaney, one of the founding fathers of aftermarket EFI. You may not know his name, but his contributions to this area are substantial. Meaney used the knowledge he gained while earning degrees in math, physics, and mechanical engineering, and a stint working at Bosch, to develop his own digital EFI system.

After partnering with Accel, now a division of Holley, Meaney brought the Accel/DFI system to market. Accel/DFI was the only serious player in the domestic EFI aftermarket during the early 1990s. Meaney left in 1996 and went to work for Fel-Pro, where he developed the SEFI8LO EFI system, which is now known as FAST. He also worked for Holley and developed the Commander 950 system. He founded BigStuff3 in 2003.

BigStuff3 offers its Gen III Pro SEFI system for the 6.1L Hemi. Interestingly, no other applications are listed, although there is no reason it couldn't be used with an early 5.7L as long as MDS was deleted. It comes

with a PCM, main wiring harness, injector harness, wideband oxygen sensor, and a 6-foot communications cable. This system does not accommodate DBW control or the VVT and SRV found on later engines. The system has sequential control for eight cylinders and has peak-and-hold drivers for low-impedance injectors. Injector phasing and individual cylinder fuel and spark compensation are standard. The system will drive the dumb coils found in Gen III Hemis. It uses a speed-density algorithm for tuning with the Windows-based calibration software.

The GEN III Pro is compatible with 1- to 5-bar MAP sensors and uses a GM idle air control (IAC) sensor. It controls fuel pumps in a staged configuration based on TPS input. The system has individual cylinder fuel and spark compensation, a built-in 2-step rev limiter, a turbo starting-line timing curve, and many optional features, including 4-stage dry nitrous activation, an integrated CO_2 boost controller, engine torque management, Racepak interface, Flex Fuel compatibility, sequential control of up to 24 injectors, barometric pressure compensation, transmission control for the GM 4L60E/80E, and external data logging.

Edelbrock Pro-Flo 4+

Edelbrock has offered EFI systems for several years and recently entered the Gen III Hemi market with its Pro-Flo 4+ system. This system offers DBW control, VCT, and SRV runner control preset at 4,800 rpm (non-adjustable). The system is available for 2013-and-newer 5.7L, 6.1L, and 6.4L engines and is billed as self-tuning with no laptop tuning or dyno sessions needed.

Edelbrock's E-Tuner software can be used with the supplied Android-based tablet or a smartphone. A speed-density fueling strategy is used with MAP and IAT sensors included. A nonadjustable alternator control is built-in and supplies 13.8 volts. Fan control, fuel pump control, and knock sensor harnesses are available as extra-cost add-ons. Factory high-impedance injectors, coils, the throttle body, and pedal must be used with this system.

The Key to a Successful Boosted Build

For the Gremlin project, the original plan had been to use a carburetor-style OCP dual-plane intake with an MSD Atomic TBI and MSD 6013 6-Hemi controller. This would have worked well for the intended usage of high-school transportation, but as the project grew into something more, I knew it wasn't going to be adequate for our purposes.

We needed aftermarket multi-port EFI, especially because there were going to be turbos in our future, and I wanted complete flexibility in the build. Today, there are a few TBI-type units that are designed for boost, such as the Super Sniper, but at the time, that wasn't the case. Even today, my choice would be the same.

The key to a successful boosted build, beyond selecting the correct parts, is data. I knew most systems would limit me in that respect. I wanted the ability to add sensors for normal engine functions, like oil and fuel pressure, but also keep tabs on oil temperature for the engine, transmission, and differentials. Exhaust gas temperatures (EGTs) will also be monitored, as well as coolant temperature and pressure for the air-to-water intercooler, boost and dome pressure, and tank pressure for the onboard CO_2 system.

Beyond that, traction control (driveshaft speed sensors), shock travel sensors, the ability to power multiple pumps (two fuel, one AAW coolant, and two for differential and transmission coolers), a fire suppression system, and a dozen other functions will be needed. I am a fanatic when it comes to uncluttered vehicle wiring, so I really wanted to be able to do all of this with a minimum of add-on boxes and modules.

I normally like to overbuild a vehicle so that I don't have to go back and fix things, such as stronger differentials and better clutches, later. This also applies to electronics. I want to do this once and be able to accommodate any future changes easily as well as drastic changes in horsepower level.

For this reason, the ability to manage multiple injector stages with high or low impedance was critical. The ease of changing the setup down the road to accommodate different engines was also a factor. This car belongs to my son, and while it is being built with a Gen III Hemi in mind, I want to make any future powertrain changes as simple as possible. The current engine is a stock bottom end 5.7L Hemi, and the only internal changes are opened ring gaps, a mild Comp Cam with beehive springs, and a valve job with staked valve seats. This is being treated basically as a running mock-up. A much more durable, all-forged version with better cylinder heads and possibly a Dart block are in the plans once we have worked out the bugs.

To this end, I chose the Holley Dominator. Yes, I work in Holley's tech department, so no surprise, right? This decision was made several years ago—long before I worked for Holley. I chose to work for Holley because I believe in their parts and their system approach to a build. In any event, the Dominator is the only ECU discussed that will handle every foreseen and unforeseen task that we will ask of it.

For the early Gen III Hemi, I chose the following components:

Part	Part Number
Dominator ECU	554-114
Main Engine Harness	558-115
Main Power Harness	558-308
Coil Harness	558-311
Coil Driver Modules	554-122
EV1 Injector Harness	558-211
J2A Auxiliary Harness	558-401
J2B Auxiliary Harness	558-402
J3 Auxiliary Harness	558-403
J4 Auxiliary Harness	558-404
NTK Wideband Oxygen Sensors	554-100 (2)
3-Bar MAP Sensor	554-107
100-psi Pressure Transducer	554-102 (3)

The main harness has provisions for a GM LS-style TPS and the IAC. If DBW is needed, another harness has to be added. In our case, we are using Holley's Hi-Ram intake and a GM pattern throttle body so no re-pinning of sensors will be necessary. Note that while the Dominator ECU can control smart coils, it requires the coil driver modules to operate the Gen III Hemi's coils. These modules simply plug into the coil harness. Full installation and setup of the Dominator are covered in a later chapter.

ENGINE AND TRANSMISSION MOUNTING

Since the Gen III Hemi engine mounts are different than those on the earlier Mopar engines, you need to change the mounts to accommodate your swap. In some cases, such as swaps that retain the original transmission, no transmission mounting changes are needed, but those swaps are in the minority. In most cases, both will need to be changed. In some, they'll need to be fabricated.

Engine Mounts

In the early days of the swap, only the most popular vehicles had bolt-in engine mounts available to accommodate the Gen III Hemi. The A-Body, B-Body, and E-Body Mopars received most of the attention. Since then, bolt-in units have become available for the C-Body, M-Body, and J-Body Mopar passenger cars, as well as for the popular Dodge Dakota and D100 trucks and the Jeep YJ and TJ.

For the sake of clarity, I will concentrate on the mounts from TTI, Schumacher Creative Services, Bouchillon Performance, and Hooker Blackheart. The TTI mounts closely resemble stock mounts on these cars and carry over the biscuit or spool

This is a TTI spool-type mount for an A-Body application on the passenger's side. This type of mount requires oil filter relocation.

No modifications are required for the driver-side spool mount.

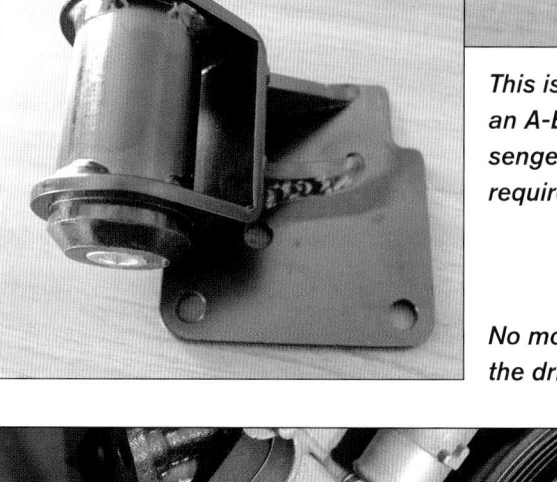

This 5.7L engine was set up for an E-Body application. The oil filter doesn't have to be relocated, but a 45-degree mount like this Ram/Dakota mount is needed for clearance. The stock straight style found on passenger-car engines doesn't work.

designs as applicable. Schumacher uses a spool type on all of its mounts. Bouchillon resells TTI mounts, as do many of the Mopar parts vendors, but it does have its own full-size Dodge truck mounts and lists more applications for the TTI mounts than TTI itself does in some cases, which is why they are included. Hooker's mounts for A-Body and E-Body engines have not yet been released, but the mounts for 1966–1972 B-Body cars use a biscuit-type mount. Dakota mounts are of a spool-type design. The D100 uses an original-style biscuit mount, and the Jeeps use a GM-derived clamshell-type mount.

With any of these mounts listed, the engine installation is a straight bolt-in, which means that no drilling, welding, cutting, or other modification is required. This allows the novice to correctly mount the engine without any guesswork or fabrications skills.

Transmission Mounts

There's something you will notice regarding bolt-in aftermarket engine mounts for the Gen III Hemi. Other

TTI Engine Mounts

Part Number	Type
57MMA	1967–1972 A-Body
57SMA73	1973–1976 A-Body
57SMB625	1962–1965 B-Body
57MMBE	1966–1972 B-Body, 1970–1974 E-Body
61MMBE1	1966–1972 B-Body, 1970–1974 E-Body with stock or Borgeson PS
57SMB73	1973–1974 B-Body

Schumacher Engine Mounts

Part Number	Type
A67H8	1967–1972 A-Body
A67H6	1967–1972 A-Body (6-cylinder K-member)
BC57H	1966–1972 B-Body, 1966–1973 C-Body, 1970–1974 E-Body
BC57HAC	1966–1972 B-Body, 1966–1973 C-Body, 1970–1974 E-Body (also accommodates low-mount air-conditioner)
A73H8	1973–Up A-Body, B-Body, C-Body, F-Body, M-Body, J-Body
97DAKH	1997–2004 Dakota

Bouchillon Engine Mounts

Part Number	Type
GENIIIMMBE	1966–1972 B-Body, 1970–1974 E-Body, 1967–1972 C-Body
61MMBE1	1966–1972 B-Body, 1970–1974 E-Body with stock or Borgeson PS
57MMA	1967–1972 A-Body
57SMA73	1973–1976 A-Body
57SMB73	1973–1974 B-Body
9011	1972–1993 Dodge full-size truck and Ramcharger (V-8 or Slant 6)

If you're using TTI, Schumacher, or Bouchillon mounts, TTI headers are recommended. They have part numbers to fit most swaps. However, be aware that some designs require a specific starter location. The TTI headers for the Duster are made for a driver-side starter, which the 545RFE has.

Hooker Blackheart Engine Mounts

Part Number	Type
VK090030	1966–1970 B-Body; includes transmission crossmember and engine mounts; requires BHS536 adapter for 8HP70, BHS535 for NAG1, BHS534 for A727
VK090242	1970–1974 E-Body; includes transmission crossmember and engine mounts; requires BHS568 adapter for A727, BH569 for NAG1, BHS for 8HP70, BHS591 for 8HP90, BHS592 for Tremec TKX and TKO
VK090245	1973–1976 A-Body; includes transmission crossmember and engine mounts; requires BHS573 for A7 or TKX, BHS574 for NAG1; TKX requires BHS588 transmission cr member/torsion bar support, N/ requires BHS578 crossmember/t sion bar support
VK090029	1972–1993 Dodge D100 2WD; includes transmission crossmem and engine mounts
VK090168	1987–1996 Dodge Dakota 2WD includes transmission crossmemb and engine mounts
VK090169	1997–2004 Dakota 2WD; includ transmission crossmember and engine mounts; requires BHS52 adapter for 8HP70; BHS527 for NAG1; BHS528 for TR6060; BHS529 for 545RFE, 46RH, 46RE BHS530 for A727
VK090170	1997–2006 Wrangler TJ; include transmission mount and engine mounts (uses original crossmember); includes adapter for 545RF and transfer case
VK090235	1987–1995 Jeep Wrangler YJ; includes transmission mount and engine mounts (uses original crossmember); includes adapter 545RFE and transfer case
VK090255	1973–1987 Chevrolet/GMC C10 2WD; includes trans crossmember and engine mounts; require BHS526 for 8HP70 passenger-c transmission; BHS585 for 8HP7 8HP90, 9HP75; BHS527 for NA BHS528 for TR6060; BHS529 fo 545RFE, 46RH, 46RE; BHS530 f A727; BHS563 for Ford TKX wit RM-8076 bellhousing

If the engine came from an LX-series car (a Charger, Challenger, Magnum, or 300C), change the pan and pickup. Swap pans for mid and rear sumps are available from Milodon, Holley, and Stef's.

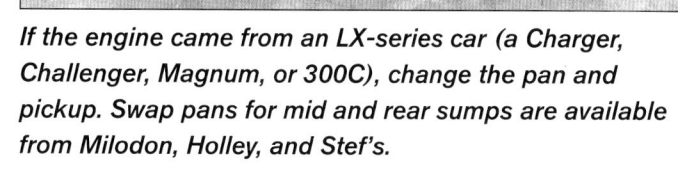

Older Mopar passenger-car swaps require a mid-sump oil pan, such as part number 302-61 from Holley. This one is for VVT engines. A non-VVT version is available under part number 302-60. (Photo Courtesy Holley)

Truck engines use a rear-sump pan. This one is an OEM piece sold by Holley. The part number is 4893207AA. (Photo Courtesy Holley)

than Hooker, no one offers a transmission crossmember to go with the engine mounts. If you use a factory transmission (as is common in many of the TorqueFlite applications

B&M offers the only aftermarket shifter for the NAG1: the Magnum Grip Pro Stick. It is part number 81188. (Photo Courtesy Holley)

or the later-model Dakotas and Jeeps), the factory transmission crossmember can likely be retained. Some modification may be necessary if the engine isn't in the stock location.

What should you do if you are changing to a different transmission? If it is an aftermarket manual transmission, companies such as Silver Sport Transmission offer their own crossmembers and everything else needed to swap the popular Tremec transmissions. They also have crossmembers for the popular

A41 automatic transmissions (essentially a GM 4L60/65E). If you have something else, you can use a universal crossmember, which works best if you are dealing with a full-frame vehicle or one with subframe connectors. You can also use a modified OEM piece or fabricate a new one. If you use anything other than a stock transmission, you'll likely have to make some modifications to the transmission tunnel to get it in, but this is one more fabrication step to consider.

The first major consideration when researching which mounts to buy is the availability of aftermarket headers. Very few stock exhaust manifolds will work with the typical swap, so tubular headers are often recommended, if not required.

For the TTI, Schumacher, and Bouchillon mounts, TTI headers are recommended. While the mounts are not identical between TTI/Bouchillon and Schumacher, they are very similar in fitment. Hooker, being an exhaust company first and foremost, has its own line of headers specifically designed to work with its mounts. While some other headers may fit with another manufacturer's mounts, when the manufacturer produces its own header or has a recommended header isn't wise and can result in fitment problems. In any case, consult the manufacturer of your chosen engine mounts for a header recommendation. Most are listed on their websites.

1973 Duster 6.1L Hemi Swap

The 1973 Duster pictured in this chapter is a great example of a typical swap candidate. The Duster was in decent shape but tired. The engine had little power and leaked oil, and the 904 transmission had seen better days. The suspension was worn out, so the car wasn't much fun to drive. My customer originally planned to swap in a later 360 Magnum V-8 from a Dodge truck, which would have been fairly simple mechanically, but he also wanted the reliability of EFI. The Magnum's EFI system isn't well supported in the aftermarket, so we discussed a Gen III Hemi swap.

My customer obtained a low-mileage takeout assembly from an 300C SRT8, which has the 6.1L version of the Hemi, and an NAG1 automatic overdrive transmission. I quickly drained his original engine and transmission of fluids, removed the radiator to prevent any damage, and pulled the old 318 and Torque-Flite from the top with a conventional engine hoist. If I planned to use an aftermarket replacement suspension system, I would have dropped the whole assembly out from the top on a lift, but since I needed to check clearances on several items, I wanted to leave the K-member in place for the time being.

Keep in mind that while this particular swap covers an A-Body, the process is similar to what is done with any torsion-bar-equipped Mopar passenger car. The main difference is that the A-Body allows far less room to work than most, and therefore more clearance issues have to be addressed. The B-Body, C-Body, and E-Body cars have much more room and fewer clearance issues.

Due to the complexity and cost of keeping the NAG1 transmission, which includes a slip-style driveshaft, wheel speed sensors, and other electronic headaches, I chose to go with a 545RFE from a 2005 Dodge Ram. The 545RFE is a very large transmission, but it didn't require a lot of supporting hardware (like the NAG1), and it had a conventional slip yoke. It was also fairly simple to adapt to the existing floor shifter in the car. The NAG1 required keeping the original SRT8 shifter, which I did not have, and frankly it would look goofy in an otherwise-stock interior.

Regardless of mounts used, putting a Gen III Hemi into a Mopar passenger car of this vintage requires a mid-sump oil pan. The front-sump-style LX body pan will not work, and there are no factory pans that accommodate this swap. However, aftermarket pans are now available from Milodon, Holley, and Weiand. At the time of this swap, only the Milodon was available, and it worked out well. Made of gold iridited sheet metal, the Milodon pan has a race car appearance and is easily installed with factory hardware. They come with their own windage tray, and a special pickup is required. You will also need their braided stainless dipstick for this pan. The stock dipstick will not work.

For mounts, I chose TTI, since it offered long-tube headers that worked with the swap. The factory SRT8 manifolds flow well but won't fit. I ordered the non-coated version, due to time constraints (they didn't have coated ones in stock) and because I anticipated having to modify the headers and wanted to get everything worked out fitment wise before having them coated. Gen III Hemis are pretty tight in an A-Body, and I expected that some minor dimpling or other modifications may be necessary. Please note this application required a driver-side starter due to the transmission choice, and the headers required this anyway. I used a Mopar Performance mini starter, which is the same as on the Dodge Dakota.

With the engine mounts installed, the first obstacle was apparent. The stock oil filter location won't work with an A-Body. I used a block-off plate from Modern Muscle and an oil filter relocation kit. Once that was done, the mounts bolted right up, much like a stock engine mount would. The next obstacle, and one I anticipated, was the steering box. Mopar power-steering boxes are huge, and no amount of header banging was going to work. I considered a Borgeson power-steering box since it is more compact, but the customer chose to use a rebuilt manual box instead. This required some changes to the stock power steering-style column and a different coupler, but once that was completed, the header fit.

At this point, I hadn't even bolted up the transmission since I knew considerable cutting was in order. After unloading the torsion bars to take tension off the crossmember (and it was coming out anyway), I took careful measurements off of the engine position and transmission and got to work. The seats, carpet, firewall insulation, and heater box were all removed for this operation, and all the glass was covered to prevent any damage from flying sparks. The tunnel area and the top portion of the torsion bar crossmember had to be removed. Since I kept the stock-style suspension, all of this had to be replaced and made as stiff or stiffer than before. Once the transmission was bolted up, some trimming was done, and the transmission was jacked up and centered on the engine.

Once I ensured the driveline was parallel to prevent unwanted vibration, a new transmission crossmember was made from a leftover part from a previous build. It was attached to the weld-in subframe connectors I previously installed. With that completed, I then bent a piece of steel tubing to arc around the top of the transmission and connected the remaining stubs of the torsion bar crossmember channels. This was securely welded in place and boxed back in, and new sheet metal was formed to replace the old tunnel.

Once the welding was completed, all seams were seam-sealed to prevent corrosion and the entry of any exhaust fumes into the passenger compartment. Frankly, the tunnel modifications were the most difficult part of the whole process and is something that needs to be weighed when choosing the transmission for a torsion-bar-equipped vehicle. There are aftermarket tunnel replacements available now from companies like US Car Tool, but welding is still required, and some fabrication skills are necessary to achieve a successful installation.

With the engine and transmission bolted up and the headers in place, I put the vehicle back on the ground and checked the steering. There was some rubbing of the tie rods on the headers, even with all the correct parts being used for the manual conversion, so the headers were carefully massaged for clearance. I don't really

1973 Duster 6.1L Hemi Swap

The stock 318 looked nice, but it was tired.

The first order of business is to drain the radiator and remove it to avoid damage to the core from the engine removal.

The carburetor was removed, and a lift plate was installed to pull the engine. This plate is a Happy Hooker from TPIS. It was originally intended for pulling Gen II Chevrolet LT1 engines, but I have redrilled it for numerous patterns over the years.

The engine and transmission were pulled as a unit because I didn't plan to use either.

The 6.1L engine came with an NAG1 transmission. I planned to use it at the time, but I wanted to remove it for now because the amount of cutting needed to accommodate it in the tunnel was unknown. The convertor was also removed at this time.

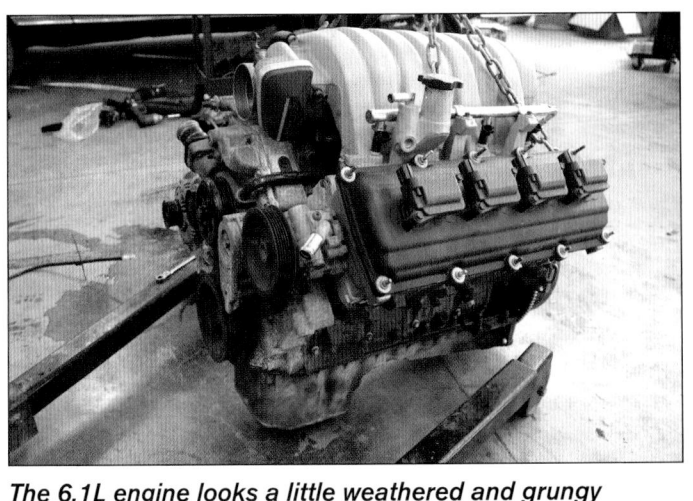

The 6.1L engine looks a little weathered and grungy despite the low miles. This was corrected before installation. The LX-style oil pan has to go.

The Duster has spool-type mounts. The TTI mounts bolt up just like stock mounts with no modifications to the K-member required.

The mounts for an A-Body do not clear the stock oil-filter housing, so this needs to be removed and the filter relocated.

The driver-side TTI mount fits with no issues. Note the 6.1L casting in the side of the block.

The clearance issue with the stock oil filter location is obvious. This isn't TTI's fault. Rather, it's a function of making the stock mounting system work with an engine that was never intended for the chassis.

This filter relocation kit from Modern Muscle/MMX is typical of aftermarket offerings. The block-off plate installs with the provided bolts, and the two brass fittings are screwed into the 3/8-inch NPT ports above the oil-filter area. The silver fittings adapt them to AN -6. The blue push-lock-style fittings and hose can be used to relocate the oil filter to a suitable place.

The old LX-style pan was replaced with a mid-sump Milodon pan, such as this on a 5.7L engine. The pickup, windage tray, and dipstick were also changed in favor of Milodon pieces. The mount shown is an older Holley mount for a B-Body or E-Body application.

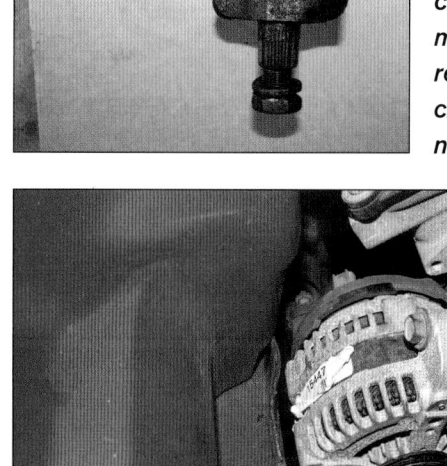

Something to consider with A-Body swaps is that the bulky power-steering box has to go. A Borgeson power box fits with headers, but the customer in this situation chose to use a rebuilt manual box. This required a few minor changes to the original steering column.

With the engine mocked up, a few problem areas are apparent. The first to address is the steering box. Master cylinder clearance is tight, but it is okay with the manual discs.

Alternator clearance was tight to the frame rail, as I had suspected. The pinch weld wasn't bent for clearance; it was already like that.

The air-conditioning compressor has been removed because it won't be used in this non-air-conditioning car anyway. The power-steering pump will be removed and replaced with a "delete" pulley because I am using a manual box. There is plenty of room for the radiator and fan package.

The engine barely clears the stock heater motor. Removing the valve cover requires loosening and moving back the whole heater assembly at the very least.

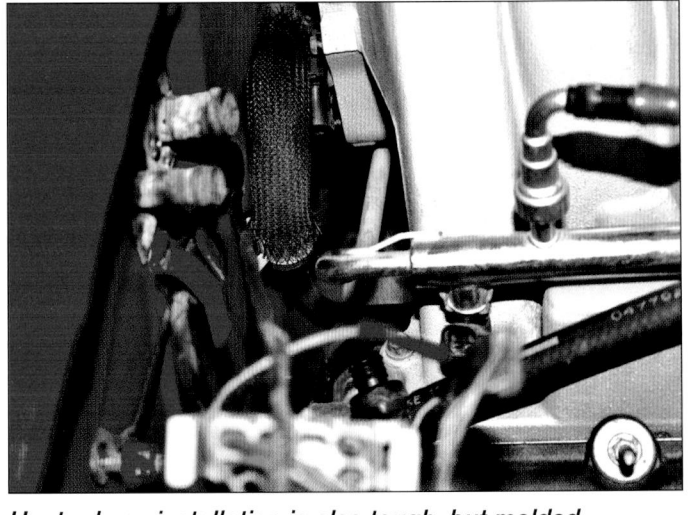

Heater hose installation is also tough, but molded 90-degree ends work well here.

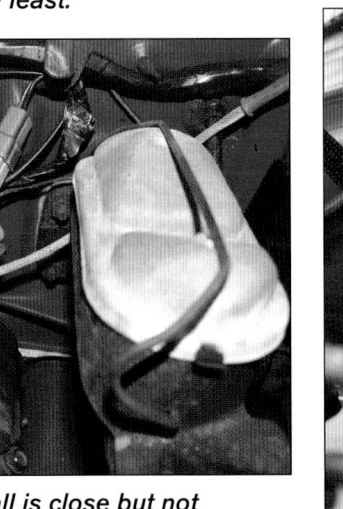

The wiring bulkhead on the firewall is close but not touching.

Wiper motor clearance looked like it might be an issue, but we were lucky here.

The new manual box is much less bulky than the power box, but clearance is still tight.

The Milodon pan clears with no issues.

Based on a few measurements, some preliminary cuts were made in the tunnel area. I planned to use the NAG1, but that idea was abandoned for complexity and cost reasons.

The headers are mocked up and clear everything well considering the limited space.

You can see from this angle that the top portion of the tunnel support had to be removed. The remnants of it are still visible to the left of the tailshaft.

The rear main seal was replaced for good insurance while I could get to it easily.

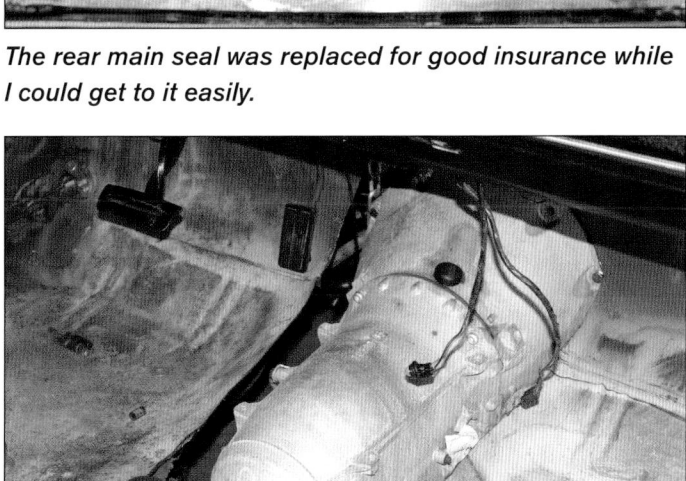

The NAG1 fits well with the top section cut off of the tunnel. The plan at the time was to split the tunnel, widen it slightly, and reinstall the transmission.

Keep in mind this swap was done at a time that very few NAG1 swaps had been accomplished, so the cost and complexity was a bit of an unknown. For those reasons, it was suggested we use a 545 RFE transmission from a 2005 Ram. This transmission is much larger than the NAG1.

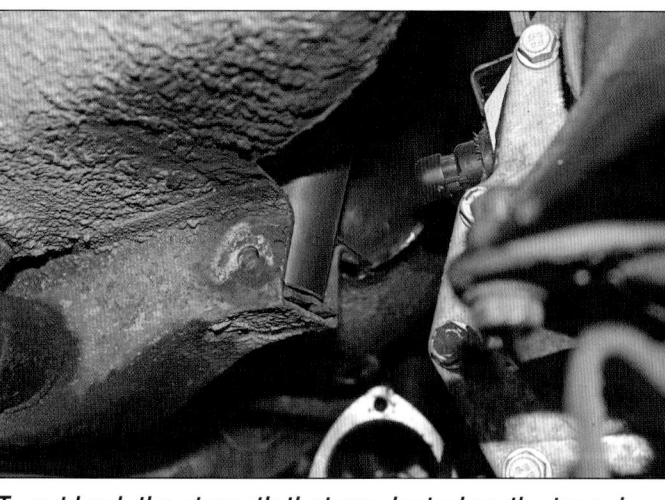

To put back the strength that was lost when the tunnel support that ties the torsion bar crossmember pieces together was removed, a piece of round tube was bent to fit and welded in place.

The torsion bar is very close to the area that was cut out. Putting things back together stronger than before is a necessity due to the increased size and weight of the transmission. There was no aftermarket solution at the time.

Regarding the torsion bars, the clearance was tight with the TTI headers, but they didn't touch.

To further strengthen the torsion-bar crossmember and stiffen the car overall, subframe connectors were fabricated and welded in place.

With the bottom side welded and a new crossmember for the transmission fabricated (they can now be purchased from Holley), it was time to weld the tunnel back into place. I chose to use new metal for this.

The old K-member was pretty crusty, and the wear items were all shot, so the entire assembly was removed after the initial mockup.

Some repairs were needed to the K-member itself before it was powder coated.

The engine cleaned up pretty well and was treated to some spray-can detailing with Hemi Orange for the block, cast aluminum for the aluminum parts, and semigloss black for the pullies. The oil filter relocation kit has been installed.

Take notes for yourself throughout project.

Oil filter relocation fittings are installed. This is what came with the kit, but a pair of -6 AN to 3/8-inch NPT adapters look cleaner.

Assemble the K-member before installing it from the bottom. If you don't have a lift, install the engine from the top after installing the K-member.

The 545RFE is a really large transmission, which makes it less attractive for swapping applications. It worked well for these specifications.

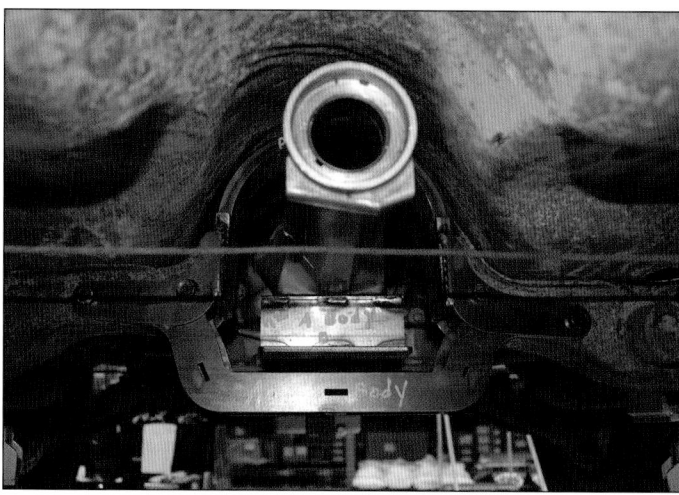

This adapter plate allows an 8HP70 transmission to bolt up to a Holley crossmember. (Photo Courtesy Holley)

Only Holley makes transmission crossmembers for these swaps. Most use the same basic crossmember with add-on adapters that are available for various transmissions to make future changes easier. (Photo Courtesy Holley)

This Mopar B-Body has a 4L80E transmission installed with a cleanly executed transmission crossmember. This was custom built by RMR Dreamcars.

The crossmember of this 1970 'Cuda was custom built for the Viper-spec T56. The engine is also from the Viper. The extreme length of the engine, combined with engine set-back, required the crossmember to attach to the subframe connectors.

Hurst offers a tunnel-patch kit for a variety of Mopar body-styles and transmissions to make their installation a little easier. (Photo Courtesy Holley)

Hooker Blackheart's transmission crossmember hoops put needed strength back into the tunnel once the original support is cut for transmission clearance. (Photo Courtesy Holley)

fault TTI for this clearance issue. Mopars of this era have very loose tolerances, and stacking them often results in some minor problems. If you are starting with coated headers, keep them wrapped in thick plastic during mockup, and tape up any areas before hammering to prevent damage to the coating. In our case, they were uncoated, so this was not an issue.

Once all clearances were checked, I removed the engine, transmission, and subframe. The K-member was cleaned, sandblasted, and powder coated before it was assembled with all new ball joints, bushings, and tie rods. The headers were ceramic coated with Cerakote. The engine was detailed and painted before reinstallation. Reinstallation was accomplished from the bottom as an assembly, which cuts out a bit of aggravation. I used a lift and a motorcycle jack for this, but the same can be done with good jack stands and a floor jack.

With today's emphasis on increased handling, steering, and braking ability, many potential Gen III Hemi swappers are using an after-market suspension. While suspension systems are beyond the scope of this book, I will go over them as they pertain to the Gen III Hemi swap.

Suspension Modifications

Traditional Mopar cars of the muscle car era and beyond, like our Duster project, came with a torsion bar front suspension that is well loved by the Mopar faithful. They are easily adjustable, can be swapped out

Initially sold under the Gerst name, QA1 now produces this suspension for many classic Mopars. These units are lighter than stock and come with modern rack-and-pinion steering, improved geometry, and coilover suspension, which allows more room for header clearance.

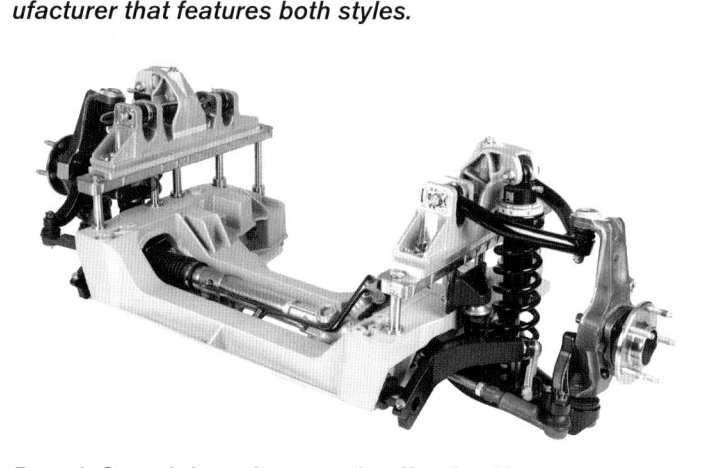

QA1 offers front suspensions that retain torsion bars for those who are so inclined. I'm not aware of any other manufacturer that features both styles.

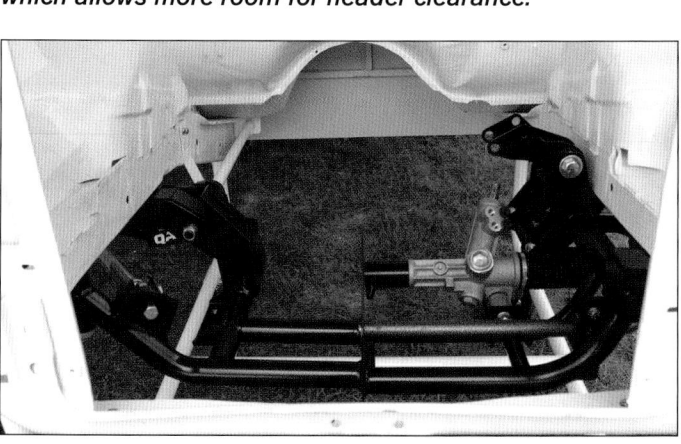

The low profile of the round-tube construction of the QA1 provides plenty of room for exhaust and charge-pipe plumbing to make these units desirable for anyone contemplating forced induction.

Detroit Speed doesn't currently offer the Aluma-Frame suspension for Mopar applications, but RMR Dreamcars has successfully modified these units for use in Mopar B-Body and E-Body cars. They were originally intended for 1964–1970 Mustangs. (Photo Courtesy Holley)

for stiffer variants as required, and offer acceptable handling. They can still be tweaked to levels far beyond what Chrysler's engineers ever intended and work very well. However, they can be a problem in some applications.

First, the location of the torsion bars is parallel to the ground, from the front of the vehicle all the way back to transmission mount. This isn't an issue with exhaust manifolds, but large-tube headers compete for this same space. The resulting tight clearances, and in many cases, interference, compromise the header design and the ease of installation and service. The typical well-designed long-tube LSx-swap headers can be bolted on in 15 minutes. This is not due to the LSx, but it's the GM chassis with plenty of room. This just isn't possible with a comparable Gen III Hemi header on a torsion bar chassis, particularly some of the tighter ones like the A-Body. Installing them from the bottom on the engine and K-member becomes the best way to install them.

Second, if you plan to use a larger-case transmission, such as an 8HP70/90, 545RFE, or NAG1, you have to cut away the center of your torsion bar crossmember and build a stronger replacement that accommodates your transmission. It needs to be strong either way, but the additional load put on it by the torsion bars is eliminated if you eliminated the torsion bars.

The most common solution to this dilemma is a bolt-in aftermarket front suspension clip. These clips are sold by many companies, such as Reilly Motorsports (RMS/AlterKtion), Gerst Suspension (now a division of QA1), Magnum Force, Control Freak, and others. They are all designed to

replace the stock K-member and use coilover shocks (QA1 is available with torsion bars) and double arms rather than torsion bars. They also use rack-and-pinion steering. These features greatly increase the amount of room available for headers and accessories and eliminate some of the problems found in the typical swap. They can be ordered with mounts for most popular engines, including the Gen III Hemi. The manufacturer can typically provide guidance on headers that are known to work with their clips. A swap header made for the vehicle application with a stock suspension should work in most cases.

While not quite a bolt-on, RMR Dreamcars successfully used the Detroit Speed Aluma-Frame front suspension in B-Body and E-Body Mopars. This suspension is different from any other offering in that it uses an OEM-style cast aluminum cradle that bolts into the modified frame rails and eliminates the need for intrusive shock towers. The tubular A-arms are more conventional and mate to DSE's own forged aluminum uprights that use Corvette hubs.

If your swap recipient of choice isn't a traditional Mopar or one of the handful of trucks or Jeeps covered by bolt-in mounts, you'll need to be a bit more creative. Enrique Ojeda, the owner and builder of a Hellcat-swapped Buick Grand National, used a set of universal LS-style mounts and re-drilled the holes to fit his 6.2L block. This may be an easy way to go for someone with a non-Mopar chassis. You can buy LS swap mounts for just about any specific chassis, even non-GM ones. The universal style can be made to work with just about anything with a saddle-style front crossmember. This is ideal for someone who wants to do

a swap in an alternative bodystyle but has limited fabrication skills.

Some chassis, particularly narrower ones from the 1920s through the 1940s, can do well with a universal mount like those sold by Speedway, Tin Man, or Welder Series. Each of these mounts comes with the block side already fabricated and consists of a bolt-on plate with a steel-plated, round urethane bushing to build the ears to attach to your frame rail and hardware. This type of mount is similar to the ones that came with our Gremlin's Control Freak front suspension. Control Freak provides a Gen III Hemi engine mount option for its Mopar-based suspensions, but since ours was the first to go Gen III Hemi, no mounts were available for the chassis end of the mount. This wasn't a big deal because I planned to set the engine back farther than normal anyway.

1972 Gremlin X 5.7L Hemi Swap

The 1972 AMC Gremlin X pictured belongs to my son and is a perfect example of a project that has grown far beyond the original plan. Initially conceived as a simple rebuild to drive to high school, I had a few basic requirements for the car. It needed to have an EFI engine, and I didn't want to stick with the original 304. A manual transmission was a must (it came with an automatic), and I wanted modern steering and suspension and four-wheel disc brakes.

After briefly considering a Chevy LSx-based engine, I located a relatively inexpensive, low-mileage 5.7L Hemi for a good price and decided to go that route instead. My son's sale of another vehicle funded the purchase of a Tremec T56 Magnum

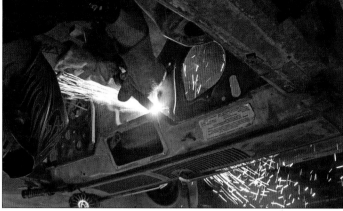

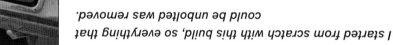

The Gremlin has a front suspension similar to an early Falcon/Mustang or Chevy II with shock towers that protrude into the engine compartment. The Control Freak crossmember is installed using existing bolt holes.

It's not necessary to cut out the firewall of a Gremlin/Hornet chassis. I wanted the better handling and more room ahead of the engine for a future turbo setup. Without cutting, you need a rear-sump pan to position the engine farther forward.

I started from scratch with this build, so everything that could be unbolted was removed.

6-speed manual transmission and a Quick Time SFI bellhousing from my friend Jeff Kauffman at Silver Sport Transmission.

He also purchased a complete bolt-in IFS from Control Freak Suspension, as I had always heard good things about them, and they had a kit specifically for the Gremlin. I installed several similar Mustang II–based suspensions in my shop, some more universal than others, so this was a good, bolt-in solution to bring safety and great handling to the Gremlin. This particular kit uses Viking coilover shocks, Wilwood Pro Series spindles, and a manual rack and pinion from Flaming River, along with custom-built tubular control arms, a bolt-in crossmember, and all the hardware needed for installation.

Our initial mockup of the Control Freak front crossmember and the 5.7L Hemi showed a problem. Our mid-sump Milodon pan (the engine was originally going into an E-Body) would not fit. A rear sump pan was available that might have afforded enough clearance, or I could have notched and reworked the Control Freak crossmember. Instead, I removed a portion of the firewall for clearance and placed the engine farther back. This would improve handling and provide a bit more room for the radiator and fans. Our headers, which came with the engine, were early long-tube Hooker headers for Gen III Hemi swaps (pre-Blackheart) in B-Body and E-Body cars. They fit perfectly.

With the Control Freak engine mounts bolted up and the engine suspended, I carefully measured until the engine was correctly positioned in the car. The bellhousing and transmission were attached so that proper clearances and driveline angle could be established. In our case, it was positioned down about 3 inches toward the rear. Once everything was properly positioned, and there was adequate clearance for the headers, some measurements were taken between the eye of the engine mounts and the crossmember. Those measurements were then transferred to stiff cardboard and checked against the vehicle before being cut out in mild steel plate.

The basic design of the mounts is very simple. I used a piece of 3/16-inch flat bar stock to connect the crossmember tubes and tacked

This photo shows the rough initial cuts made with a plasma cutter. By this stage, we planned on a new custom firewall, so everything was removed.

The Hemi fits rather nicely at this point and is roughly mocked into place. There is no interference with the shock towers.

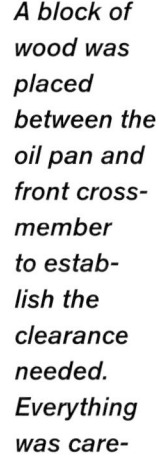

A block of wood was placed between the oil pan and front cross-member to establish the clearance needed. Everything was carefully measured to ensure that the engine was centered for the best clearance. Production cars are often offset for steering-box clearance, but that wasn't an issue here.

Alternator clearance is definitely an issue with this setup. I planned to build a custom bracket to mount a GM 1-wire-type alternator, but as the project changed direction, I devised another solution.

I chose a Tremec T56 Magnum for this project and a Quick Time blow-proof bellhousing for safety. The transmission wasn't installed yet at this stage. However, once the transmission was installed and the driveline angle was determined, a crossmember was fabricated and mounted.

Control Freak provided the engine side of the mounts. However, the company didn't have the crossmember side because no one had ever done this before, to Control Freak's knowledge.

When this engine was last mocked up in the Gremlin, it had a Milodon pan. The stud location for the pickup did not have to be changed in this case because we had already done it for the old pan.

The pickup uses an O-ring to seal to the oil pump and is bolted down at the pump and one of the main caps. This varies according to the style of pan that you remove and install. Purchase a new main-cap bolt and stud from the dealer if you have to change the location of either. Note that VVT and non-VVT pumps/pickups are clocked differently.

The pan rail is cut for an O-ring-style gasket (supplied). Simply bolt down the pan using the factory sequence and the supplied hardware.

Carefully remove any gasket or sealer residue from the rails on the block.

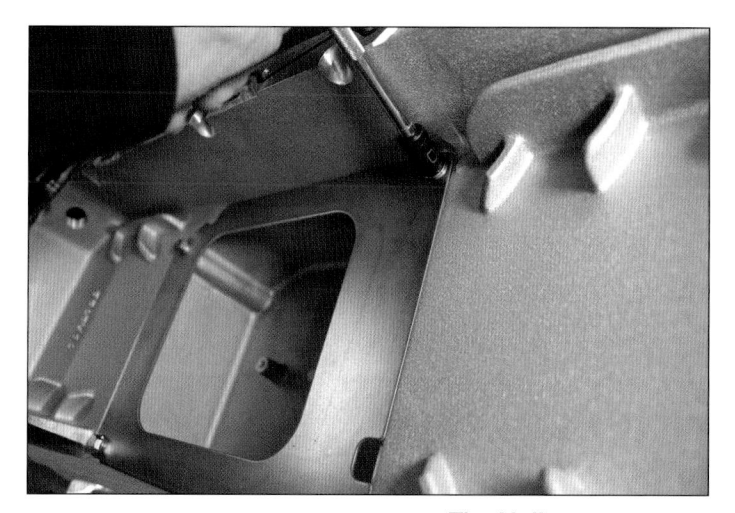

The Holley pan comes with a baffle that is bolted in place at all four corners.

The two threaded ports at the front are for oil drain-back. These will be plumbed to the twin turbochargers.

Simple mounts were built from flat stock and will be fully boxed in and cleaned up later.

The engine mounts leave plenty of room for the Hooker full-length headers on the driver's side.

Clearance around the oil pan is very good with it hanging only slightly below the crossmember. Even if a wheel was lost, it will not be the lowest point, so the slight loss of ground clearance is worth it for a lower center of gravity.

Passenger-side clearance is very good.

that in place. Then, I tacked on the ears of the mount. Once everything was tacked, the crossmember assembly was unbolted and the mounts were finish welded. The next step was to box in the ears for additional strength and round off the corners for a nicer appearance.

While Silver Sport Transmission now offers a bolt-in crossmember for AMC applications, they didn't at the time I did our initial mockup. Because of our engine setback, some modification may have been required. Equipped with a JD Squared tubing bender, I could have

Engine height with a production-style EFI intake isn't an issue, but the Holley Hi-Ram installed here will cause hood clearance issues. The cowl panel still needs some trimming to allow the top to sit in the proper position.

bent our own crossmember from steel tubing, but since my shop had done many swaps over the years, I had a leftover transmission crossmember from an LS swap that could be easily adapted. The existing mounting pad was correct for a GM transmission, so that wasn't an issue, but the overall length was far too long for our Gremlin. I was fortunate that cutting down both ends of the tube and welding on a piece of steel angle was all that was required to put the transmission in its proper place. Drilling mounting holes in the angle and corresponding holes in the subframe to accommodate threaded inserts allowed us to bolt the transmission crossmember up to the Gremlin's front frame rails.

Custom Engine Mounts and Motor Plates

Somewhere between a bolt-in front suspension and full fabrication, RMR Dreamcars of Hudson, Florida, perfected the use of the Detroit Speed Aluma-Frame front suspension in B-Body and E-Body cars. Intended for the 1964–1970 Mustang, this unit has many advanced features, like an OE-quality cast aluminum subframe that sandwiched the original rails bolted into the original Mustang, a splined sway bar, and aggressive front suspension geometry found on all of DSE's products. While some fabrication and cutting are required, this is much easier than a fully custom-built suspension. Gen III Hemi engine mounts will have to be fabricated.

Even without advanced fabrication skills, if you can install the premade mounts, you can likely build the whole assembly from scratch with very little effort. Whether or not that is worth the time and effort to do so is a question you'll have to

Coated in wrinkle-finish black in this photo, the DSE Aluma-Frame looks like an OEM installation. There is plenty of accessory drive clearance, and the steering rack is well protected from road hazards.

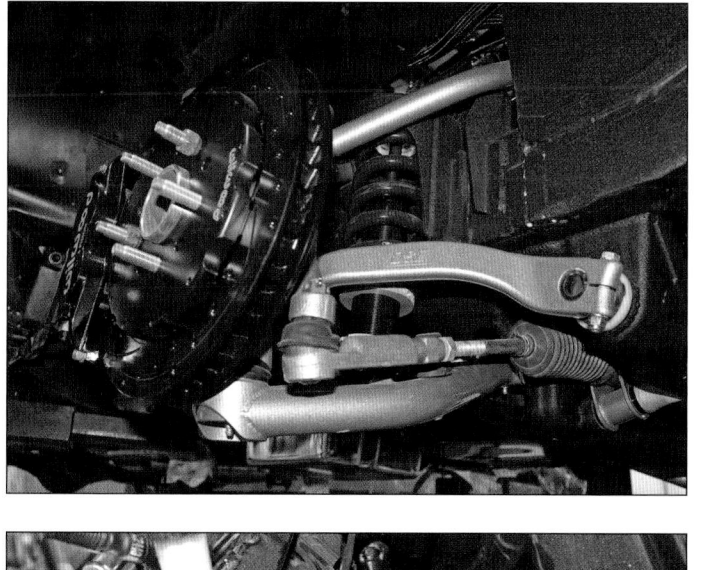

The splined sway bar is nicely integrated. The tubular A-arms are beefy, which is a good thing for street-driven cars. Weight isn't everything. The rack-and-pinion set is a readily available Mustang-type unit.

Control-arm clearance to the headers can be a headache at times, but there is plenty of room here.

decide on. But if your time is worth less to you than money, or you have access to a well-equipped metal fabrication shop, you can make mounts just as nice, or nicer than any of the commercially available ones. You'll need appropriate flat-plate steel, tube for the bushing mounts, and urethane or rubber bushings to fit your tubing size.

Huge Wilwood brakes with 6-piston calipers will bring this B-Body to a halt quickly.

Alternator clearance is very good. You can see by the valve cover that this is a Hellcat engine.

RMR's engine mounts are simple but effective.

Depending on the nature of your build, a motor plate may be in order rather than a conventional mount. The primary reason for a motor plate is rigidity and to prevent twist in the chassis (usually in a race application). This serves to solidly mount the engine and transmission and effectively make them a structural part of the chassis rather than something bolted into it. A side benefit is that if the transmission needs to come out, it can without disturbing the engine. A motor plate can often be easier to install in a tube-chassis car due to increased room for exhaust headers freed up by the absence of a side engine mount.

This is also a major plus for any turbocharged vehicle with forward-facing headers, as the header tubes can be routed on the bottom side of the exhaust flange rather than at the top since the side engine mounts are now out of the way. This may be impossible in a Gen III Hemi application due to other obstructions like shock towers or brake master cylinders and boosters.

Another advantage is that stress on the block is minimized over a conventional motor mount, which can increase engine life in high-powered applications.

A mid-plate is typically used between the engine and transmission bellhousing to add further support. Some applications may forgo a transmission crossmember, but I recommend retaining it, along with a rubber or polyurethane (not solid) mount.

The disadvantages of a motor plate system are few, but they need to be taken into consideration. A primary one is that while they do free up room for headers, no header companies make headers specifically for a motor plate application. The mid-plate can often be in the way as the typical headers are swept back further to clear the now-unused motor mount location. You may have to modify headers, have custom ones built, or build your own. Another factor is your accessory drive. Gen III Hemi motor plates are attached at the water pump bolt holes on the timing cover so the water pump and water pump pulley are going to be spaced out by the thickness of the plate. There is no aftermarket solution currently for spacing the damper a corresponding amount, so maintaining a factory-style alternator, power steering, and the mechanical water pump is pretty much out. I am aware of only one company, AEI, that makes a motor plate for the Gen III Hemi. Theirs is available either set up for a Gen III Hemi-style Mezierre electric water pump or a more common and less expensive big-block Chevy-style pump. They also have an option for a reduced-size Denso alternator. For a drag car and some street cars, this is all you need. Swappers who are building for road racing, autocross, or drift probably have to look elsewhere for the time being.

As with more conventional engine mounts, you can build your own motor plate. The typical plates are cut from 3/8-inch aluminum. While most of us don't have a plasma table or laser cutter in our home shops, most areas have shops that will cut one for you for a reasonable fee if you provide the dimensions.

The process is fairly simple. Mock up your engine precisely in the desired location. If you have existing engine mounts, you can leave them in place for this portion of the project. With that done, determine the overall width and height desired and make a pattern to those dimensions from thick plywood or MDF. You can use stiff cardboard, but you don't want your pattern to flex, so use something more substantial. Once you have cut the rough pattern, put it in place in front of your engine and determine what can be removed for header clearance. Mark off any other areas that can be cut away for clearance or appearance purposes. Leave as much material as possible in the alternator mounting area since you won't know exactly what will be required there at this point.

This is the tricky part, but it doesn't have to be too bad. Get some

RMR built a custom crossmember to accommodate the 4L80E transmission and restore the integrity of the chassis. This is much stronger than the previous sheet-metal stampings.

The 4L80E adapter plate requires the use of a driver-side starter.

This motor plate is by AEI and is similar to the one being used for the Gremlin project. Note the dry-sump oiling system and the lack of a water pump. Plates can be cut for just about any combination and chassis style.

threaded transfer punches in M8x1.25 and screw them into the water pump bolt holes. They are relatively cheap on Amazon. You don't need to put one in every hole, but the more you have the better as they are the most

accurate way to transfer the bolt hole locations to your motor plate.

Take a piece of plywood or MDF that fits the measurements you took previously and position it on top of your frame rails where it will be attached. Press the wood into the points of your transfer punches and tap it with a hammer in their general location. Make sure you have the pattern lined up where you want it. Remove the pattern and drill the pump mounting holes. If you use a Gen III Hemi–style electric water pump, you'll need to drill them all.

Position a gasket over the drilled holes and mark around the inside perimeter so you know what needs to be removed. If you plan to use a BBC electric pump, you can do enough to secure the plate. You then have to determine proper placement of the BBC pump and what needs to be removed to allow coolant to pass through. The mounting holes should also be marked for the pump, as well as for the thermostat housing of choice (small-bock Mopar ones are commonly used for this) or an AN-style outlet. Once your pattern is made and all hole sizes determined, the pattern can be duplicated by your local metal fab shop. A 3/8-inch aluminum is typically used for this application.

Keep in mind that holes for the BBC water pump and the water outlet or thermostat housing will need to be equipped with threaded steel inserts (Heli-Coils). Some mounting holes for the plate may wind up under the water pump housing, so those holes should be counter-sunk to ensure proper gasket seal without interfering with the pump housing.

With the plate secured to the front of the engine and the ends resting on the frame rails for support, you'll need to fabricate support brackets for the plate. Simple L-shaped brackets with a couple of 3/8-inch holes in each should be sufficient. If your car is caged, attach the bars to the plate. You can use a conventional transmission crossmember for sup-

port at the rear, but a mid-plate is also an option. This is a plate that serves to support the back of the engine and the transmission. In some cases, it allows the engine and transmission to be removed separately without additional support needed. It can be as simple as tabs welded to a steel bell-housing, or a machined billet work of art that ties into the firewall and bolts in with the bellhousing. Most flywheels are offset enough to not be an issue, but in some cases pilot bearing engagement can be, so a longer one may be required.

Remember what I previously mentioned in regard to changing the

direction of a project? In the case of the Gremlin, I had just begun making changes. This project has sat for a long time since the initial mockup due to a lot of factors. One of them is my son has been away for four years serving in the USMC. During that time period, his and my own interests moved away from building a nice street car.

Drifting increasing in popularity was a definite influence. Ken Block's *Hoonicorn* Mustang was an inspiration for the direction I chose to take with this car. I am old enough to remember the IMSA look of what today seems like an early version of

The Art Morrison front clip uses C5/C6 Corvette suspension components and is only 28 inches between the frame rails. This spec, along with the 2x4 rail size, was given to AEI to make the motor plate.

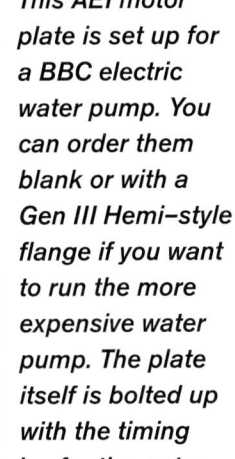

This AEI motor plate is set up for a BBC electric water pump. You can order them blank or with a Gen III Hemi–style flange if you want to run the more expensive water pump. The plate itself is bolted up with the timing cover through-bolts that go into the block. The other bolts holes for the water pump are also used to seal the water passages. During the final installation, don't forget a gasket or silicone sealer here. A kit with a reduced-size alternator and bracket can be ordered from AEI.

pro touring but without the excessive billet do-dads and creature comforts and with heavily flared fenders covering wide (for the time) rubber.

I also remember when *Big Red*, the absolute most impressive 1969 Camaro ever built, started doing things conventional wisdom said was the territory of supercars. Those influences and others have helped us make the decision that I want to push the limits of this car, not just in the power area (1,000-plus-hp street cars are pretty common these days), but in handling, braking, and a style not often applied to cars like this. When completed, I want to be able to participate in everything from drift to road racing to land speed and rally. While drag racing isn't a focus,

it might be fun to take to Drag Week. This car isn't being purpose built for any one discipline, but instead, I want to have fun and do that as safely as possible.

One of the first decisions made was to incorporate twin turbos to pump up the Hemi. The boost will be kept low as I learn the car and tune it, but I fully expect to make 600-plus wheel hp even in the initial mild version. While off-the-shelf turbo headers for Hemis aren't yet available, they are available for the GM LSx, and the port location between those engines is very close.

I ordered a set of Flowtech 304SS forward-facing headers and got a set of Hooker 3/8 flanges for the Gen III Hemi with the intention of removing the old flanges and welding on new ones. It looks like it will work out fine, but I had another problem. The engine mounts are in the way when I tried to run the headers in the down-and-forward position. With the shock towers in place, the headers couldn't be flipped and run in the up-and-forward position either. I could build a motor plate to alleviate the problem, but for a car that hopefully will run at Pike's Peak, I felt I needed a lot more suspension than could be easily bolted into the Gremlin's unibody.

To that end, I looked hard at aftermarket choices in suspension that

were better suited to our new purpose. I realized that to get the handling I wanted, along with durability and commonly available heavy-duty replacement parts, something based on Corvette C5/6/7 geometry and uprights was a great way to go. There are a lot of options available in the aftermarket for something like this, but after some research I decided on a front clip from Art Morrison that uses C6 Corvette components. Their clip is designed for use with coilover shocks, uses a Detroit Speed rack and pinion, and can use factory Chevrolet forged aluminum control arms and uprights. With the width I need, custom billet steering arms by Morrison are being provided.

The installation of this clip and the building of the rest of the chassis is beyond the focus of this book and requires a book in itself to properly document. However, I wanted to show the installation of a motor plate in a Gen III Hemi application from start to finish. Actual mounting of the proper plate will be covered here, and the accessory provisions will be covered in Chapter 7. The plate I am using is from AEI and has provisions for a BBC electric water pump. The mid-plate is still in the works, but it will completely encircle the bellhousing and provide a mounting flange for attachment to the firewall.

Since the factory Gen III timing cover is equipped with integral accessory brackets, those need to go. A little time spent on a mill or with a 4.5-inch grinder with a cutting disc and flap wheel can remove all of the unneeded brackets. This is required so that the plate fits flush to seal the coolant passages.

To secure the plate to the chassis, simple tabs can be welded to the frame rail, and a hole can be drilled through the plate to accommodate a bolt. Once the front roll-cage bars are installed, another tab will tie the top of the plate into the tube.

CHAPTER 5

FUEL SYSTEM

One of the most important aspects of any engine project, whether carbureted or fuel injected, is proper delivery of fuel. The typical pre-EFI vehicle used a mechanical fuel pump mounted directly to the engine and a feed line from the tank. Some later models had return or vent lines as well but were still simple in concept.

Mechanical pumps are generally reliable and do an excellent job of pulling fuel from the fuel tank. Although, some of the current parts-store replacement pumps are questionable. The pickup arrangement in the tank doesn't matter, except for more specialized applications, such as racing. The main concerns are proper pressure, which is sometimes controlled by an external regulator, and sizing, which is 5/16 to 3/8 in most cases.

Beyond that, not much thought has to go into a mechanical setup. Unfortunately, a stock Gen III Hemi has no provision for a mechanical fuel pump. The only aftermarket method of installing one was through use of a now-discontinued timing cover from Mopar Performance that accommodated an AMC-style distributor and had a boss to accommo-

date a mechanical pump. This setup wasn't popular when available, and it is doubtful that many swappers will use it, so concentration here will be on electric fuel pumps.

Carbureted Electric External Fuel Pumps

The vast majority of electric pump setups for carbureted vehicles use an external fuel pump. Holley, Carter, Mallory, MagnaFuel, Aeromotive, and others have made pumps for years for the street and race markets. It is likely that if you have an electric pump on your vehicle, it is one of these brands. In most cases, no significant changes are needed when going to the Gen III Hemi as long as the line size and pump volume are adequate for the new powerplant.

If you are starting from scratch with either a fuel tank or cell, you'll need at minimum a 100-micron prefilter (remove the sock filter from the tank), an electric fuel pump, a 40-micron post-filter, and a fuel-pressure regulator. Some lower-powered pumps are preset and do not require a regulator. It still isn't a bad idea to have one.

While it is not required, I highly

Holley's Red Pump electric fuel pump (part number 12-801-10) and its big brother, the Blue Pump, have been used by hot rodders for the last 50 years and are still popular today. No regulator is required, but it can be added if desired. This pump is only compatible with gasoline (no E-85 or methanol). (Photo Courtesy Holley)

recommend using a bypass-style return regulator, as it will allow you to run a return line to the tank. This can help minimize any vapor lock or fuel percolation issues by keeping the fuel moving and allowing it to cool after passing through the engine compartment. This wasn't always a common thing on the typical carbureted street car, but with today's awful pump gasoline with its federally-mandated ethanol content, I highly recommend it for any carbureted vehicle. This is especially critical if you live in a warmer climate. The return line should be routed as far from the pickup as possible with a dump tube inside the tank to minimize any fuel pump cavitation issues. This is more of an issue with higher-pressure EFI pumps, but it needs to be considered.

Before picking all the other components, determine what line size is needed to feed your engine adequately. For purposes of this book, 3/8 inch (-6AN) will be a minimum. For a carbureted application, this will be adequate to 600 hp. Use 1/2 inch (-8AN) up to 800 hp and 5/8 inch (-10AN) up to 1,000 hp.

Calculating Fuel-Pump Flow Requirements

Once you have the line size determined, you need to determine what fuel pump your engine requires. This requires some basic calculations. This process is the same whether your engine is carbureted or fuel injected.

First, you need to know how much horsepower you plan to make. Estimate it on the high side to run the pump at a lower duty cycle. Pumps are normally rated in either gallons per hour (gph) or liters per hour (lph). Pay attention to what pressure was required for the output, as that is critical, especially with EFI where the number can vary greatly.

You also need to estimate the Brake Specific Fuel Consumption (BSFC) for your engine. This refers to the efficiency of the engine and is the rate of fuel consumption divided by the power produced. This is typically in the 0.45 to 0.5 range for a naturally aspirated engine, 0.6 to 0.65 for an engine using nitrous oxide, and 0.6 to 0.75 for a forced-induction engine (supercharged/turbocharged). E85 and methanol numbers are higher, and keep in mind that not all electric pumps are rated for non-gasoline fuels.

In this example, I am assuming a 450-hp carbureted engine with 0.5 BSFC.

$$GPH = (Max\ horsepower\ x\ BSFC)\ /\ 6$$
(6 pounds is the average weight of a gallon of pump gas)
$$(450\ hp\ x\ 0.5\ BSFC) = 225$$
$$225\ /\ 6 = 37.5\ gph$$

If you need to convert the GPH figure to LPH, multiply it by 3.7854118. Liters per hour is more common with EFI pumps, though many of the larger EFI pumps are rated in gph.

With this in mind, select a pump that exceeds that GPH/LPH figure as a margin of error and is best suited for the line size. A larger-than-needed fuel pump isn't really an issue with a return system. In the example, the 37.5 gph requirement is easily covered by just about any rotor/vane–style pump, even after figuring in the desired fuel pressure. A pump such as Holley's 12-801-1 Red pump leaves lots of room for growth, but a more basic pump like Carter's P4594, rated at only 50 gph, will suffice in this application.

Mounting Considerations

The typical electric fuel pump for a carbureted application is externally mounted. If it is a rotary vane-style, it needs to be installed upright (motor vertical). To ensure a longer pump life, install it below and as close to the tank as possible to ensure it is gravity fed. This will minimize cavitation. It should be mounted securely to the chassis and never in a closed area like the trunk. Rubber mounts are a good idea and often included with your pump.

Route the fuel pump power lead (typically red) to a 12-volt ignition source and use an inline fuse (typically 15 amps is enough) and relay. This isn't always required, but it is a good idea with any electric fuel pump installation. An oil pressure safety switch, like Holley's 12-810, is always a good idea since it will shut off the pump in the event of an accident or if the engine is killed for any reason.

Follow the manufacturer's recommendations for wire size and keep voltage drop in mind. Err on the side of larger than needed wire. Your pump will run better and last longer. Be sure the ground is run to a good chassis ground free of dirt, rust, paint, or coatings. Many fuel pump issues can be traced back to a bad ground.

When using any electric fuel pump, safety should be a consideration because it will continue to run if there is an accident or engine failure and the ignition circuit is still hot. Holley's 12-810 fuel pump pressure safety switch installs into an oil port and shuts off power to the pump if it reads less than 5 psi. (Photo Courtesy Holley)

EFI External Fuel Pumps

With EFI external pumps, there are a few minor differences, but most of the previous applies. You will need a 10-micron post-filter as opposed to the 40-micron filter used with carburetors. Typically, the pumps are a roller vane design and cylindrical in shape so that they are easier to mount than the rotary vane type. Instead of a direct ignition switched source or toggle, the pump is, in most cases, going to be triggered by a switched source coming from the ECU and run through a relay (some EFI harnesses may include this relay) to avoid damage. Wiring from the relay to the pump should be at least 10 gauge.

That said, I really don't like external EFI fuel pumps in a continuous-duty application like a street car. Due to the high pressures involved, they work harder than the typical carburetor-style pump and have more of a tendency to overheat. Ever go on a long cruise like *Hot Rod* magazine's Power Tour and see cars on the side of the road with someone under the back end? Driving for hours at a time, sometimes in heavy traffic, and in the summer heat is a true test of a fuel pump. Any issues in the installation are going to reveal themselves.

The biggest issue is that very few OEM fuel tanks are well suited for an external pump in that the fuel pickup is typically on the top of the tank. Fuel has to go through a prefilter, straight up to the top of the tank, and then be gravity fed into the pump. If you have a sock filter in the tank and a prefilter, remove the sock filter because it creates too much restriction. You may have seen complaints online about junk external pumps, and how the person has installed two or three and they keep failing. There are offshore copies of Walbro pumps that are to be avoided, but when I see this, it is almost always a poor installation. I'm okay with them in some applications, like early Mustangs where the stock pickup location is better suited to an inline pump, or fuel cells or tanks with a fabricated sump or pickups put into the lowest portion. I'd still take an in-tank pump over these, even in cases where I have to fabricate my own.

Why do manufacturers sell these pumps and package them in universal fuel systems kits for use with their entry-level EFI systems? There are a few reasons, one being that they are cheaper and they can sell them at a lower price point. Another is that there is a misconception that exter-

nal is better because it is easier to change. While that may be true, it is far easier to not have to change the pump at all. People don't want to have to drop the fuel tank to install it. They are most likely going to have to drop it anyway to remove the sock filter and add a return. I'd rather do it once, do it right, and move on to something else. A final reason is that it isn't practical to make a bolt-in internal fuel pump for every application. One thing that working for Holley has taught me is that people will put EFI on anything.

Carbureted Electric Internal Fuel Pumps

External electric fuel pumps have been the only choice for many years, but that has changed as more people realize there is another way. With the advent of many bolt-in EFI fuel tank systems, from a variety of sources such as Holley, Aeromotive, and Tanks Inc., the process of installing a pump in the tank has become simpler. EFI systems typically operate at 43 to 60 psi, so how does that work? For one thing, a bypass regulator designed for a carbureted application or one that can be used for both carb and EFI with a spring change is needed. You also need a return line that is as large as your feed to handle the extra fuel flow without creating back pressure on the pump. Keep in mind that since the system only has to provide 6 or so psi for the typical carb setup, the horsepower capabilities are greater than they normally would be in a true EFI application.

If there isn't an EFI tank system or fuel pump module available for your tank or fuel cell to use the above method, there are still some options. Holley's 19-365 is similar to its EFI

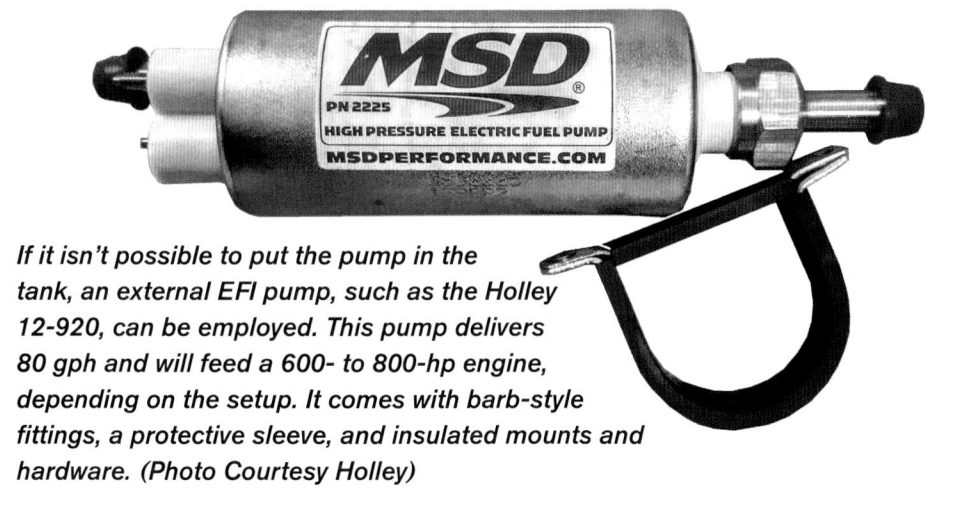

If it isn't possible to put the pump in the tank, an external EFI pump, such as the Holley 12-920, can be employed. This pump delivers 80 gph and will feed a 600- to 800-hp engine, depending on the setup. It comes with barb-style fittings, a protective sleeve, and insulated mounts and hardware. (Photo Courtesy Holley)

If you already have a good original or reproduction fuel tank, there are several options for making it EFI compatible. This one is in the 1973 Duster.

retrofit fuel pump module kits and will install in the top of any tank with a flat top surface and a depth of 7 to 12 inches. It uses an internal regulator that is preset for 6 psi and is replaceable with one of Holley's Sniper-style regulators if you ever decide to go EFI. The pump is rated at 340 lph and will support 900 hp in the carburetor application. Due to the internal regulator, there is no return line, so it is an easier installation. Aeromotive offers a similar unit under part number 18201. Unlike the Holley unit, it requires an external dead-head regulator (part number 13201).

Another option is Holley's Dominator line of inline fuel pumps. This line includes both single and dual pumps in a shared case and can be used for either EFI or carbureted applications. This is a high-horsepower-type pump and can be run externally. It also works well in a submersible application. This lends it well to custom fuel cell installations or in tanks with a large enough access hole to install it.

If your project vehicle was originally EFI equipped and is now carbureted, a carburetor-style return regulator can be used to accomplish the same thing as the above modules while retaining the return line, which provides some benefit. Any factory regulator in or on/near the tank obviously has to be discarded.

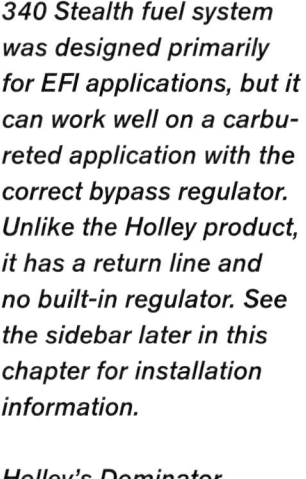

Aeromotive's Phantom 340 Stealth fuel system was designed primarily for EFI applications, but it can work well on a carbureted application with the correct bypass regulator. Unlike the Holley product, it has a return line and no built-in regulator. See the sidebar later in this chapter for installation information.

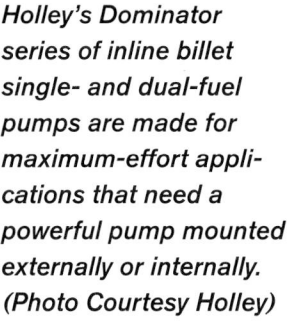

Holley's Dominator series of inline billet single- and dual-fuel pumps are made for maximum-effort applications that need a powerful pump mounted externally or internally. (Photo Courtesy Holley)

Holley's Sniper Diecast 340-lph in-tank retrofit fuel module (part number 19-365) is unique in two ways: it is designed for a carbureted application, and it is returnless. (Photo Courtesy Holley)

EFI Internal Electric Fuel Pumps

Considering that many Gen III Hemis are swapped into vehicles that already have an EFI system, such as Dodge Dakotas, D100s, Jeep TJs, GM and Ford vehicles, imports, and others, you may not have to do much to accommodate your swap's fuel requirements. Check the rating of the stock-style pump. If it is lower, a performance version is often available that will bolt in with minimal hassle. For the popular D100 and Dakota swaps, Holley makes a bolt-in fuel pump module in either return or returnless styles in 255- and 450-lph versions.

I am seeing more Gen III Hemi swaps into GM vehicles like the 1982–1992 F (Camaro/Firebird) and G-Body (Monte Carlo, Regal, Cut-lass, Grand Prix, etc.). While not all of these vehicles came with EFI since the vast majority were carbureted, a factory-style EFI pump hanger assembly from a parts store will fit most of the applicable tanks. Use an appropriate pump, like the 255-lph Holley 12-914, and you are set. It works for the above-mentioned vehicles, as well as many other vehicles from that era such as Fieros, TBI-equipped trucks (don't forget to replace the low-pressure hoses with high-pressure ones), and others.

For older vehicles, many companies now offer EFI-rated fuel tank conversions. Holley, Tanks Inc., Aeromotive, and Spectra Premium are the most commonly used. Be sure that the tank you choose has an appropriately sized pump, will work with your existing fuel pressure gauge, and is set up as a return or returnless system as desired. I prefer return systems for higher horsepower (over 500 hp) applications. If you plan to run a returnless fuel system that doesn't have an in-tank regula-tor, keep in mind that you will still need a return line from the tank. It will just be much shorter than in a true return-style system.

If you have a good original or repro tank, you can keep it. Holley offers a line of Muscle Car EFI Modules for most popular applications that will replace your stock sending unit and retain the fuel level sender. These are returnless units with a built-in regulator and are great for applications under 500 hp. This makes it easier to retrofit restored vehicles where running a return line could be an issue. For those desiring a return setup, this isn't the best choice. You can add a return to the tank and eliminate the regulator, but I'd suggest one of the return-style tank setups instead.

If your application isn't covered, or if you have a more specific usage in mind like road racing or autocross, custom tanks from companies like Rick's Tanks are an option. Most are stainless steel and have options you won't typically find in an off-the-shelf

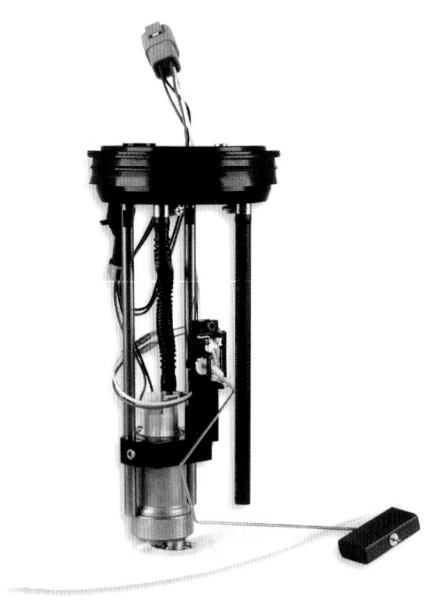

Are you planning a Gen III Hemi swap in a 1991–2004 Dodge Ram, Durango, or Dakota? If you want a pump module that will feed all but the healthiest Hemis, Holley has you covered with up to 450-lph pumps. (Photo Courtesy Holley)

As much as it pains the LSx crowd, plenty of GM vehicles have received Gen III Hemi swaps. Many of these vehicles had EFI (some were TBI), but all you really need to do it is update the pump to a high-pressure in-tank one, such as Holley part number 12-914, and use the correct EFI/TBI hanger. (Photo Courtesy Holley)

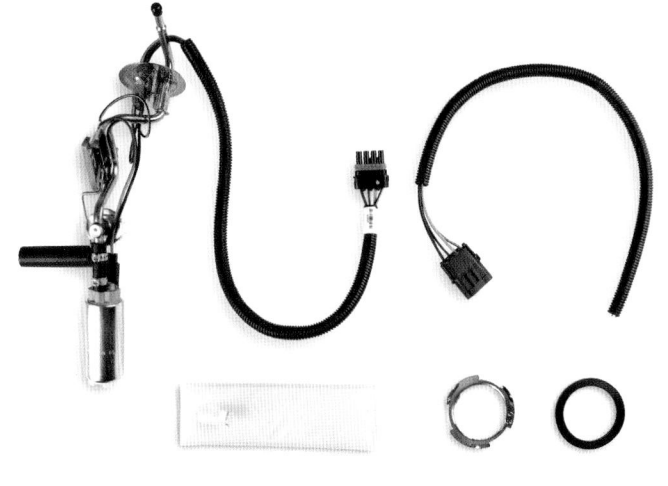

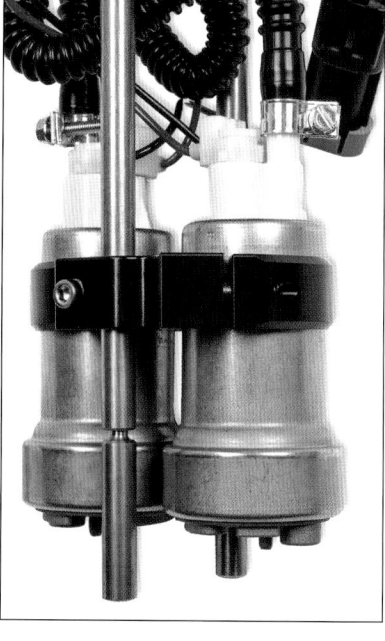

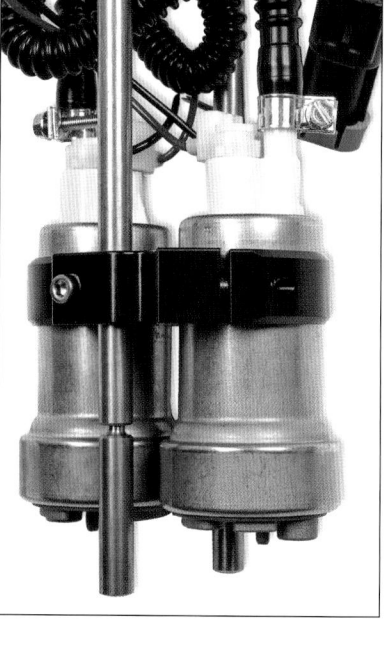

If you have a good tank, in most cases, you can buy an OEM-style fuel-pump module. Most include a 255-lph pump and Holley HydraMat, so fuel starvation when going around curves is eliminated. This one is part number 12-319 for 1963–1976 Dodge and Plymouth A-Body models. (Photo Courtesy Holley)

This tank kit from Holley (part number Vk040057) is for 1968–1970 Dodge/Plymouth B-Body cars. Holley offers some tanks for non-Mopar applications with a return system. You can easily identify the return style by the aftermarket-style separate fuel-level sender. (Photo Courtesy Holley)

The Holley 12-147 dual 450-lph fuel cell pump assembly supports 1,750 hp and bolts into any 12-bolt-flange fuel cell. (Photo Courtesy Holley)

Fuel filters should be matched to the line size. Holley part number 12-570 has -10 AN O-ring boss (ORB) ports. (Photo Courtesy Holley)

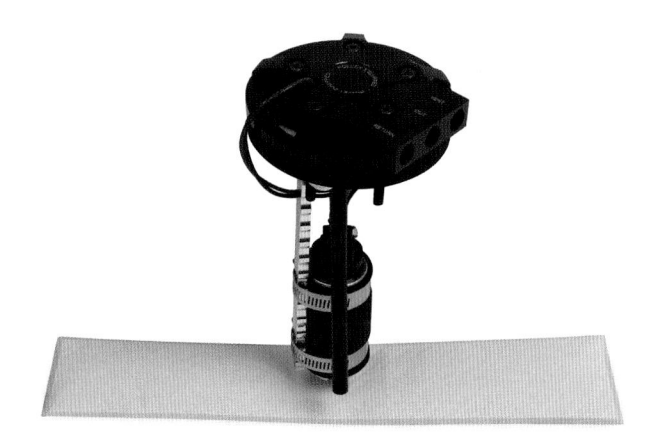

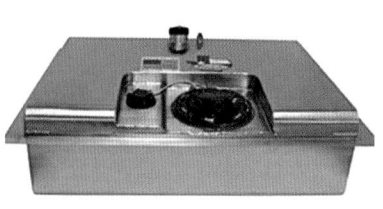

If you want a turnkey, custom stainless-steel tank for your project or want to add a PWM-style pump, do so with a tank from Rick's Tanks. They are high quality and can be built to virtually any specification. (Photo Courtesy Rick's Tanks)

Similar to the module previously mentioned for carburetor applications, Holley part number 12-130 is made for applications where an OEM-style module isn't available. They come with HydraMat pickups and a wide variety of pumps. (Photo Courtesy Holley)

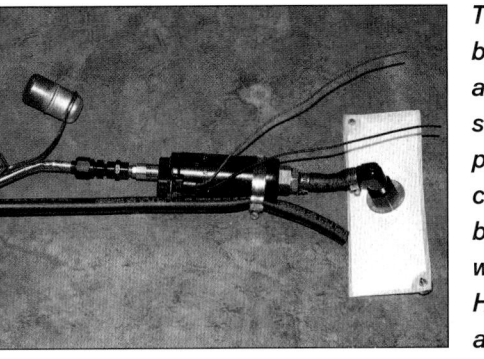

This pump assembly started as a reproduction sending unit/pickup for an older carbureted vehicle but was modified with a fuel pump, Holley HydraMat, and return line.

tank system. For example, they can accommodate factory-style GM pump modules and offer single or dual pump hats to handle just about any horsepower level. They will be far more expensive than your typical stock-style EFI tanks.

What if you have a good, usable tank but no bolt-in pump assembly is offered?

This problem has been addressed by both Aeromotive and Holley. Both units install by cutting a hole in the top of the tank and bolting it in. Aeromotive's offering is the Phantom Stealth system, which uses a foam baffle/basket to retain fuel for the pump assembly. This unit has been available for many years and is what I used on the Duster swap project. It is offered with single or dual pumps, as a return or returnless-style, and in carburetor or EFI versions.

At the time, there was no bolt-in EFI tank available for the A-Body Mopars, so this was a great option. Holley's system, the Retro-Fit Fuel Pump Module, is a bit different in that it doesn't use a baffle system. Instead it uses Holley's HydraMat, which is a fuel reservoir system that looks like a conventional fuel sock but uses surface tension and fluid wicking to let fuel in and keep it inside the reservoir. Not every version comes with HydraMat, but it can be retrofitted to any in-tank pump assembly. Holley's

system for conventional tanks is a single-pump system, but with pumps as large as 525 lph being offered, you are covered for up to 1,200 hp with EFI. They offer a stainless shim that allows it to be installed in a poly tank, and there are kits to change from a return to a returnless system.

If you plan to use a fuel cell, Aeromotive offers a wide variety in its Stealth line that uses all of its popular pumps preinstalled in aluminum fuel cells. If you already have a cell and just want to retrofit an electric pump, you can use Holley's Fuel Cell EFI Pump Modules. They are similar to the Retrofit Fuel Pump Modules above but are specifically designed to replace the fill cap plate on 6- and 12-bolt flange fuel cells. Unlike those designed for a regular tank, there are dual pump options available, even with the brushless VR Series pumps that allow up to 4,400 hp in an EFI application. No, that isn't a typographical error. Of course, any cell can be modified with an-in tank pump, but with the engineering already done for you at a reasonable cost, there really isn't much reason to do so.

Fuel-Pressure Regulators

Fuel-pressure regulators typically come in two basic types: deadhead/non-return and return/bypass regulators. For a low-horsepower carb

application, like an internally stock early 5.7L truck Hemi with a carburetor, you really don't need a regulator in many instances, but I prefer to run one for the fuel pressure control it provides. As mentioned previously, I am a fan of return systems on EFI systems, and I recommend one in a carbureted application as well. Gen III Hemis can provide a tight fit even in some engine compartments, and that just adds to the heat. Heating the fuel can cause vapor lock or fuel percolation, and a dead head–style regulator adds to the problem since excess fuel and fuel vapor can't be directed back to the tank. For this reason, pass on dead head–style regulators if it all possible.

The typical bypass regulator is best installed after the carburetor. With a fuel log arrangement, fuel flows in one end of the log, feeds the carb bowls, and has a port at the rear for a return line. This line is plumbed into the side of the regulator and out the bottom to return to the tank. If you plan to do an EFI swap on your Gen III Hemi later for cost or other reasons, you can purchase a return regulator that can accommodate both carbureted and fuel-injected applications with a simpler spring change.

Holley's 12-880 comes with the lower-pressure spring installed and -6 AN (3/8-inch) O-ring boss (ORB) ports that will work well for most applications, whether carb or EFI. Holley offers other similar regulators with different port size arrangements (NPT and AN). They are machined from 606-T6 billet aluminum for durability. They are also boost referenced so they can be used in a forced induction application. In an EFI application, run the pressure side of the pump into one fuel rail, cross

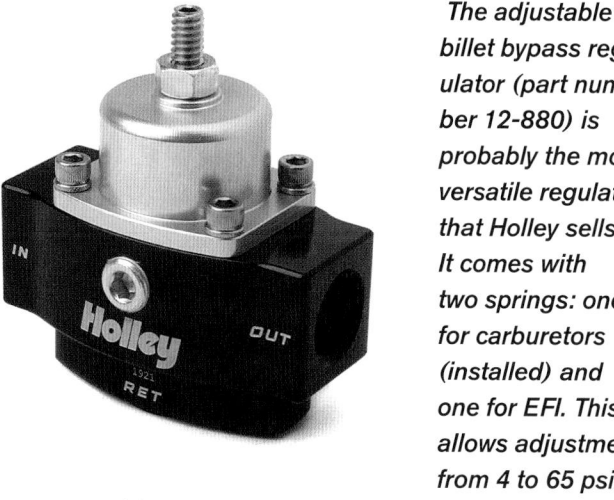

The adjustable billet bypass regulator (part number 12-880) is probably the most versatile regulator that Holley sells. It comes with two springs: one for carburetors (installed) and one for EFI. This allows adjustment from 4 to 65 psi. They come with a 1/8-inch NPT-gauge port and a fitting for boost reference. (Photo Courtesy Holley)

This Aeromotive regulator was used on the 'Cuda build and is shown with an ORB-style fitting as used with most regulators.

The Corvette filter/ regulator works with stock-style plastic lines, but most use fittings like these to adapt it to -6 AN. These are Fragola, and all the major fitting companies have them.

The Gremlin's fuel-pressure regulator is a Holley four-port VR Series and is adjustable from 40 to 100 psi.

over to the other rail, and exit into the fuel-pressure regulator, just like the carb application.

A third, less-common type of regulator is the filter/regulator assembly. The first of this type to be of interest to engine swappers is the one found on C5 and C6 Corvettes, which is mounted close to the tank. While not a true returnless system, it is billed as such and has been popular with both

Holley's answer to the filter/regulator is its diecast filter regulator (part number 12-888). Unlike the Corvette piece, the filters are replaceable without replacing the whole unit. They are offered in several fitting sizes. (Photo Courtesy Holley)

LSx and Gen III Hemi engine swappers due to its versatility. Preset at 58 psi, this unit has an inlet and return on the tank side, and it has an outlet side on the other.

The tank-side fittings are the typical male push-lock style commonly found on EFI fuel rails. The return is 5/16 inch, and the feed side is 3/8 inch. The outlet side uses a female fitting. Plumb these with either stock-type plastic fuel lines or convert to AN fittings. They have the filter built in and are meant to be replaced since the filter can't be serviced. These are available at any parts store. I typically use Wix part number 33737. Holley offers their take on this, but rather than a totally disposable unit, theirs uses a replaceable element and has a choice of either 3/8-inch NPT or -8 AN ORB (O-ring) ports. They are preset at 59.5 psi. Since both types eliminate the benefit of a return line, only use them for applications under 500 hp.

Fuel Lines, Hoses, and Filters

Using the suggested line size previously mentioned for your horsepower level, you should know what size line you require. The choice of material type will be dictated by a lot of factors, including application, intended usage, and budget. For example, a later-model vehicle with existing plastic lines that are adequately sized for the Gen III Hemi can be retained, and any modifications needed can be made with repair kits from Dorman, which are commonly available in any auto parts store.

A classic vehicle with good restoration market support may have repro lines available in an adequate size (most big-block muscle cars used a 3/8-inch line) that can be purchased in pre-bent form in either mild steel or stainless. In many cases, you can double up the lines and use one for a return to make the installation easy.

The flex lines can be made from your typical parts store EFI-rated fuel hose or an aftermarket EFI hose like Earl's Vapor Guard. As an alternative, the hard line can be flared with AN 37-degree flares and AN fittings and hose used. I recommend sticking with a Teflon-lined hose for better longevity. If no repro fuel lines are available, they can be made with bulk tubing in steel, stainless steel, aluminum, or a copper/nickel alloy tubing. Tubing benders, flaring tools, and a good tubing cutter are recommended if going this route. If you are doing standard automotive 45-degree flares, you'll need a double flaring tool. For AN flares, a 37-degree flaring tool is needed.

A word of warning: when trying to flare 3/8 or larger tubing in steel or stainless steel, you need a very good flaring tool. A heavy-duty manual one will work, but I prefer a hydraulic tool or one of the turret-style units as sold by Eastwood Company or Earl's. They aren't cheap but will save a lot of frustration.

Why not plumb the whole system in either EFI-rated rubber hose or AN Teflon hose? You can, and many do, but my preference is to use as much of a hard line as possible. For one thing, it is less expensive though more difficult to install. When the hose invariably has to be replaced, there is less of it to mess with. This is true even of AN hose. It doesn't last forever. In fact, it makes it tougher to see issues with the hose deteriorating due to the braided nylon or stainless-steel covering.

Regardless of what material you choose for fuel lines and hoses, always clean them out properly with air and solvent to ensure that no debris winds up in your filters or injectors.

Fuel-Pump Controllers

Fuel-pump controllers, such as the part number 16303 Fuel Pump Speed Controller kit from Aeromo- tive, have been around for a while in the hot rodding community. They became popular as larger fuel pumps were needed. Aeromotive's offering uses a manual switch, RPM signal from the ignition, or both to control a pulse modulation signal to the pump. Cutting voltage can damage a pump so they pulse it so no damage is done. The duty cycle is reduced during periods of low demand. In their words, this minimizes fuel heating and vapor-lock problems by matching the duty cycle of the fuel pump to engine RPM. At low demand, the FPSC slows the fuel pump down to reduce the chance of suction side cavitation and vapor lock. When demand increases, the FSC returns the fuel pump to 100-percent duty cycle for maximum flow. It's like an automatic transmission for your fuel pump.

This is a great addition to any street-driven car with large pumps as long as they are PWM compatible. Check with Aeromotive to be sure yours is. Normal return systems with filters and regulators are still used

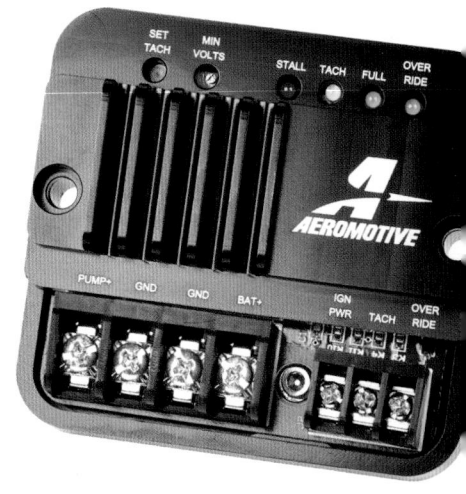

Aeromotive's billet fuel-pump speed controller (part number 16306) allows PWM or switch control over the fuel pump or pumps. (Photo Courtesy Aeromotive)

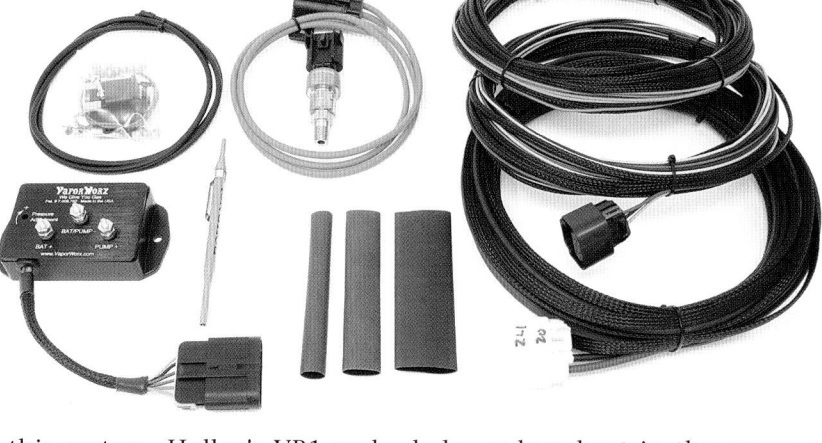

VaporWorx offers many solutions for PWM control. This particular kit is designed to work with the popular CTS-V2 fuel modules and both OEM and aftermarket engine management. These modules are commonly used in custom fuel tanks, such as those from Rick's Tanks. (Photo Courtesy VaporWorx)

with this system. Holley's VR1 and VR2 brushless pumps come with a controller, but no separate controllers are available at this time. They aren't typically used in street-driven cars and are beyond the scope of this book.

Facing the same issue with today's high-horsepower supercharged new cars, the OEMs have turned to true pulse width modulation (PWM) technology. PWM, simply put, is the equivalent of turning a switch on and off at a high rate of speed. Instead of limiting voltage or relying on a switch or RPM signal, the PWM controller uses a fuel pressure sensor to modulate fuel flow. This

helps reduce heat in the pump and increase its life. Considering that vehicles like the Hellcat make more than 700 hp and still need to be reliable for 100,000-plus miles, this is a huge advantage over the typical fuel-pressure regulator. In fact, no regulator or return line is needed, and the only filters in the system are in the OEM modules. There is just a pressure line between the tank and fuel rails.

At present, there are few PWM systems being used in swap applications. But this will be a major change in the hobby as it becomes more popular. While OEMs have used this for years, it is slowly catch-

ing on in the performance aftermarket. VaporWorx is the leader in this technology and offers kits based on the fifth-generation Camaro LS3 and ZL1 and the Cadillac CTS-V2. Rick's Tanks offers fuel tanks with these pumps and can build them for nearly any application.

Aeromotive has teased swap tanks available with the Hellcat PWM pumps to fit 1968–1976 A-Body, 1964–1972 B-Body, and 1970–1974 E-Body cars, but they are not available as of now. Interestingly, they can be run without a PWM controller if desired as long as a proper return-style regulator is used. The Hellcat PCM has one built in. This is perfect for the various Hellcat-based crate engines.

In-Tank EFI Solution

When this 1973 Plymouth Duster's 6.1L Hemi swap was underway, no one had a bolt-in EFI tank available, so I had to improvise.

I started with a stock reproduction tank and sending unit and added an Aeromotive Phantom 340 Stealth fuel system (part number 18688). This required cutting a hole in the tank (be sure to clean it out well afterward), measuring the depth, and cutting the bracket assembly to length. The baffle assembly was then installed, followed by the retaining

Here, the Duster's tank was cut open and holes were drilled using the supplied template. The plastic inner ring has been installed along with the foam baffle. Cleaning inside the tank was by far the most time-consuming part of the job.

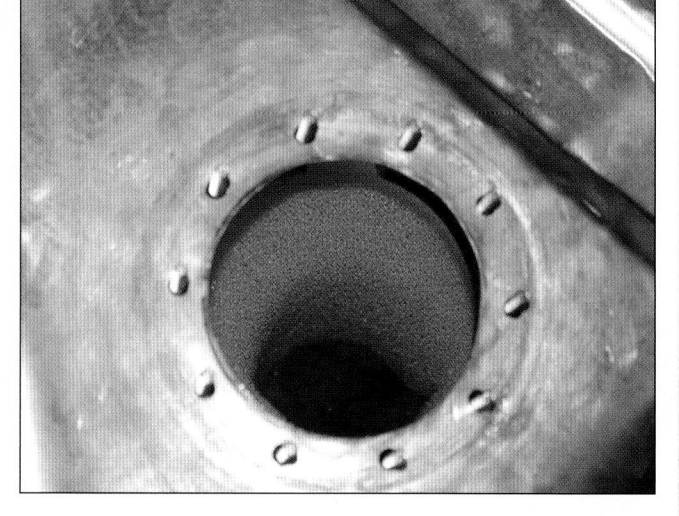

In-Tank EFI Solution *continued*

ring, gasket, and pump assembly. Tighten it down, and you are finished with the installation.

Keep in mind that the unit does stick up a bit. You can either shim the tank down slightly or build an access panel in the trunk for easier future service. While there are better ways to do this now for this particular vehicle, this is a great example of what you can do if you have a vehicle with no aftermarket in-tank EFI solutions.

This method provided a return line, but I chose to use a Corvette filter/regulator assembly (Wix part number 33737) and Fragola AN adapter fittings to minimize its length and simplify plumbing. I used AN fittings made for fuel rails with a plastic insert that locks onto the flare. Don't be afraid to put a little force on these fittings. They need to be on tight. Otherwise, they might come off. The rest of the system was done with -6 Earl's Pro Lite 390 hose, a 3/8-inch aluminum line, and an Aeromotive post filter.

The foam gasket has been installed. The nicely labeled ports for return, vent, and outlet are seen here. The pump support has already been shortened to fit the tank. This is an easy step with a cut-off wheel.

The pump module is securely bolted down. Go around twice to be sure because the foam will give a bit. Once tightened down, the locknuts keep it secure. Overall, it's an easy installation.

The unit protrudes a bit from the top of the tank. You can shim the tank down slightly, dimple the trunk, or make an access panel to cover it. I did the latter to avoid any damage to the lines from anything in the trunk.

The Corvette filter/regulator was securely attached to the frame rail. Some of the undercoating was removed to allow proper mounting.

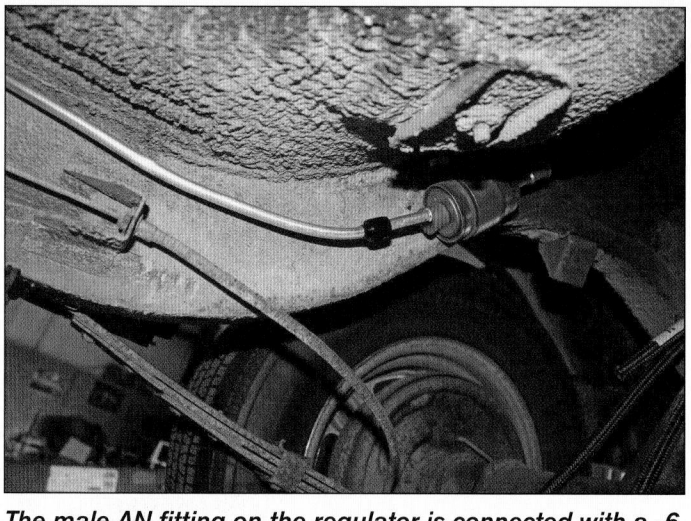

This photo provides a view of where the filter/regulator is mounted. Put it away from the exhaust and any moving parts, such as the rear suspension. The line is 3/8-inch aluminum with a -6 AN tube sleeve and nut along with a 37-degree AN flare.

The male AN fitting on the regulator is connected with a -6 tube nut and sleeve on the flared fuel line.

Custom Fuel System

In some instances, a conventional fuel OEM-style fuel tank just won't do. This 1970 Barracuda is a great example. Because the rear leaf springs were moved inboard, larger tires installed, and the 3-inch dual exhaust routed, there was no longer room for a fuel tank.

To solve this issue, a steel box was fabricated and installed in a hole in the trunk floor, and an Aeromotive Eliminator Stealth Fuel Cell was installed. The cell comes completely assembled with a 340-lph pump and sending unit and feed, return, and vents with rollover valves. They are available in a variety of configurations and fitting sizes to fit nearly anything.

In this application, intrusion into the trunk was minimal. An Aeromotive bypass regulator and filters were also used, and all lines were AN hose or aluminum hard line. This made for a very simple fuel system that will last a long time. ■

The fuel cell is much deeper than it appears. Rather than bolt it to the top of the trunk floor (as is commonly seen in many street cars), I cut a hole in the trunk pan and welded in a fabricated steel box to protect it on the bottom. The flange was welded in place and finished in LizardSkin like the rest of the floor pan. Rivnuts were installed so that the straps can be easily removed for service.

Custom Fuel System *continued*

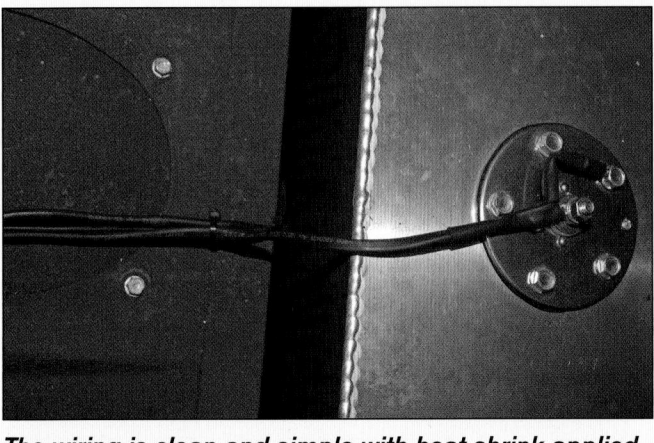

The wiring is clean and simple with heat shrink applied over all connections and where the wire is exposed. Leave enough visible for wire identification. I typically do this on all wires that pass through the trunk, under carpet, or under the vehicle. It looks good and adds some protection.

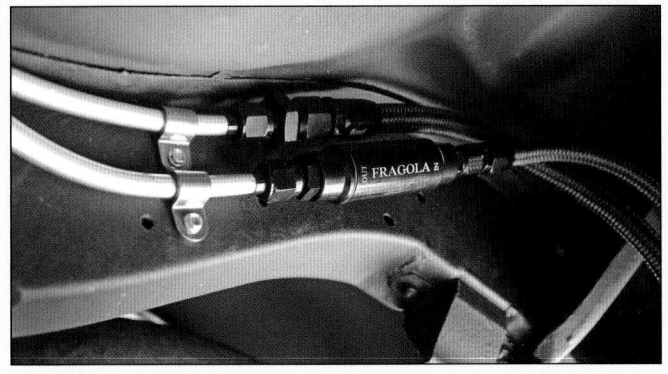

This photo shows the 'Cuda's fuel line plumbing over the axle. I prefer to keep my filters close to the engine because it minimizes the chance of debris from inside the fuel line or hose from getting into an injector. Even if it is new, you'd be surprised by the amount of gunk that is inside a fuel line or hose—especially once you cut it with a wheel. Always clean out the lines before a final installation.

The 'Cuda's engine compartment was a bit crowded, so I mounted the bypass regulator under the car. This is just behind the torsion-bar crossmember, which was heavily modified due to engine setback and the Viper T56 transmission. This car didn't retain its torsion bars. It had an aftermarket K-member with coilover Viking shocks from Magnum Force.

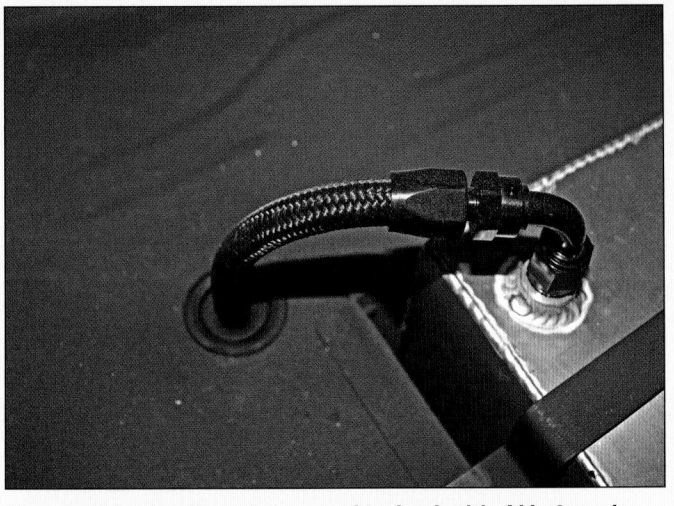

The dual fuel cell vents were plumbed with AN -6 and routed below the car. They should not vent inside the vehicle for safety reasons.

Aluminum 3/8-inch hardline was run up the subframe connector and secured with billet clamps.

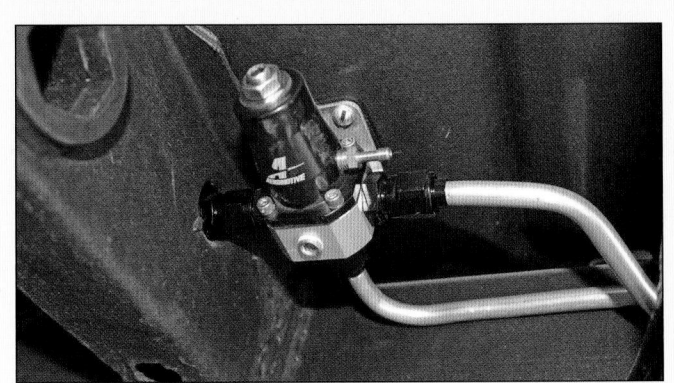

EXHAUST SYSTEM

As mentioned in Chapter 4, the vehicle and mounts you select will dictate (in many cases) what you can use on the exhaust side. Since the cast-iron exhaust manifolds found on most Gen III Hemis flow reasonably well, many people want to use them, especially for a daily driver or budget build that doesn't need every last bit of horsepower. Some people don't like tubular exhaust headers due to bad experiences with warped flanges, leaking gaskets, and bent collector flanges from scraping on speed bumps and driveways. Others want a less-expensive alternative in what can be a relatively expensive engine swap.

When the 6.1L SRT8 engine arrived, one of my employees commented the manifolds looked like they flowed well and maybe I could reuse them. Thanks to information I had gleaned from online forums and Facebook groups, such as G3 Hemi Swap, I knew that wasn't going to be the case for our A-Body. This was easily confirmed. There was no way these manifolds would work. One would think anything that fit in the relatively small engine compartment of an LX-series car, such as the 300C that ours came from, would easily fit

in the typical Mopar muscle car, but no such luck.

The 5.7L Hemi log-style manifolds found on the LX cars may fit in some limited applications, but in most cases, any of the traditional A-Body, B-Body, C-Body, and E-Body cars use Jeep log-style manifolds. The earlier ones are square port. The newer ones are D-port and tend to flow a little better. The D-port Jeep manifolds are available from Rock Auto under part numbers 53013858AD (right) and 53013857AD (left) for under $290 per pair.

If you are swapping into a truck, Jeep, or vehicle with a larger engine compartment, you may have better luck making your existing manifolds

fit. Due to production tolerances and the wide variety of equipment, engine mounts, and other factors, I hesitate to offer specific advice on exhaust manifold fitment beyond this. I *will* say that if you are using stock manifolds, be sure to get the flange and a short section of pipe with them, as the flanges are not readily available to exhaust shops. DIY Hemi has flanges available for some applications, so check with them if yours are missing.

Hooker Blackheart recently released high-clearance, cast-iron exhaust manifolds for Gen III Hemis in the following vehicle types: 1966–1972 B-Body, 1970–1974 E-Body, 1987–1997 and 1997–2004 Dakota,

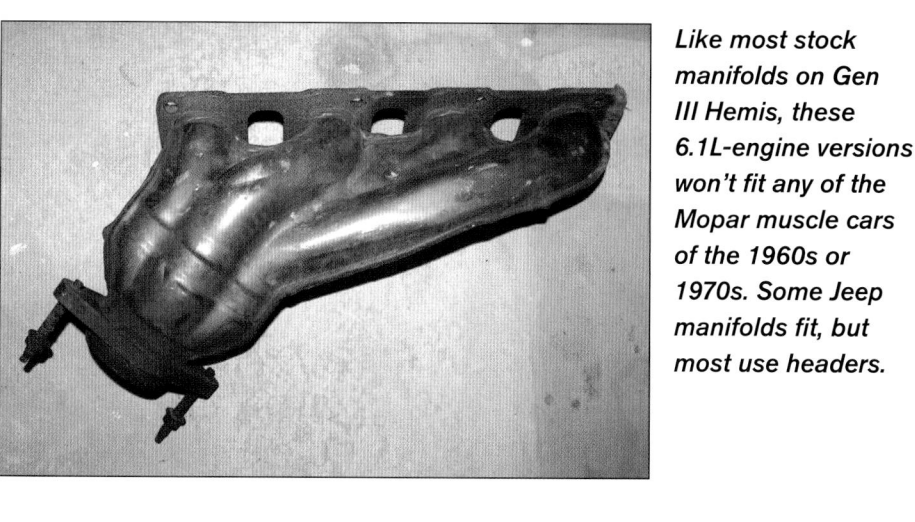

Like most stock manifolds on Gen III Hemis, these 6.1L-engine versions won't fit any of the Mopar muscle cars of the 1960s or 1970s. Some Jeep manifolds fit, but most use headers.

For truck applications, there is often a little more clearance for manifolds. Passenger-car versions rarely fit. Paul Terlosky's 1978 D300 used Jeep manifolds on its Hellcat engine.

and 1972–1993 Ram. These are log-style manifolds with a 2.5-inch outlet that turns down just ahead of the firewall. Hopefully, A-Body versions and turbo versions with V-band connections and crossovers, like they offer for LSx applications, will be offered in the future.

Headers

If you want headers for your swap, there are a lot more choices. As stated previously, if your swap is using bolt-on engine mounts from any of the sources previously listed or one of the aftermarket front-end packages that replaces the torsion bars with coilovers, look to their recommendation for headers. TTI, Schumacher, and Bouchillon all recommend TTI headers.

Interestingly, TTI lists the same headers for A-Body, B-Body, and E-Body cars with variations to accommodate different circumstances. TTI offers several different headers, and you'll need to make sure they fit all aspects of your requirements. For example, for the A-Body, B-Body, and E-Body applications they list, there are long-tube headers in 1¾-inches and 2-inches. Some require a

driver-side starter, while others specify the passenger's side. This is determined by the transmission choice, as the starter can be mounted on either side. With the A-Body applications in particular, watch for the steering type. Some require a manual box, and others fit with the Borgeson power box. None fit with the OEM power-steering box. For B-Body and E-Body applications, all box types will clear.

If you are using a coilover conversion, TTI offers a few part numbers for those applications. Rack clearance isn't an issue, whether manual or power. Conveniently, TTI lists the front-end packages they confirmed to fit. All of its long-tube Gen III Hemi headers come with oxygen sensor bungs welded in, 3-bolt-style collectors (their 1⁷⁄₈-inch shorty headers have ball-and-socket-style collectors), and are available in either bare mild steel, satin silver ceramic coated, or polished ceramic coated. If you have any doubt regarding which header you need, full product details are listed on its website.

As a part of its engineered swap systems, the Hooker Blackheart division of Holley came up with its own line of headers. By the time you read this, Hooker will have headers available for A-Body, B-Body, and E-Body cars, as well as 1972–1993 Dodge D100, 1987–2004 Dodge Dakota, and 1987–2006 Jeep YJ and TJ models, and possibly a few others. All of the headers are constructed of 18-gauge 304 stainless steel for the primaries and have 3/8-inch flanges in the same grade. The A-Body, B-Body, and

These long-tube 304 stainless-steel headers (part number BH2358) are from Hooker Blackheart. Primaries are 1⁷⁄₈ inches with three collectors. They fit 1966–1972 B-Body and 1970–1974 E-Body cars.

Use Several Factors to Determine Headers

The 1973 Duster received a set of TTI long-tube headers (part number 61HC). This set was selected for two reasons: it accommodated the driver-side starter necessitated by our 545RFE transmission, and it cleared the manual steering box the customer selected. I originally planned to use the Borgeson power-steering box and needed part number 61WPA. Overall, the headers were of very nice quality with precise mandrel bends. The flanges were 3/8-inch thick and laser cut. Since I didn't want to wait to have the headers coated by TTI, I ordered them bare, which is my preference when dealing with a header I haven't installed before. Any issues can be noted in the mockup and corrected before the coating goes on.

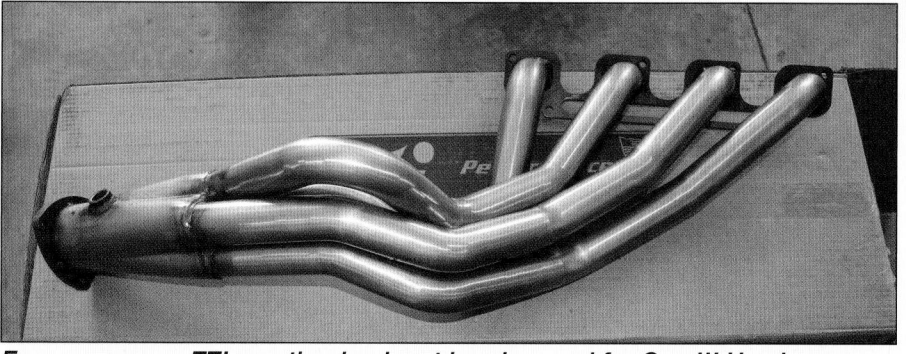

For many years, TTI was the dominant header used for Gen III Hemi swaps because they were designed around the only production mounts available at the time.

Since the car had factory power steering, I had a little work to do before installing the engine. The power steering box was removed and replaced with a remanufactured manual box. This was straightforward enough, but Mopar used a different steering column in power steering cars, so an adapter from Mancini Racing was needed to attach the box to the column. The column was a bit stubborn, but eventually everything was mated up. The power steering pump had already been removed from our 6.1L engine.

The headers themselves bolted up with no issues, but when I went to install the steering linkage, another issue was apparent. There was some slight interference that had to be rectified with slight clearance of the header tubes. While I was not aware at the time, the Firm Feel fast-ratio pitman arm that was purchased with our manual steering box was the culprit. This is noted on the TTI site, although I'm not sure it was at the time our installation was done.

The primaries spread out fairly wide to clear about any automatic transmission you want to run. Clearance around the oil pan is good.

The customer didn't want a shiny header finish, so I coated his headers with a dull exhaust ceramic coating from CeraKote. This finish requires a rough surface for adhesion (sandblasting is preferred) and can be sprayed on like a typical automotive paint. It is much thinner, so be careful not to cause runs. Many of CeraKote's finishes are over cured, but this particular one is air dried, so no large ovens or special equipment are needed. This is an economical way to coat your own exhaust or anything else at home as long as you have an area to safely spray it. Materials cost, including sandblasting, was under $200.

Once the slightly modified, coated headers were dry, they were reinstalled on the engine that was painted and detailed on a fully powder-coated and rebuilt K-member and reinstalled in the vehicle.. ■

Use Several Factors to Determine Headers *continued*

Passenger-side torsion-bar clearance is ample. You should be okay even with larger bars than were used in this 318.

The steering, brake lines, and torsion bar all fight for space on the driver's side. Clearance is adequate.

Center link clearance is good.

Idler-arm clearance is sufficient. Note that all of the front suspension is being rebuilt before final assembly.

This is another view of the torsion-bar clearance. It is tight but workable.

Torsion-bar clearance here is more than adequate.

The passenger-side collector is very close to the frame rail but does not hit. Hooking up the exhaust system will not be a problem.

Oxygen-sensor clearance looks tight in the photo, but there is enough room. I prefer to see more angle on the sensor: 2 o'clock is ideal.

The driver-side collector clears everything well. The cable to the right is for the speedometer. It is hanging loosely at this point and will not be a concern for the final installation.

E-Body headers, as well as the 1997–2004 Dakota headers, are a long-tube design created specifically for the individual chassis. All others are mid-lengths, with the exception of the Jeep applications. While referred to as mid-lengths, they are what most consider shorty headers. All of the long-tube and true mid-length versions come with oxygen sensor bungs welded on both sides. The Jeep shorties have a Y-pipe available with the oxygen sensor provisions in it. The Jeep headers have 1¾-inch primaries and connect to the available Y-pipe with supplied V-band clamps. All the other headers use a slip-fit-style collector. Interestingly, all the headers are designed to allow clearance for starters on either side and give maximum room with a variety of transmissions.

I spent a day with the engineers who created the Hooker Black-

Some swaps are so tight that it is difficult to even see the headers. The Boosted Motorsports Hellkota Dodge Dakota is equipped with Hooker Blackheart swap mounts and headers.

Larry Rose's 1970 Challenger has gone through many stages, and I have photographed several of them. It is now Hellcat powered. His car is equipped with TTI headers, which work well with the RMS/Alterkation front suspension.

Hooker calls this a mid-length header, but the primaries are as long as many of its long-tube designs. This is a D100 chassis.

This 4WD Dodge is a Holley development vehicle and has a set of prototype headers for this swap. This is different than the 2WD headers because the transmission and transfer case are not moved in this swap for cost and simplicity.

heart engine swap systems, and I was very impressed with what they have accomplished. These headers are beautiful, and they fit. I mean no offense to other manufacturers and hesitate to mention this because I do work for Holley (Hooker Blackheart's parent company). Looking at the clearance around the headers on several different development vehicles, I was struck by how much room there was around them. It is quite obvious that a lot of time was spent not just ensuring fitment but also ensuring adequate room for service. I have worked on plenty of vehicles where something as simple as a starter replacement required removal of the header, which often led to jacking the engine off its mounts. Most Gen III Hemi headers are tight enough in this area to be a problem. If your project car changes at some point, like if you go to a different transmission that requires you to switch the starter to the other side, then you have to buy another set of headers. It's not the case

here since the headers are designed to clear the starter on both sides.

The headers themselves are not the whole picture. Because Hooker makes the engine mounts, the transmission crossmember with adapters for most popular transmissions, oil pans in both sheet metal (Weiand) and cast aluminum (Holley), radiator and fan packages (Frostbite), and accessories and brackets, they can ensure all the various parts work together. The end user has guaranteed fitment as long as they don't deviate from the recommended parts. In fact, it is possible to source nearly every aftermarket part needed to complete a Gen III Hemi swap from the Holley family of companies.

I'd love to provide other sources for headers for swap applications, but as far as headers designed for a specific mount in a specific chassis, this is it. Doug's Headers were designed for Street & Performance mounts and may work with others, but Mark Campbell, the owner and founder of Street

& Performance, passed away several years ago, and the company did not continue after his passing. This was a great loss to EFI swappers everywhere, as Street & Performance was a leader in the swap hobby and produced many high-quality parts. I had the opportunity to speak to Mark on several occasions, and I was always struck by his friendly demeanor and willingness to help others.

The popularity of the Gen III Hemi has led to swaps in many non-traditional applications and into full custom builds with fabricated chassis from companies like Art Morrison, Schwartz Performance, Scott's Hot Rods, Detroit Speed and Engineering, and The Roadster Shop. All of these have their own challenges and performance goals, so finding a header that works can be difficult. In some cases, the headers previously covered may work. Definitely try them if your vehicle is laid out in a similar fashion. If not, don't get discouraged or feel like the only way you can complete your

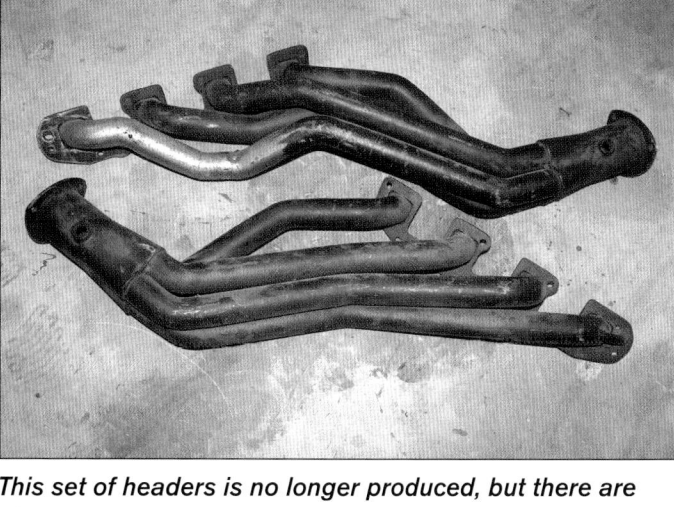

This set of headers is no longer produced, but there are plenty of them out there. Made by Hooker, they were designed to work with TTI/Schumacher-style mounts for B-Body and E-Body cars. This set was modified to clear a Borgeson power-steering box. They were mocked up on the Gremlin project when it still had the factory fender wells in place, and they fit well.

This amazing Monte Carlo SS from Schwartz Performance has its trademark chassis and a set of beautiful stainless-steel long-tube headers. Unfortunately, you can't see them due to the large carbon-fiber wheel tubs. (Photo Courtesy Schwartz Performance)

If you want to build a set of headers, start with a set of flanges (such as these from Hooker) and an assortment of U-bends and J-bends. Otherwise, use a kit from Motion Raceworks or another reputable vendor.

swap is by building or having some else build a set of custom headers. Headers of all descriptions are available for these engines in their OEM chassis. If you only have room for a shorty header or a log style, you can likely find one designed for a late-model application that will work.

Manufacturers like Stainless Works and Kooks make high-end stainless headers for many late applications in shorty and long-tube arrangements. Flowtech, BBK, Gibson, and others also offer Gen III Hemi applications so don't feel like you are locked into an expensive header just because it is a little out of the ordinary.

Building a set of custom headers isn't as difficult as it used to be, and sometimes there isn't a lot of choice. Laser-cut flanges are available from several sources, and the needed tubing, collectors, V-bands, and other components are widely available from most exhaust companies and specialty retailers like Motion Raceworks. Header kits have become more common as well and contain just about everything a potential builder needs. Header construction is a book in and of itself, but there are fortunately many videos online regarding this subject. Some of the better ones are from Trick-Tools.com, Reckless Regal, and Finnegan's Garage.

At a minimum, you'll need a method to cut the tubing (a band-saw works well), a welder, and the ability to use it (MIG will work, but TIG is preferred). If you're using stainless-steel tubing, use a regulator capable of back-purging the tubes with argon gas to prevent sugaring of the welds. Building headers takes practice, even if you are a decent welder, so you may want to get some extra tubing to practice on if you aren't used to welding tube.

Exhaust

Unless you already have a good exhaust system suitable for the power level anticipated (2.5 inches minimum in a dual system, or 3 inches in a single), you'll need a new exhaust system.

TTI makes exhaust systems that work for the A-Body, B-Body, and E-Body cars in 2.5-inch and 3-inch versions using Dynomax Super Turbo mufflers. You can also order systems without mufflers if you want to substitute a different muffler. All of its systems are aluminized steel that is CNC mandrel bent. They have H-pipe and X-pipe options. Some modification may be required, even when using their headers, since these systems are not swap-specific and can be used with virtually any engine.

Hooker Blackheart offers 304 stainless-steel systems designed for an easy bolt-in installation in the vehicles for which they offer mounts and headers. For the 1972–1993 D100 and D150, they have both single 3-inch and dual 2.5- or 3-inch systems. A-Body, B-Body, and E-Body systems are offered dual only in either 2.5-inch or 3-inch. Jeep TJ and YJ systems use a 2.5-inch Y-pipe and 3-inch single exhaust. They currently do not offer exhaust systems for Dakotas but that may change soon.

If your vehicle is one that isn't listed above, or you want something different, virtually any brand of exhaust system can be easily adapted to work with your Gen III Hemi swap as long as it is properly sized. For most cars, this should not be an issue. If you are dealing with a custom chassis or have made major changes to an existing one, like a 4-link rear suspension or IRS, you may have to custom build at least part of the exhaust system.

Many exhaust companies, such as Flowmaster and Magnaflow, manufacture builder kits that have the components typically needed to build a system, minus mufflers, with plenty of extra bends and straight sections to fit about any situation. If you go this route, make sure you secure the pipes well; especially stainless steel, as it will grow when heated. Stay as far away from brake and fuel lines as possible and take any emergency brake cable routing into consideration. Careful routing around the fuel tank is also required as you do not want to heat the fuel.

Exhaust systems are often offered in several configurations. This D100 system from Hooker Blackheart has a 3-inch single exit and is a direct bolt-in with Hooker headers.

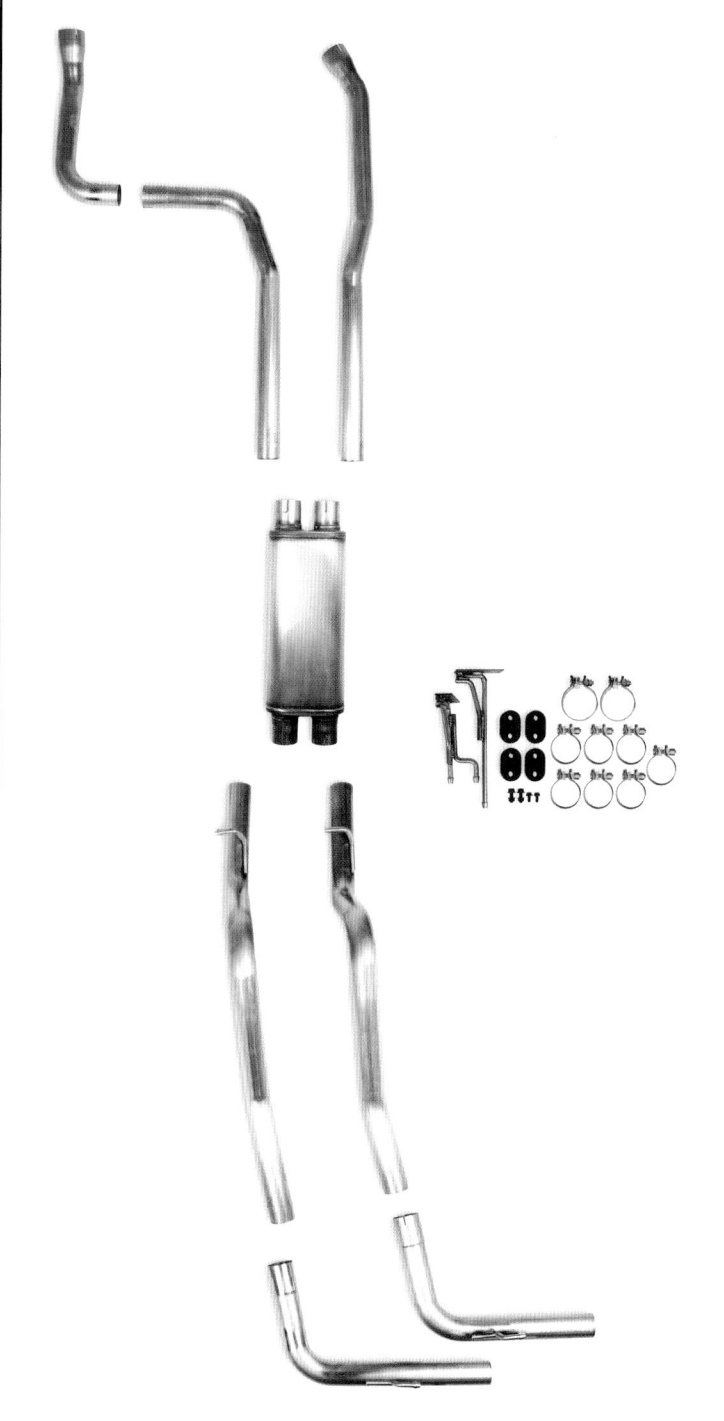

The Hooker Blackheart offers complete exhaust systems to fit most of the applications where it offers headers. This one is for 1975–1993 Dodge D100/D150 trucks.

Creative Header Applications

I visited the shop of Mike Staveski of Lexi J, Inc./RMR Dreamcars and was blown away by the quality of workmanship and problem-solving skills. This shop became famous under its old name, Time Machines, for doing several Viper V-10 swaps into Mopar muscle cars.

When the Gen III Hemi came on the market, it started using them instead. Some of the project cars still use the Viper chassis, which is excellent but with Gen III Hemi power. Projects like these, and others with non-typical suspension choices, have led to some very creative application of headers designed for other cars. A few of those are included here. While you may not be doing a similar

swap, you might see something that will work for your own vehicle.

One of my favorite cars from this shop is the 1971 Viper 'Cuda built for Gil Haas. The Viper 'Cuda was built around a 2001 ACR Viper chassis and has a 392 Gen III Hemi engine with a Magnuson supercharger backed by a Tremec T56 6-speed manual transmission.

Another great build I saw in process was the 1963 Dodge Polara with one of the first functional Hellcat 6.2L swaps. The Hellcat engine is backed by a 4L80E transmission and uses a Holley Dominator ECU to make it all happen. This car uses Detroit Speed's X-Gen Front Suspension that was custom fitted to the Polara chassis. It's another case where there are no clear choices in what headers to use. Mike has used the Detroit Speed suspension in many cars since then and recommends it highly. ■

Custom front suspensions, such as this modified Mustang DSE unit in a B-Body Mopar, create exhaust challenges. RMR Dreamcars found a late-model shorty header that worked perfectly.

Made for LX-series cars, these BBK shorty headers fit well, have a nice finish, and are reasonably priced.

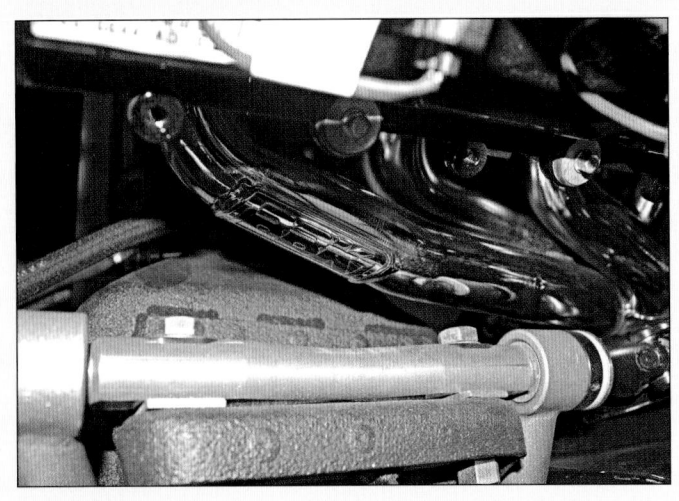

Clearance between the number-1 primary and the control-arm shaft is very good and leaves plenty of room for alignment shims if needed.

It appears that some massaging was necessary here for collector clearance, but that is minor compared to modifying a header or building one from scratch.

COMMON SWAP CONCERNS AND SYSTEM UPGRADES

Previous chapters covered the biggest issues of your Gen III Hemi swap, but as with many things, it's the details that can make or break a project. This chapter addresses those details and provides as many solutions (or at least a good direction to go in) for the more offbeat swaps. Because of the varied nature of swaps and the fact that many are going into vehicles of other makes and eras, it is impossible to cover them all.

Cooling Systems

The proper radiator for your swap may be the one that is already in the vehicle or comes stock in a more powerful version of that vehicle. Ideally, you want something large enough to adequately cool an engine of a given size and power level. The number of rows and overall width and height is determined by the space available. Air conditioning, the type of driving you plan to do, and climate can all affect the radiator choice.

A pro touring–style build destined for the Hot Rod Power Tour and a strip-only build will have vastly different cooling requirements. The radiator doesn't necessarily need to be made to accommodate the swap specifically. For the least amount of hassle and best appearance, it should have both the inlet and the outlet on the passenger (RH) side of the vehicle. If it doesn't, you may be able to make things work with factory-style molded hoses from another application or a combination of rubber and fabricated steel tubing cut and welded with the proper bends.

This Frostbite radiator fits B-Body and E-Body cars and has the proper inlet and outlet for a Gen III Hemi swap. These are available in three- or four-row versions and with or without fan packages. (Photo Courtesy Holley)

I have had good luck with odd-ball swap applications in the past by using the search function on Summit Racing's website. Under filters, you can choose material, style, with or without a transmission cooler, inlet and outlet locations, and the width and height range. I typically choose only the most important criteria and work it down from there. This search can bring up anything from stock replacement radiators for another vehicle (which is nice if you are planning to travel and ever have to replace the radiator on the road) to specific swap-oriented radiators.

Check that the inlet and outlet sizes are compatible with your engine. If you have an otherwise-perfect radiator, but the hoses on your vehicle are too large, you can buy radiator hose adapters, which are basically rubber sleeves to take up the difference. They sound sketchy, but in practice, they work well. Most swap radiators, such as the Frostbite brand from Holley and the similar ones from Champion Radiator, come with 1.5-inch inlets and 1.75-inch outlets, which make hose selection much easier. G3Hemi swap-specific radiators are currently available for A-Body, B-Body, and E-Body Mopars.

Most truck applications, particularly those with truck-sourced engines, can use the radiator, condenser (if AC equipped), and fan module from the donor vehicle. If you are building a Dakota, or post-1993 Ram or Jeep, you may be able to use the existing radiator and fans. Stock-replacement-style radiators, especially those for later models, can be especially desirable because efficient fan packages were already designed by the OEMs and can be acquired inexpensively through salvage yards or online sources, such as Rock Auto.

Even if the radiator isn't an OEM style, some careful measuring of fans on late-model vehicles can often help with retrofitting them to your existing or aftermarket replacement radiator. Many aftermarket radiators are available with electric fan packages that use either single or dual electric fans and typically have an add-on-style fan controller.

If you plan to swap your Gen III Hemi into anything that is often LSx swapped, chances are good you can use an LSx-swap radiator. These radiators typically have the inlet and outlet on the passenger's side, like a Gen III Hemi. In most cases, they use slightly smaller (1.25-inch inlet and 1.5-inch outlet) inlets and outlets. This is easily remedied with the previously mentioned hose adapters. Interestingly, Frostbite offers LSx swap radiators with screw-in -16 ORB-style inlets and outlets and appropriate fittings so you can install from 1.25-inch to 1.75-inch hoses. This can be a great problem solver.

No one to my knowledge offers swap-specific radiator hoses, which is likely due to the number of variables involved. However, if you are using an engine pulled from a donor car, the factory hoses may work or at least be modified to suit as a mock-up before buying new hoses.

If you don't have a good relationship with your local parts store counter folks, this may be a good

The radiator in this Studebaker truck is a factory-style replacement in aluminum. Most existing radiators can be made to work as long as they have enough capacity for the power level.

This car has a Griffin radiator with an overflow canister mounted along the side. Note the Gate Powergrip clamps that give a clean look with reliable sealing.

time to get to know them. Being able to walk into a parts store with a pieced-together hose or bent piece of wire and a tape measure and be let loose in the stock room to find a hose that will work isn't something that all stores allow, but I have never had a problem doing so.

The typical swap can use a stock or stock replacement–style water pump, but there are a couple of instances where that may not be possible or desirable. An electric pump may be preferred. In a drag application where the pump can run without the engine running or during specific parameters set up in the ECU, there is really no other choice. This can be very handy in a dyno cell. They can be engine-mounted units or remote universal-style pumps that install in the radiator hose, such as those from Stewart Components. With an adequate electrical system, there should be a power gain.

However, engine-mounted electric pumps for this application don't utilize a pulley, so they can't be used with a stock accessory layout. Typically, a race application will have only an alternator or perhaps a dry-sump pump or vacuum pump to drive it, so some fabrication may be needed.

Sometimes, you can find a radiator with the right dimensions but the inlet and outlet aren't the right size. Spacers, such as this, can be used to overcome the issue.

The clean Hellcat swap in this wagon used late Challenger/Charger components for the cooling system. It can be worth the trouble to make OEM components fit because they are available anywhere in case of an issue.

This dragster uses a BBC-style electric water pump. This is fairly common with any Gen III Hemis with motor plates. Meziere makes one that bolts on in place of a factory pump if you want to go electric without a motor plate or fabrication.

A passenger-car-style accessory drive is used here. This one is a VVT version (2009–newer).

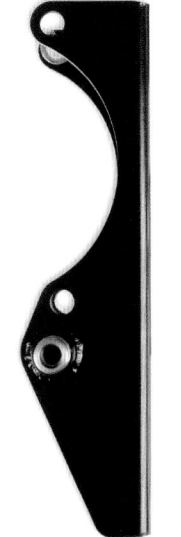

This is the truck version. Note the mechanical fan, which indicates this engine came from a heavy-duty truck. This system is very tall and works best in trucks or older cars with a high hood line.

If your alternator is a bit too tight to the frame rail with a 2009–newer car accessory drive, use Holley part number 97-369 for some extra clearance. This alternator doesn't require ECU activation like the stock ones. (Photo Courtesy Holley)

Other than that, the main drawback of an electric pump is the cost (over $600 retail for a bolt-on-style Meziere pump) and lack of availability if it needs to be replaced. Some may choose to run a remote-style pump to get around this.

Another popular application of an electric water pump is when running a motor plate. Most manufacturers of motor plates, such as AEI Inc. who made the plate for our Gremlin project, offer an option to use either the stock-style pump (whether mechanical or electric) or a big-block Chevrolet (BBC)-style pump.

Why a BBC-style pump? In addition to lining up well with the factory timing cover, the primary reasons are cost and availability. While I have used Meziere electric pumps on the street in other applications with zero reliability issues, the Gen III Hemi–specific one is going to be difficult to replace in a pinch. The BBC version is available anywhere from several different suppliers and is far more likely to be in someone's trailer at a race if you need one in a hurry. AEI offers a bracket kit as an option to run the popular 93-mm Denso alternator. You'll have to forgo other accessories, such as power steering and AC, which isn't typically an issue in a drag race application.

Accessory and Drive Systems

For the vast majority of swaps, the existing accessory drive on your engine will work, aesthetics aside. Accessory drives on passenger vehicles and some Jeeps are mounted low for clearance for the front-mounted throttle bodies. Truck engines typically have an upward-facing throttle body to accommodate high-mounted AC compressors on earlier models and alternators on later ones.

If the height and appearance of the truck's intake and accessories aren't an issue, you can use them. Whether your accessory drive is passenger-car or truck based, the low-mounted AC compressors can create clearance issues and need to be addressed.

Fortunately, the AC compressors can be deleted with a shorter belt on the passenger-car engines. I did this on the Duster project's 6.1L since it was a non-air car. Tensioner placement on most low mount truck engines makes this impossible, so you'll need to fabricate or locate an idler to go in its place.

If there are changes made with stock components, the most common one is to replace the truck accessory layout with the passenger-car version. This is usually done to convert to a stock front-mount-style intake like any of the passenger-car 5.7L/6.1L (aluminum) or 6.4L intakes. Early 5.7L and 6.1L intakes interchange directly, but to run any of the later 2009-and-up Eagle (5.7L) or Apache (6.4L) intakes, you'll need to use intake adapters like those sold by Holley and MMX to accommodate the change in bolt pattern.

I used the Holley spacers on our Gremlin's early heads when changing to the Hi-Ram intake. The timing covers are different between passenger car and truck, as are the harmonic balancer and the accessories themselves, so this will all need to be changed. VVT and non-VVT use a different cover. Note the passenger-car system will have some clearance issues at the alternator on some applications, like Dodge D100s and D150s and some A-Bodies. You can notch the frame slightly to compensate or use Holley's alternator relocation bracket with part number 97-347 for factory alternators or part number 97-368 for Holley alternators.

There are a couple of issues with the stock accessories. For one, the

Holley's power-steering pump (part number 198-104) works with 2014– newer car and truck drives and reduces pressure to avoid issues with factory power-steering boxes. (Photo Courtesy Holley)

If you want something a little flashier, CVF has a billet accessory drive available in several configurations with either a clear or black powder-coat finish.

power steering pump provides too much pressure for some systems, particularly older power steering boxes and rack-and-pinion units. The fix is either slowing down the pump (Bouchillon has a pump kit for most applications), adding a valve to reduce pressure (Heidt's makes one), or adapting a GM pump (Holley offers this for both early and late passenger-car applications).

The other issue is the alternator. The 2008-newer alternators require an input from the ECU, and the most common way to eliminate that problem in a swap is to use an adjustable external voltage regulator like the one from 1970s BMW 1600, 1800, 2000, and 2002 models. These are available on eBay from California

Alternator and Starter. To wire one, you have a ground from the regulator, a switched 12V, and one lead to the top pin of the alternator. It can also be commanded through an aftermarket ECU. Earlier alternators can use the 1970s-and-newer Mopar external voltage regulator.

If you want to use an aftermarket front engine accessory drive (FEAD), there are a few choices. March Performance makes a kit called the Style Track that uses a chrome GM-style CS130 alternator and aluminum Type 2 power steering pump along with a chromed Sanden 7176 AC compressor. The PS is on a separate bracket so it can be ordered with or without power steering. A remote reservoir is required. There isn't a conventional tensioner. This system uses a belt adjustment tool and three idlers instead. I haven't used this particular system, but I have had good luck with March products in the past. You can get this system with clear or black powder coating or with a chrome finish. This system is available only for non-VVT engines. This system does have a 1980s street rod look to it, so it isn't for everyone.

CVF Racing also offers a serpentine kit with choices of alternator only, PS and alternator, or alternator, PS, and AC. I have used a few of their kits on other engines with great success. The CVF kit is available with a GM-style CS130 140-amp or 300-amp alternator in a 1-wire configuration, a Sanden AC compressor, and Type II power steering with an optional pump for Hydroboost setups. This system can be ordered with a provision for a mechanical or electric fan. This system uses a conventional Gates-style tensioner. The look of this kit is a bit more modern and is available in either a clear or black powder-coat finish for both early and late (VVT) applications.

Holley has offered its mid-mount accessory bracket kits for GM LSx, LTx, SBC, and BBC engines for a while but recently released kits for Gen III Hemi applications in both VVT and non-VVT versions with a choice of as-cast or black-coated finish. Unlike other manufacturers' serpentine kits, Holley chose to do things in a very OEM-like way by retaining the bracketless system these engines were designed to use instead of incorporating a series of add-on brackets. This was done by starting with a new cast-aluminum timing cover assembly that addresses all the shortcomings of the original systems and does it very cleanly.

Holley's mid-mount kit is available with a natural or polished finish for VVT or non-VVT engines. This system is based around a new timing cover that functions as an accessory **bracket and pulls the accessories in much tighter while solving several problems, such as power-steering pressure and alternator wiring.**

Adding all the attachment points to it for the needed accessories was the most logical thing to do, but Holley didn't stop there. Instead of using a conventional water pump, the water pump housing is cast into the timing cover and accepts a replaceable cartridge that contains the bearing, seal, and impeller, and the water pump pulley. This makes service easy with only 6 bolts to remove. Holley also provided several ports to configure your heater hoses and Coolant Temperature Sensor (CTS) as needed and added swivel-style water inlets and outlets to make hose routing easy. The included GM-style alternator doesn't require the factory ECU exciter like the OEM unit (see Chapter 9).

The GM-style Type II power steering pump, sourced from another Holley company, Detroit Speed & Engineering, is internally valved to provide proper pressure for older steering boxes and power rack-and-pinion units to prevent leaks and the floating feeling that an over-powered steering can cause. The AC compressor is a compact Sanden SD7 unit. Because of the design, all accessories are tucked in tightly to the engine to resolve clearance issues that are often found with other accessories. A remote-mount reservoir kit is available if desired.

Air-Intake Systems

No one makes air intake systems specifically for engine swaps, but that doesn't mean you have to fabricate your own. For later model vehicles, you may be able to adapt factory airboxes and plumbing from the original engine and combine it with components from the new system. Not everyone wants a stock look or the inlet restrictions that can result with some factory pieces, so I'll present a few other options. In many cases, an aftermarket air intake system designed for a late-model passenger car or truck can be used.

The 6.1L Hemi that I swapped into the Duster in Chapter 4 came with a Mopar Performance cold-air intake that had been installed on the SRT8 300C the engine was pulled from. It fit the Duster chassis with no modifications. It used an open, conical, oiled-cotton air filter, which is

The airbox from a donor late-model Ram was used on this D100 swap. This is a cheap and effective idea if you have room.

The air intake on David Kruk's 1970 Super Bee adapted the stock boot to a second boot from a 5.7L engine with a tube going through the core support for fresh air. David is modifying this system because it is a bit restrictive, but the basic idea is sound.

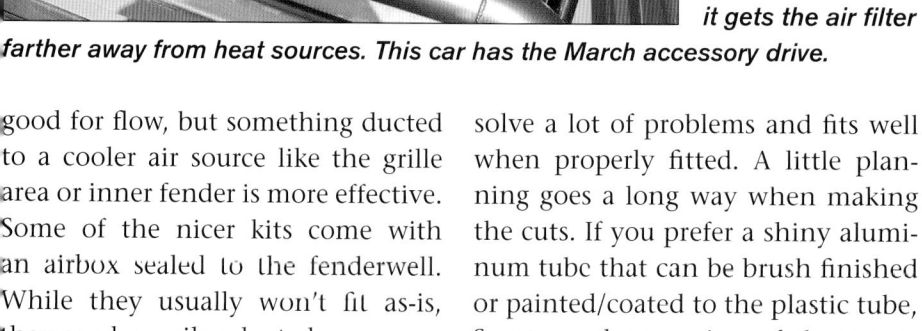

The intake tubing on this 6.1L engine is custom built with mandrel-bent tubing that is cut and spliced together. This is a great method, and it gets the air filter farther away from heat sources. This car has the March accessory drive.

good for flow, but something ducted to a cooler air source like the grille area or inner fender is more effective. Some of the nicer kits come with an airbox sealed to the fenderwell. While they usually won't fit as-is, they can be easily adapted.

Flowmaster makes an interesting kit for fabricating your own air intake system under part number 615400. It comes with a conical filter, adapters, clamps, mounting bracket, and a large, bent-plastic tube that can be easily cut and re-joined with the included silicone couplers and stainless-steel clamps. It can

solve a lot of problems and fits well when properly fitted. A little planning goes a long way when making the cuts. If you prefer a shiny aluminum tube that can be brush finished or painted/coated to the plastic tube, Spectre makes a variety of aluminum tubing, silicone couplers and bends, filters in all sizes, and anything else needed to build an air intake system for any vehicle. They even sell carburetor-style adapters, which will work with most 4-barrel throttle bodies.

Want something a little more creative? Use lengths of straight alu-

minum or titanium tubing, along with an assortment of mandrel bends and some TIG welding skills, to create the intake plumbing to exactly fit your application. It will provide a finished look that no universal kit or factory-built piece can ever outshine. Style is up to the builder. Exposed welds in a rainbow of colors or the more recently-popular pie-cut technique where a series of pie cuts are used to replace the mandrel bends or create angles that aren't possible with a tubing bender, are now the norm.

I still prefer smoothed welds that, regardless of the assembly technique, look like a single, fluid piece of tubing. Supports for the tubing can be easily made and added where necessary. Connections to the throttle body can be made with silicone couplers or V-band or Wiggins clamps. Since best results are found with only fresh, cool air entering the intake tract, an airbox should be built to direct air from an outside source such as a headlight (common on four-headlight cars), grille, or from

Project Goals

One of the biggest pitfalls of building a project car is the tendency for the project to grow far beyond what was originally intended. Sometimes this is due to unforeseen problem areas, such as well-hidden rust or poor repairs. However, ours was due to a change in project goals.

The 1972 AMC Gremlin was a fairly complete car with minimal rust, a factory 304-ci V-8, and a nice driver-quality first car for my son to drive to high school. A few early changes in the plan resulted in a low-mileage 5.7L Hemi being purchased along with a Tremec T-56 Magnum and a Quick Time bellhousing, a Control Freak front suspension, and a mix of Viper and C4 Corvette components to build our own hybrid IRS.

Fast forward a few years of the car languishing while my son served an enlistment in the US Marine Corps. The new plan was for a car that could drift and participate in road racing, hill climbs, land speed racing, and whatever else I wanted to do with it. The new goals led to the idea of using a full custom chassis built by us around an Art Morrison C6 Corvette–style front clip, C6 suspension in the rear with twin turbos, and an air-to-water intercooler. Add in the roll-cage tubing now required to legally and safely race in venues and the addition of an AWD system comprised of Nissan Skyline components and Dutchman aluminum 9-inch IRS-style housings at both ends. Suddenly, this car is a completely different animal. The factory unibody structure is gone and replaced by a removable 2x4 and 1.75 round-tube chassis. The car is now officially known as "The Gremlin-Shaped Object."

As part of these changes, a decision was made to mount the engine with a motor plate from AEI Inc. It provides more room for turbo plumbing and AWD components, is stronger, and makes servicing the car much easier. I am currently in the earliest stages of chassis construction but wanted to show the basic plan for how the plate will be mounted. More importantly, for this chapter's purposes, it shows how it affected our choice of accessory drives.

I looked at all sorts of configurations with various water pumps and components, but the obstacle that didn't have a good answer was how to incorporate power steering into the system without engineering our own complete accessory drive. I considered adapting an electric power-assist steering (EPAS) system to get around this, but tuning that type of system for our intended usage was a bit of an unknown. Most of the commonly used systems, such as the Volvo and GM units, are essentially run in a limp mode. I wanted to stick to a tried-and-true hydraulic system. This may be something to

The AEI motor plate is installed with a modified stock, early timing cover. The plate is attached at the frame rail and to the roll-cage tubing.

The motor plate is drilled and tapped for BBC water pumps. I utilized this feature to accommodate the Holley BBC mid-mount accessory drive kit.

The large bypass port will be plugged for this application

consider later, but hydraulic assist is the way to go for the time being.

Fortunately, I found a partial solution that will make the rest of this conversion fairly simple and update the cooling system at the same time. AEI offers its plate with either standard 1/2- or 3/4-inch NPT water inlets for use with a remote electric pump or a big-block Chevy (BBC) electric water pump. The outlet options are 3/4-inch or 1-inch NPT or a small-block Mopar water neck housing pattern.

I chose the BBC inlet and 1-inch NPT outlet. I should have deleted this one, but it will be plugged for our purposes. The intention was to run a reverse rotation, serpentine-style BBC pump since I need the upper pulley to run our PS pump. There are a few water pumps available that meet that need, but lining up all the required accessories, tensioner, idlers, and the crank pulley is still a problem.

The charging system needs to put out plenty of voltage for the EFI system and other electrical demands, which may be marginal with the typical reduced size race alternator. The power steering needs to put out proper pressure for the DSE rack I am using. The stock Mopar pump puts out too much pressure. I searched for anyone who used power steering in an application like ours with any water pump but came up with nothing that seemed like a good solution. It's enough to make your head spin, but I came up with a plan.

For those not familiar with the Holley mid-mount accessory drive systems, they are a custom accessory drive using GM LT1–style 150-amp alternators, Type II Saginaw power steering pumps, and a Sanden AC compressor in a unique (for the aftermarket) bracketless system that mounts all the accessories on the front of the engine and out of the way of obstructions like steering boxes, frame rails, and forward-facing turbo setups.

They use a modern LT1-style cartridge type of water pump, which is reverse rotation and provides a belt surface like any other mechanical pump. These units were first released for the GM LS and LT engines and are available for the big-block Chevy. They recently became available for the Gen III Hemi, so why am I still considering the use of a BBC system? Simple. The Gen III Hemi system uses its own timing cover with a design that doesn't lend itself to motor plate use like the BBC system does.

Our AEI plate bolts cleanly to the front of the stock timing cover after I cut off the original brackets for clearance, so I decided to stay with that plan. The BBC system is different than the late-model-style mid-mount kits in that everything is

The ATI balancer/hub assembly and lower pulley from the Gen III Hemi mid-mount kit will be used.

mounted off a water pump housing rather than a new-design timing cover. This allows the entire system to bolt up to our motor plate like it would on a BBC. Granted, I will delete the AC. Delete pulleys for SD7 compressors are readily available from Power by the Hour and others. This change will give the same cartridge-style LT1 water pump used in the other mid-mount kits, as well as a superior alternator and a PS pump that will work well with our DSE rack.

While this all sounds great, what about the belt spacing? Unfortunately, the stock Gen III Hemi harmonic balancer/pulley is not the correct depth for this system, but the ATI-sourced damper and bolt-on pulley from the Gen III Hemi kits is. I will use these parts to complete the system. ■

The Holley mid-mount kit is installed pretty much as received from Holley except for the air-conditioning compressor. I used a "delete" pulley. (Photo Courtesy Holley)

The front of this engine is a very clean design. Part of that is because there is no intake tubing in the way. The throttle body is ducted straight up into a modified 'Cuda shaker hood scoop.

inside the fenderwell. It doesn't have to be high-pressure air. The goal is to make sure the inlet temperatures are kept down so the intake air temperature sensor (IAT) doesn't make any adverse changes.

Oiling System

As previously covered, the OEM oil pans for Gen III Hemis come in front-sump (passenger car) or rear-sump (truck) designs. VVT pans and non-VVT pans are the same but use a different oil pan pickup. Hellcat 6.2L pans have a different pan bolt pattern. Aftermarket pans are available in the same layouts, plus the mid-sump design used on traditional Mopars. Milodon offers steel mid-sump and rear-sump pro-touring and drag-race pans in both bolt patterns.

Holley offers cast mid-sump pans for VVT and non-VVT applications. They are sold with the pickup, hence the different part numbers. The pans are identical. Weiand offers sheet metal mid-sump pans for the same applications. Stef's offers nice fabricated aluminum dual-pattern pans that fit both the 6.2L Hellcat and 6.4L in front-, mid-, and rear-sump versions. They also offer the standard-pattern pans with the same layout. Moroso has front- and rear-sump steel drag racing pans in both bolt patterns.

With any oil pan change, you'll likely need to change the attachment point of the pickup tube. They attach to the main cap, which has a stud on the end for this purpose. I recommend purchasing a new main cap stud from the dealer (part number 06513100AA) to ensure proper clamping.

The oil-filter housing on many Gen III Hemis, including those found in passenger cars, are mounted on the passenger side and often interfere with the frame or K-member. In some applications, like B-Body, C-Body, and E-Body Mopars, you can substitute the factory 2003–2008 Ram oil filter adapter (part number 53021610AF). It uses the same attachment point but is turned at a 45-degree angle. In many cases it will offer enough clearance.

In tighter applications, such as the A-Body, this won't work. You'll need to use a block-off plate available from MMX, Earl's, and others and install 3/8-inch NPT fittings in the two oil ports above the filter housing to plumb a remote filter. Earl's offers a kit specifically for late-model Hemi engines that comes with everything needed to relocate the oil filter. If you plan to add an oil cooler, which is especially beneficial on turbocharged applications, this is a good time to do so.

Due to crossmember clearance on the Gremlin (and for better oil control), I switched to this Milodon pro-touring pan. It has trap doors for better oil control and a 9-quart capacity. Figuring in the oil cooler, dual filters, and an Accusump, the oil-system capacity should be around 15 to 16 quarts. I will go with a dry sump as the budget allows.

Earlier in this book is an oil filter block-off kit from MMX. This one is from Earl's. There are several different versions.

Common Clearance Issues

While Gen III Hemi engines are fairly compact in comparison to some modern V-8s, particularly OHC V-8s like Ford Mod Motors, there can still be some fitment issues. A primary one is brake booster clearance. Most larger vehicles, like traditional Mopar B-Body, C-Body, and E-Body vehicles, wouldn't typically have a problem. But on A-Body or the later F-Body, M-Body, and J-Body Mopars, there isn't adequate clearance for the stock brake booster. Choices include converting to manual brakes (many of these cars came from the factory with manual brakes), a smaller street rod–type brake booster, or Hydroboost. The Hydroboost is a popular upgrade but adds weight and complexity to the system. Trucks, even Dakotas, normally don't have booster clearance issues with Holley engine mounts. This is due to movement of the engine forward from the stock location (1¼ inches on the D100 mounts). This is a trick that may help in your custom swap.

Some models, such as B-Body and E-Body cars as well as trucks, can use this Dodge 45-degree filter adapter if the filter is a problem with the passenger-car-style filter adapter. A-Body cars have to block it off and use the ports on the side of the block.

Another common problem is windshield wiper motor clearance. While it is close, it won't be a problem on most swaps with premade mounts for Mopar vehicles that use stock or aftermarket intake manifolds, regardless of manufacturer. Many cars with the wiper motor mounted in the center can cause clearance problems, particularly on Hellcat swaps, due to the size of the intake. If you run into this issue, there are a few options, but none of them are easy. In some cases, you may be able to recess the wiper motor into the cowl enough to gain clearance and modify the linkage accordingly.

I used this Canton remote oil filter block on a previous project. It provides a convenient bung for a pressure sender in the housing.

Another option is to adapt a late-model-style wiper motor from

Many older Mopars have manual disc brakes. This one has a Wilwood master cylinder that allows plenty of clearance for the engine.

This D100 uses a combination of an aftermarket brake booster painted matte black to appear stock and a later-model-style Mopar master cylinder. Note the bolts in the frame rail below. This truck has a Crown Victoria suspension swap.

Jim Cain used a Hydroboost system powered by the power-steering pump to create more clearance for his Charger's 6.4L swap.

another vehicle and fabricate linkages or cables to accommodate the change. If you'd prefer more of a pre-engineered solution, Specialty Power Windows offers a Deluxe Universal Wiper Drive kit (part number WWKXLWD-2I) that can be adapted to nearly any vehicle. For our Gremlin, which has an extreme amount of engine setback and a fairly large wiper motor, things are going to be more drastic. The cowl is split into two sections with the Hi-Ram intake sitting in between. I will likely wind up using a pair of universal single wiper kits from Speedway Automotive.

Power steering box clearance is nonexistent on A-Bodies and later

FMJ cars. You'll need to convert to manual or Borgeson power steering. Custom headers may still be required on all but the A-Bodies because clearance on some of these cars is very tight. For non-Mopar swaps, such as GM A-Body, F-Body, X-Body, and G-Bodies, S-Series, and full-size GM trucks 1967-and-newer, steering box clearance isn't an issue since the Saginaw 800 boxes are more compact than the bulbous Mopar units.

Most 1960s and early 1970s vintage Fords have good clearance for the steering boxes since they are essentially manual boxes with a power assist. But considering the poor performance and tendency to

leak of those systems, I'd replace them with Borgeson power boxes anyway. The 1974–1978 Mustang IIs, 1979-and-newer Mustangs, all the 1978-newer Fox variants, and the fourth-generation F-Bodies are all equipped with rack-and-pinion steering, so the worst case is the steering shaft may need to be re-routed. Many people will swap these engines into imports of all types, and I haven't forgotten them. Since most of those vehicles use rack-and-pinion steering, clearance isn't an issue.

Another stumbling block is with the vehicle's stock HVAC system. Compressor clearance issues have been mentioned previously. The best choice is an aftermarket accessory drive that places all the components in a more desirable location. This isn't the only issue. The HVAC

Jim's Charger has a very clean but serviceable aftermarket air-conditioning system that makes effective use of the limited space available.

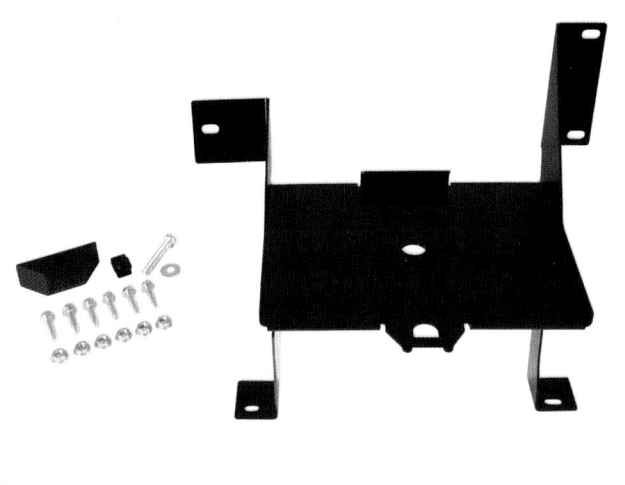

This battery tray is designed to move the battery from the driver's side to the passenger's side of the engine compartment for air-intake clearance. Part number BHS589 fits 1970–1974 E-Body models. (Photo Courtesy Holley)

components on many vehicles intrude into the engine compartment and can create interference with the passenger-side valve cover and coils. While possible, relocating coils on a Gen III Hemi isn't an easy job and adds potential spark issues and unnecessary parts, like the plug wires themselves. A better solution is to move the engine slightly forward. The adverse effect on handling is minimal. Overall, this solution makes the vehicle far easier to service. If that is not an option, the box itself can be modified. Depending on the make, some of the shrouding is plastic and can be carefully massaged with a heat gun.

If it is fiberglass, the housing can often be removed, notched with the use of some cardboard, mat, and resin and reinstalled. In extreme clearance cases or for aesthetics and a more modern system, companies like Vintage Air make AC systems that can often be installed with only the refrigerant and heater lines and a few wires entering the engine com-

partment. This can be a great way to go, especially if you are already upgrading to a newer-style Sanden AC compressor with your choice of accessory drive.

The last issue I am addressing specifically is one that is often overlooked until the final steps of the swap: the location of the stock battery. With early engines, or engines using aftermarket intakes with a straight entry to the throttle body, you can choose the side the battery is on for air intake routing. However, later Gen III Hemis have the intake manifold and air intake routed to the driver's side. If your battery is in the way, you'll have to address it.

If you have an E-Body Mopar, Holley makes a battery tray that bolts up to the passenger side (part number BHS589). Some vehicles, like GM 3rd generation F-Bodies and the 1978–1988 A- and G-Bodies, were equipped with the battery tray on either side, depending on model year and options. It is very easy to change to the needed location. Today's

smaller, more powerful AGM or lithium batteries can be more easily relocated and do not have to be positioned upright to allow even more mounting options. Trunk mounting is always an option and helps with weight distribution.

In the course of a swap, other clearance problems may occur but few are going to require difficult steps to remedy. Slightly creating clearance with a ball-peen hammer, notching or grinding brackets, and modification of new components is all part of hot rodding.

Gauges and Instrumentation

Since the earliest EFI swaps, one of the biggest questions has been, "What do I do about the gauges?" There isn't a one-size-fits-all answer to that question, especially with the varied nature of these swaps, but I will give a brief overview of the possible solutions. Much of this depends upon your chosen engine management.

Just because you run an EFI engine doesn't mean you have to use a digital dash. Greg Huizenga used conventional AutoMeter gauges in his turbocharged Cherokee.

Retaining the original gauges is often desired, whether in an older vehicle like a 1968 Charger where you want to preserve an original look in the interior or a later model such as a Dodge Dakota or a Jeep. Some installations will be far more complex than others.

To run the typical mechanical speedometer, whether OEM or aftermarket, you need a transmission that is equipped to run it, such as an A-833 4-speed or a 727 TorqueFlite—or can be equipped to provide a mechanical output. Any of the popular aftermarket manual transmissions, such as the Tremec TKO 500 and 600, TKX, and T56 Magnum, can be set up with a mechanical speedometer.

The popular 4L60E (Silver Sport Transmission sells these as the A41) and 4L80E can be equipped with a mechanical conversion available from several sources such as Bowler Transmission. Many transmissions have this type of conversion available, including the 545RFE, but the newer your transmission type, the less likely this will be an option.

For those where it is an option, it can be pricey. NAG1s, 8HP70s,

and 8HP90s will likely need a convertor to go from the electronic VSS signal to an electrically-driven servo motor. This can be done with any vehicle speed sensor (VSS)-equipped transmission. It is often easier and less expensive than converting to a mechanical-style speedometer output. AutoMeter, Dakota Digital, and others offer conversion boxes to accommodate this.

Electronic speedometers that run off of a VSS signal are more common in swaps. They are fairly easy to configure with most aftermarket EFI and transmission control and can run using the existing VSS signal from the transmission without any add-ons. Different makes may use a slightly different calibration (a different number of pulses per mile, usually a square wave signal), so this is something to watch. GM is 4,000 pulses per mile versus Mopar with 8,000 pulses per mile. Nissan is 16,000 pulses per mile.

If you need to use an older-style transmission that only has a mechanical speedometer drive available, which is common with some transfer cases for the 4-wheel-drive guys, you

can use a pass-through pulse generator from Dakota Digital to get around the issue. If you use an electric aftermarket speedometer, most of these are set up to use a very wide range of VSS signals and come with instructions on how to calibrate them so complex calculations and altering the square wave signal through resistors or other means isn't necessary.

If you start fresh with new aftermarket gauges, a GPS speedometer may be a good choice. These do not require a mechanical or VSS connection. It just needs a GPS antenna. This option is becoming far more popular due to its simplicity.

Tachometer hookup is very simple with this swap. Most harnesses, whether OEM style (Hotwire, DIY Hemi, Mopar Performance, etc.) or aftermarket (Holley, FAST, MS3, etc.), will have a 12-volt square wave tach signal wire. If not, tap into the primary lead of one of the coil wires and

Gauges, such as this speedometer from Holley, are linked to the ECU instead of using separate sending units. (Photo Courtesy Holley)

Holley's Pro dashes, such as this 12.3-inch unit, are infinitely programable but only work with Holley EFI. (Photo Courtesy Holley)

The RacePak IQ3 shown here is compatible with Holley, AEM, Electromotive, Haltech, Motec, MegaSquirt MS-3, and other EFI. (Photo Courtesy Holley)

use the MSD part number 8918 tach signal GMR pickup. This converts the low-voltage, high-current pulse to a clean square-wave signal to power a tach or shift light. This is great for a modern tachometer, but earlier factory and some aftermarket tachs that are current triggered may need a tach adapter like MSD part number 8920.

Before getting into the other gauges that are commonly used with G3 Hemi swaps, an easy way to display all the functions monitored by your ECU, whether it is a factory or an aftermarket ECU, is through the controller area network (CAN) bus. CAN is your engine's nervous system. It allows microcontrollers and devices to communicate with each other. What does this mean for the swapper looking to hook up the gauges? The biggest benefit this brings is that additional sending units and wiring do not have to be added as long as the functions being monitored are already monitored.

Speedhut is one of the few gauge manufacturers that offer gauges that communicate with most factory ECUs. They will not work with aftermarket ECUs unless they follow the OEM CAN protocol. They will not

work with Holley EFI. Holley does offer its own CAN gauges that are compatible with its EFI systems.

Dakota Digital is known for high quality gauge panels tailored to a variety of vehicles. They cover the popular 1968–1970 Mopar B-Bodies, as well as 1970–1974 E-Bodies. Jeep applications from 1955–1981 are also covered. They also offer panel systems for GM, Ford, VW, Toyota, and universal applications and individual gauges. Using the appropriate BIM module, the gauges can communicate with your OEM or aftermarket ECU. They have modules for Holley, AEM (now a Holley company), Edelbrock, FAST, Haltech, MegaSquirt, and MSD Atomic.

Want something a little better suited for a race car or more easily packaged in custom installations? Holley has a few choices, but to take advantage of the CAN function you have to run a Holley ECU. The 7-inch Digital Dash (part number 553-106) works with any Holley EFI system and is fully customizable with a 7-inch low-glare, high-brightness, high-contrast, full-color touchscreen. It has a virtual switch panel, can control and play back data logs, and has

user defined alarms, shift lights, and other features. This is one of Holley's older offerings, but it works well.

A standalone version is available for those using non-Holley ECUs, though you'll lose the CAN functionality and have to run sensors and wiring. Holley's newer offerings, which are sold under the Pro Dash banner, are available in 6.86- or 12.3-inch versions. They allow real-time tuning, monitor up to 238 values, and have many of the same features as the regular digital dash. They also have 12 multi-configurable inputs and 4 switched ground outputs. The layout is determined by your needs and design skills with a high degree of customization available. Like the 7-inch Digital Dash, there are standalone versions available so you can use this with any ECU but without the CAN functionality.

Racepak's IQ3 Display Dash will work with any 2008-later OBDII systems and the most popular aftermarket ECUs, including Holley, Fuel Tech, MS3, FAST XFI, BigStuff3, MoTeC, AEM, and others. This is a much simpler system than the Pro Dash but offers a built-in data logger and the ability to monitor up to

28 inputs on four pages. Shift lights, warnings, and gear indicators are also offered. A full line of accessory sensors, including shock travel sensors, driveshaft speed sensors, and others are available to tailor the Racepak to your specific needs.

What to do if you like your original or aftermarket gauges and don't want to change them to a modern gauge panel? A perfect example is an otherwise restored car with a G3 Hemi swap. Due to differences in voltage and the possibility of changing the signal to the ECU if equipped, it isn't a good idea to tap into existing sensors to feed the gauges. This is where CAN is a nice feature. Instead, the best way is to add the sensors for your existing gauges, whether mechanical or electric. Sometimes, this is easier said than done.

Most older OEM sensors have NPT threads and can be a bit larger than the newer OEM sensors. In some cases, it may be possible to use adapters from AutoMeter or Equus from the factory, which is especially handy with non-US sensors that may be metric. If you are not using the oil ports on the passenger's side of the block, they can be used for an oil pressure gauge tap. The two threaded ports are 3/8 NPT. If you are using a carburetor and don't need the factory coolant temperature sensor (CTS) located on the water pump housing on later engines and in the block casting behind the top of the timing cover on earlier engines, you can remove it and install your sender there.

The CTS is also 3/8 NPT, so most factory and aftermarket senders can be easily adapted. I suspect most of the engines being converted to a carb are early ones, so it is a simple task on those engines. For the others, since

there isn't much room for a T-fitting, I suggest one of the two options: either drill and tap another section at the top of the water pump housing for your gauge sender or run a 3/8 NPT to AN adapter and plumb in a remote sensor block. Motion Raceworks and Holley both offer these.

Voltmeters are a simple matter to connect. You simply need a source of battery voltage regardless of what engine is being used. If your vehicle is equipped with an ammeter, have it converted to read voltage (gauge conversion specialists like Redline Gauge Works can help with this) or replace it in favor of a voltmeter. An ammeter essentially has a battery fed circuit that is live at all times, typically unfused, and was designed for relatively low-powered charging systems for cars with few electrical demands. This can be catastrophic if there is an issue. It usually results in an electrical fire that can easily destroy carpet and padding typically found under the dash of your vehicle.

Other gauges, such as transmission temperature, boost, and fuel pressure, assuming it's not covered by the CAN like with a carbureted swap, are straightforward as with any other installation.

Drivetrain Upgrades

Depending on what vehicle you start with, you may need to upgrade the drivetrain. Assuming that you have matched your engine's desired power level with the transmission, the largest concerns are the rear axle assembly and the driveshaft.

For traditional Mopars, an 8¾-inch rear or a Dana 60 is going to be preferable. The 7¼-inch (usually found in A-Body, E-Body, M-Body, and J-Body cars with either slant six or small V-8 power) and 8¼-inch (1972-and-later A-Body, B-Body, F-Body, M-Body, and J-Body cars, and half trucks and vans) are inadequate for any serious performance usage. For GM vehicles, the 8½-inch 10-bolt or the 12-bolt (heavy-duty 14-bolt rears and Danas found in three-quarter and 1-ton trucks are also fine) are preferable. Don't even consider keeping a 7½ inch or 7⁵/₈-inch 10-bolt unless it has been beefed up substantially. IRS-equipped Corvettes are okay with the possible exception of the very early Dana 44 found in the late C3 Corvettes and the Dana 36s found in automatic C4s. Fords should have an 8.8-inch (found in everything from Fox Body cars, such

The Dana 60 is a great choice for a solid rear axle for your project. They can handle Hellcat power levels quite easily and have a great aftermarket. This one is a factory E-Body unit.

Independent rear suspension is a popular option for today's pro touring–oriented builds. This one is from Speedtech, and it offers Mopar versions as part of its chassis upgrades.

as the Mustang, to trucks and SUVs) or 9-inch bolt. The IRS versions are also fine.

For solid axle cars with an inadequate rear, there are several options. Plenty of rear end specialists like Moser, Strange, Gear FX, Currie Enterprises, and Quick Performance offer retrofit rears based on the popular 8.8- and 9-inch Ford, 12-bolt Chevrolet, and Dana 60. These can typically be ordered ready to bolt in to most popular chassis or in a more universal form with a specified width. Different housing ends and axle bolt patterns are available to accommodate most stock brakes and wheel bolt patterns. Usually these are offered in everything from housing and axle packages to complete assemblies with a choice of gear ratio, differential type, axle spline count, housing ends, wheel bolt patterns, and brakes. Just about any combination is available. As you can imagine, the price goes up substantially for the complete, ready-to-bolt-in units.

For those looking for a more low-buck solution, today's best bet isn't the popular 9-inch Ford recommended in the past. Most people today want gearing in the 3.27–4.10:1 range, a limited-slip differential, disc brakes, 31-spline axles, and a width that works well without going to a narrowed housing and custom axles. They also want a

relatively lightweight housing with good availability of service parts at reasonable prices, reasonable weight, efficiency, and the ability to hold a reasonable amount of power in stock form. You won't find that in a salvage yard 9-inch.

Most of them left in yards are in trucks, and all of them have drum brakes and need narrowing. This seems like a large bill to fill, but the 8.8 Ford, particularly the ones from 1997–2004 Ford Explorers, does it all. The width is acceptable as-is for most 1950s-era vehicles through the present. If narrower is needed, the unequal-length axles make narrowing one side using a second short-side axle with junkyard parts possible. They can be lengthened just as easily. The axles are already in the popular 5x4.5-inch pattern, same as traditional Mopar/Ford), and can be re-drilled to other patterns easily enough. These rears can be found in everything from muscle cars to Jeeps and street rods and are quickly eclipsing the 9-inch Ford for all but the most powerful combinations. The gear selection is huge, as is the choice of differentials, so it's easy to match one to your specific requirements.

There are many other non–Big 3 vehicles that are receiving these swaps. The vast majority are 1970s-newer cars and several that have a factory IRS. For many, like the Nissans/

Datsuns from the earliest 240Z up to the newer 370Zs and GTRs, there is a great degree of interchangeability. It isn't unusual to see one of these cars with a differential from a much later V-8 (Infiniti) or turbocharged application. In the case of 350 and 370Zs, Winters quick-change differentials are swapped in with the factory-style CV axles. Like Nissan, BMW has a great deal of crossover with drivetrain components. Mazda RX-7 builders and Porsche 928 and 944 owners often use components from turbocharged models if they weren't factory equipped.

Forums and social media groups can be a great source of information on drivetrain upgrades for your specific vehicle, so utilize these resources, as I do not have the space to cover all the possibilities. In many cases, there is an upgrade available using factory or mostly factory parts that doesn't require a lot of fabrication or expense.

IRS swaps to handle the power are a lot more common than they used to be, but it's still not something for the faint of heart unless you have deep pockets or a lot of time and fabrication skills. Speedtech, Heidt's, and others have bolt-in units and sub-frame assemblies that can be grafted into your existing chassis. Most chassis suppliers like Schwartz Performance, The Roadster Shop, Speedtech, and others have IRS options. Most of these are based on the 9-inch Ford. Homebrewed swaps using components from late Mustangs, Chargers/Challengers, Camaros, and C5/6/7 Corvettes (usually with another differential since they are transaxle applications) are also popular. Any of these will hold the power of a stock or mildly modified Gen III Hemi without issue.

SUPERCHARGED AND TURBOCHARGED SWAPS

Many years ago, when this book was in its initial planning stages, the addition of a forced-induction chapter wasn't something I considered. However, since then, boosted Gen III Hemi swaps have become quite common with many of them being Hellcat or Hellcat-based (Redeye, Helephant, Demon, etc.). Some have used take-off blowers from these engines or aftermarket superchargers from Whipple, TorqStorm, ATI ProCharger, and others.

Turbocharged swaps, such as Greg Huizenga's 5.7L Hemi Cherokee, aren't quite as common. But with the ever-increasing popularity of turbos and the power potential they provide, they will become a larger segment of the swap community. This section isn't intended to cover every aspect of these installations or the engines themselves. Instead, they give you a better idea of what needs to be done for a successful swap.

The first documented Hellcat swap using factory electronics was done by Diversified Creations for the Roadkill *1968 Charger General Mayhem. The build was well documented, but the sad part is that it now has a 440 back in it. More power? Nope. It's just more* Roadkill, *and it's what owner David Freiburger wants. To each his own.*

General Mayhem was built with most of the factory electronics and under a time crunch, so lots of late-model Challenger parts made their way into the car. There are better ways of doing things now.

Hellcat Engines

If you're lucky enough to start with a Hellcat engine, you already have a great foundation for a forced-induction build as long as your power goals aren't significantly more than the factory rating. As in most cases with late-model factory offerings, the weak point is the connecting rods. While some list the rods as being forged, the engineers refer to them as powder-forged. They are fine up to 850 to 900 hp (or so) due to an upgraded material over other factory Gen III Hemi rods. Beyond that, you'll need a good set of forged rods.

The stock pistons are unfortunately cast and use the same second and oil rings as the Apache 6.4L engines with a PVD coating on the first compression ring. The skirts are graphite coated, and the piston pins are treated with diamond-like coating (DLC). The compression ratio is 9.5:1. When it comes time to replace rods in these engines, most will use a drop-in rod-and-piston package from companies such as Modern Muscle Extreme. In the past, going to a stronger piston-and-rod combination meant that the engine had to be torn down, even at low mileage, to rebalance the

This Monte Carlo SS by Schwartz Performance rides on one of its chassis and forgoes the ubiquitous LSx for a Hellcat engine. (Photo Courtesy Schwartz Performance)

The Schwartz Monte Carlo SS's huge front tubs cradle the Hellcat engine. It is run off of a Mopar Performance controller. (Photo Courtesy Schwartz Performance)

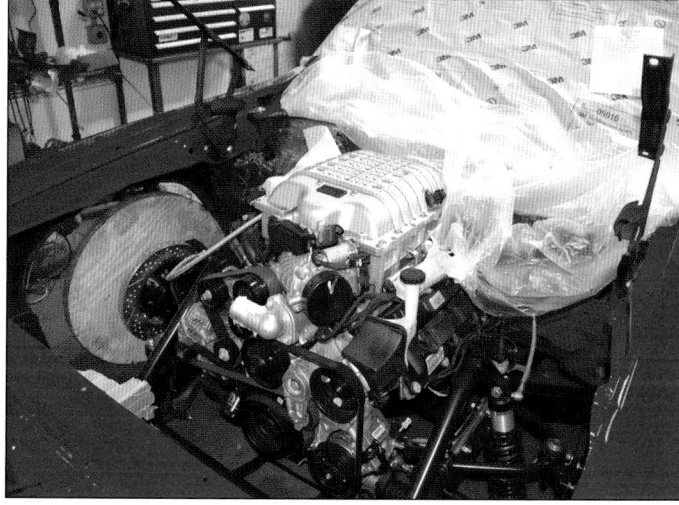

Schwartz Performance does more chassis conversions on Mopars now, and this one is in the assembly stages. You'll need a good chassis and braking to take advantage of all the power from a Hellcat. (Photo Courtesy Schwartz Performance)

The Drag Pak version of the Hellcat engine is one that you aren't likely to see in many swaps. Although it is rated at 630 hp by the NHRA, the real figure is around 1,300 hp.

A total of 354 ci, a 3.0 Whipple supercharger, and an ice tank in addition to the normal heat exchangers make this a very potent package.

Dakota Hellcat swaps are getting more popular. This one uses factory electronics.

engine. This is time-consuming and costly. Backlogs at the machine shop can stretch out this simple step for months.

Fortunately, there is a solution: drop-in rods and pistons. Drop-ins are specifically designed to maintain the factory balancing and allow piston/rod replacement without full teardowns and engine removal.

The crankshafts, based on the Apache forgings, have their fillets rolled under a higher-than-normal load to increase strength, and the machined surfaces are induction

hardened. Higher-load-capacity bearings and optimized clearances for the application are also part of the package.

Unless going with a longer stroke, there is no reason to replace the crankshaft with an aftermarket piece. However, those wanting to push well over 1,000 hp are advised to increase the displacement by stroking the engine. David Weber of MMX prefers a 4-inch-stroke Molnar crank with 2.100 GM rod journals due to the overlap between the rod and main journals. This overlap pro-

Brake booster clearance is very tight in the Dakota chassis. This truck has a manual transmission with a clutch master cylinder (likely a TR-6060).

vides the needed strength to transmit all that power without flexing or failing. This stroke also allows the retention of the factory 6.2-inch rod length to eliminate the side-loading that is common with long stroke/short rod combinations.

Redeye/Demon/Super Stock versions of the Hellcat engine use a larger version of the IHI supercharger (2.7L, up from 2.4L in the Hellcat) to boost power from the standard 707/717 hp (depending on year of the engine) up to 797/897 hp. Both rotors were increased in size by 28 mm, and boost was raised from 11.6 to 14.5 psi. The front bearing plate was also upgraded. To add extra airflow, a much larger airbox with a conical-style filter in place of the original Hellcat panel filter was added. A dual fuel pump and larger injectors replace the standard ones used in the Hellcat. This amounts to 510 pounds per hour of fuel flow (1.36 gpm).

With all these external upgrades, the engine itself wasn't left alone. The block, which comes with a distinctive red paint, is made of a higher-strength cast iron with 4-bolt

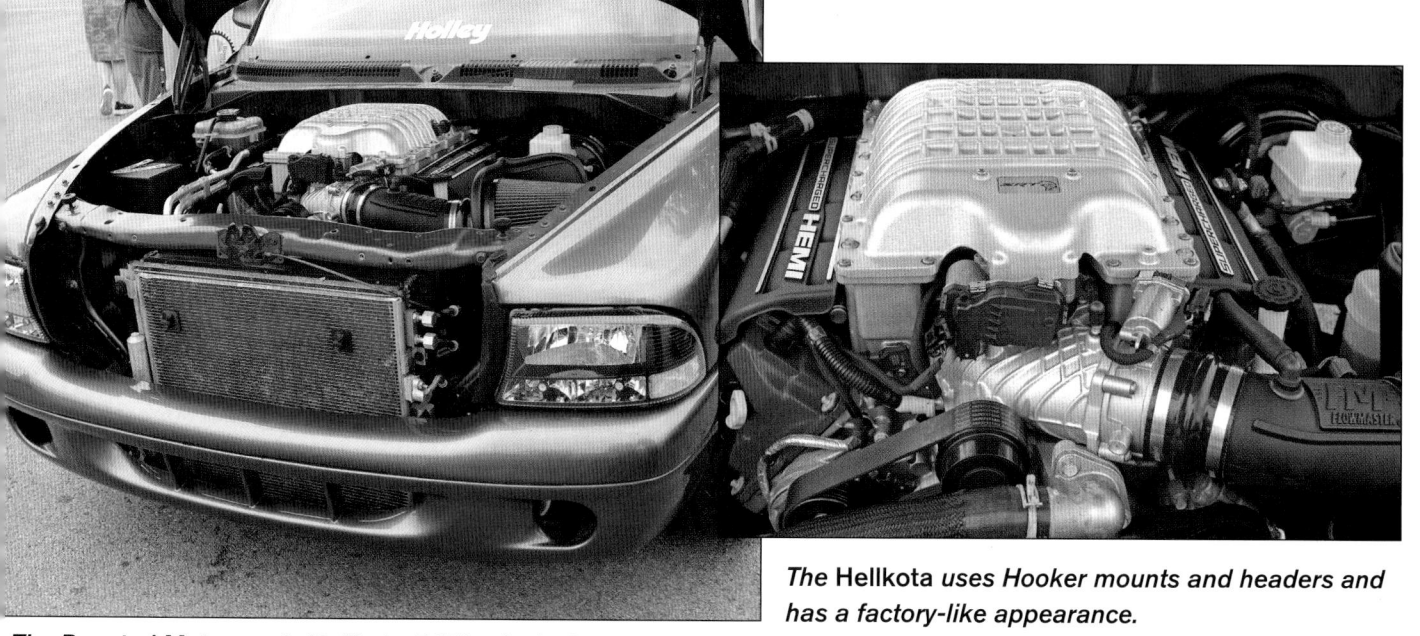

The **Hellkota** *uses Hooker mounts and headers and has a factory-like appearance.*

The Boosted Motorsports **Hellkota** *R/T is nicely done. It uses the Hellcat engine and 8HP90. The factory dash, instruments, shifter, console, etc. are all used from the donor vehicle. It uses factory electronics.*

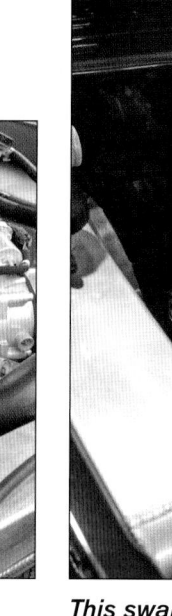

This Hellcat swap uses the Mopar Performance controller, which is the most common method to control these engines. Note the JLT catch can. This is a nice touch for any boosted engine.

This swap was underway at RMR Dreamcars when I visited several years ago. Most RMR Hellcat swaps at that time used a Holley Dominator ECU and GM 4L80E transmission so that one ECU could control both.

steel main caps. The block is honed with deck plates and fitted with higher-strength forged rods (the strongest used in any Gen III Hemi engine), pistons, and crankshaft. It also has an improved cam profile with 0.561/0.551 lift and 224/240 degrees duration at 0.050-inch lift. The heads are likewise fitted with higher-strength valvetrain components to handle the extra lift and duration. A high-flow oil pump was also added, and the SRT Chiller system was developed to plumb refrigerant from the AC system into the intercooler.

If you have one of the Demon/Redeye/Super Stock engines, you aren't likely to need to upgrade anything for durability.

Regardless if you are using a crate engine or a salvage yard take-out, there are a few things to keep in mind when planning your swap. First, most swappers are using factory Hellcat heat exchangers, coolant reservoirs, and hoses where possible.

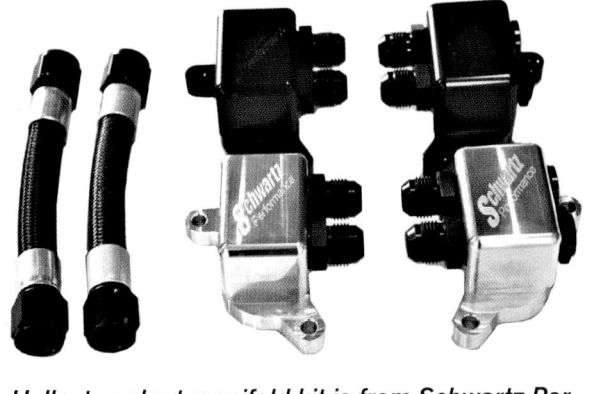

This Hellcat coolant manifold kit is from Schwartz Performance. As with everything else Schwartz does, it is high quality.

The Speedtech AAR 'Cuda Fast Fish has an 807-hp Hellcat Redeye engine that is backed by a T56 Magnum and Dutchman 9-inch. An aftermarket coolant manifold at the rear of the supercharger is used.

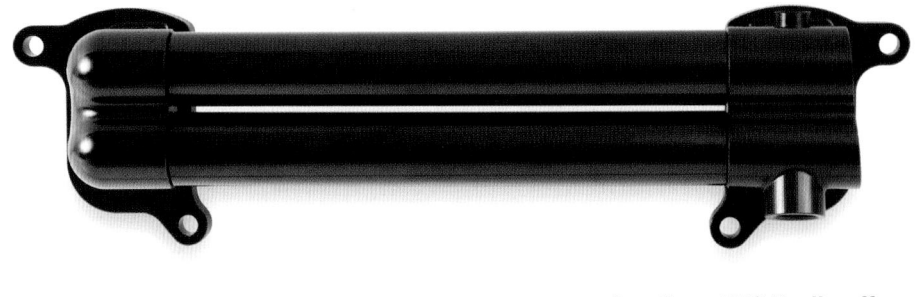

Need the clearance but want to run factory hoses rather than AN? Earl's offers fittings to accept them (part number AT785013ERL). (Photo Courtesy Holley)

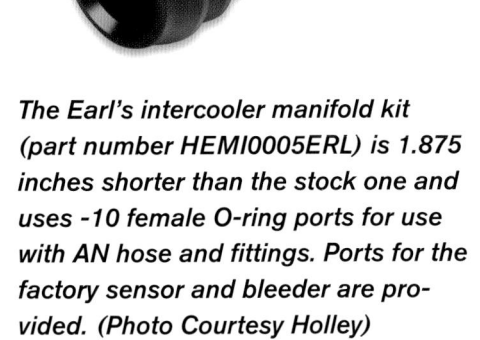

The Earl's intercooler manifold kit (part number HEMI0005ERL) is 1.875 inches shorter than the stock one and uses -10 female O-ring ports for use with AN hose and fittings. Ports for the factory sensor and bleeder are provided. (Photo Courtesy Holley)

This follows the "keep it simple, stupid" (KISS) principle and provides a good baseline even if you change things around later. One exception is that many swappers find interference issues from the intercooler manifold at the rear of the engine.

Earl's offers a replacement log-style unit that is 1.875 inches shorter than the factory one and has -10 O-ring inlet and outlets. This unit also has provisions for the factory coolant sensor and bleeder port. Schwartz Performance has its own unit, which looks much different but serves the same purpose. It uses a pair of billet aluminum housings, connected by AN hoses, and shaves over an inch off of the factory spec. Like the Earl's unit, it also has provisions for the temperature sensor and bleeder valve. The Schwartz unit offers more possibilities for hose routing.

6.4L Engines

The 6.4L engines come with hypereutectic pistons and powdered-metal connecting rods. Hypereutectic pistons are great for naturally aspirated engines and milder boosted engines and provide a long service life, but in this case they have some limitations when it comes to boost. The compression ratio is the highest of the Gen III Hemis at 10.9:1. While this is a concern, it isn't the biggest issue. The biggest issue is that the tight ring gaps from the factory can lead to the rings expanding to the point of touching and breaking ring lands in a boosted application. Some have opened the ring gaps on the stock pistons to alleviate this, but most go to a drop-in piston and rod combo to address the strength issues of both the rod and piston, lower the compression ratio to allow more boost, and a more appropriate ring gap. Block strength for the truck BGE blocks is on par with the Hellcat block.

The 6.4L engines have the advantage of a strong forged crankshaft from the factory. Cylinder heads are

Not all supercharged Hemis are Hellcats. This one is equipped with a Magnuson MagnaCharger.

This Magnuson-equipped 'Cuda, which is in progress at RMR Dreamcars, has a catch can, as should any boosted car. Oil residue is best left out of the intake.

very similar to the 6.1L heads and have excellent flow right out of the box.

5.7L and 6.1L Engines

Rods and pistons in the 5.7L and 6.1L engines are similar to the 6.4L but with a slightly lower 10.3:1 compression ratio. At the very least, the ring gaps should be opened up, but considering the cost of doing so with gaskets and all associated fasteners, which in factory form are torque-to-yield and one time use only, drop-in piston and rod assemblies make more sense. There are many who report reusing the bolts without issue, but that's a chance I don't take. I'm rarely that lucky!

The 5.7L engines come with a nodular iron crankshaft, and the 6.1L engines have a forged steel crankshaft. While crank issues with these engines are rarely noted, upgrading a 5.7L's crank to the 6.1L version with an identical stroke is a good addition to any boosted 5.7L build. Stroker kits for both, with all forged components, are available if desired.

While the 5.7L early heads are very good by modern standards, the later 2009-and-up Eagle castings are better, as are the 6.1L heads. These are a common upgrade on the earlier engines, and pistons are available to better suit these heads for a boosted application. As is, the Eagle heads will boost compression on an early engine to over 12:1, which is inappropriate for even most naturally aspirated builds.

Regardless of which Hemi engine you have, go back to high-quality fasters and gaskets after any of these modifications. The factory hardware works fine for most streetable forced-induction builds, but I prefer to go with ARP head bolts or head studs when the chassis allows (it can be difficult to remove the heads in the car in some cases) and Cometic MLS head gaskets.

While I'm not going to wade into the benefits of turbos over superchargers or vice versa, I want to cover some of the packaging issues that come with both and let you decide what is best for your application and budget.

Superchargers

Superchargers in the Gen III Hemi world are typically one of three types: roots, twin screw, or centrifugals. Roots blowers trace their history back the farthest and include the popular 6-71 and 8-71 GMC-style blowers as sold by Weiand, BDS, and others. The (X)-71 series blowers are rarely seen on Gen III Hemis. Most roots-style blowers used on these engines are based on the Eaton design. The factory superchargers found on most GM and Ford applications, as well as MagnaChargers and Edelbrock versions, are based on Eaton roots-style blowers. They work well but are not as efficient as the twin-screw superchargers like the Hellcat's IHI 2,380-cc unit, the newer Eaton TVS, or units sold by Whipple and Kenne-Belle. Roots blowers build boost pressure against the sides of the supercharger casing.

Twin screws actually compress air between the rotors, which improves efficiency and reduces heat soak.

Centrifugal superchargers that resemble a turbocharger minus the

Larry Rose's 1970 Challenger RT/SE

Larry Rose's 1970 Challenger RT/SE has been a regular at events like the Hot Rod Power Tour and Holley Moparty events for many years, so I've been able to witness its transformation.

I first saw it in 2014 and took some of the photos seen here. The Challenger is built around Reilly Motorsports' Alter-Ktion front suspension and Street-Lynx 4-link rear. It initially had a 6.1L Hemi with a Magnuson supercharger. The transmission at that time was the popular Tremec T56 Magnum. When the Hellcat engines first came out, Larry decided to make the change and was one of the first to do so with the 8HP90 transmission. Why the automatic? The gearing offered lets the Challenger take advantage of every bit of available power and is more comfortable for long trips. ■

This is the first time I saw Larry's 1970 Challenger RT/SE on the Hot Rod Power Tour in 2014. I believe this stop was in West Virginia.

The Challenger had a nice 6.1L Hemi with a Magnuson supercharger and a T56 Magnum at the time.

Custom emblems tell everyone this isn't a 440 RV motor.

The small plastic reservoir to the left of the master cylinder is the reservoir for the T56 Magnum's hydraulic clutch.

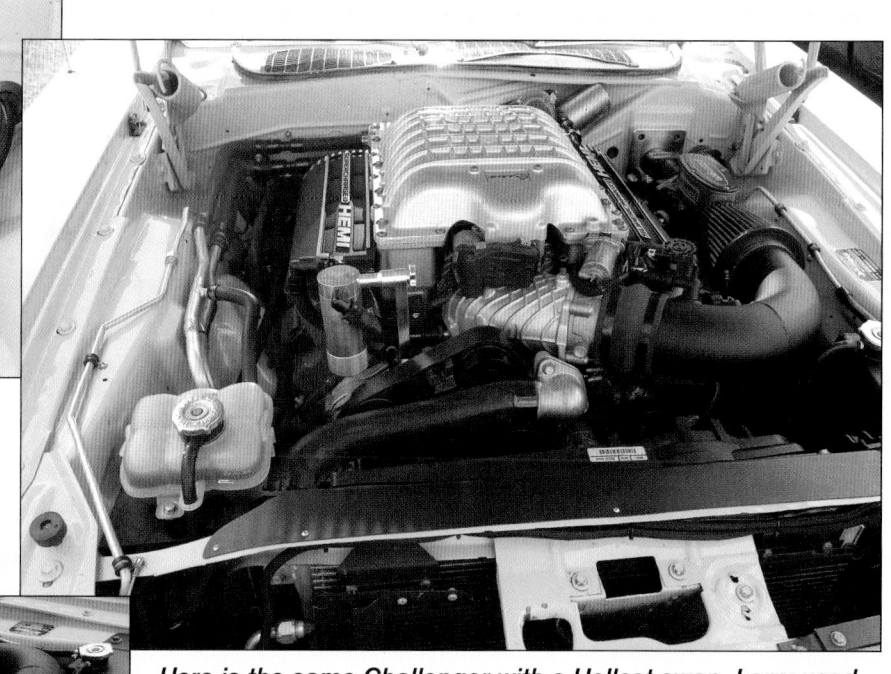

Here is the same Challenger with a Hellcat swap. Larry used a 8HP90 transmission, and he was one of first to make it work correctly in a swap application. The clutch reservoir is gone, and the car now has Hydroboost.

Larry blacked out the supercharger lid, which gives it a more sinister look.

The Challenger's engine position left just enough room to clear the Hellcat's water manifold. For those who don't have clearance, there are aftermarket solutions.

Kenne Bell superchargers have been around for a long time but are rarely seen on Gen III Hemis. They work very well in my experience.

This Roadrunner was built on a Viper chassis and has a Steve Morris–built 6.4L Hemi with a 3.6L Kenne-Bell supercharger and a G-Force 6-speed.

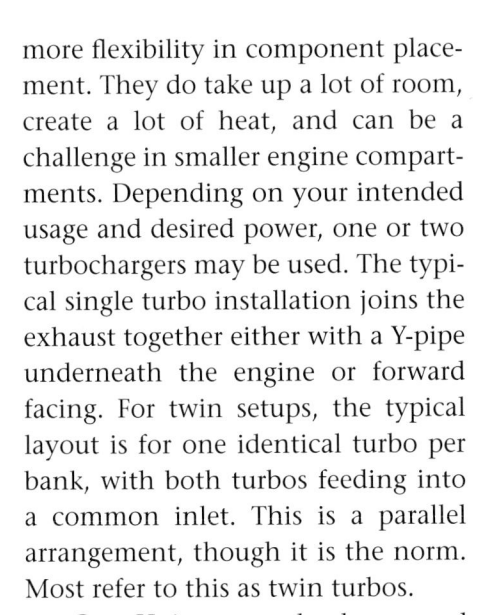

Centrifugal superchargers aren't as common as they once were, but they can make very good power. This one is in a late-model application, but it is included because the placement of the supercharger allows it to fit most earlier chassis.

exhaust side use an impeller to draw air into the compressor housing at high speed and low pressure. The diffuser then converts the airflow to low speed and high pressure 9 boost, which is fed into the engine.

All of the supercharger types are belt driven, though it is possible to drive a centrifugal directly off the crank. This is most often seen in race applications to reduce the side load placed on the crankshaft and eliminate belt slippage issues, which adds some complication to the accessory drive but typically isn't much

of an issue in a swap application. The brackets to attach the centrifugal superchargers can be quite large in some cases and interfere with the hood, frame rails, or shock towers on some models. Exhaust implications are minimal. You just need enough exhaust flow to support your desired power level.

Turbochargers

Turbochargers, which use exhaust gas to drive a turbine, can be very complex in their setup but allow

more flexibility in component placement. They do take up a lot of room, create a lot of heat, and can be a challenge in smaller engine compartments. Depending on your intended usage and desired power, one or two turbochargers may be used. The typical single turbo installation joins the exhaust together either with a Y-pipe underneath the engine or forward facing. For twin setups, the typical layout is for one identical turbo per bank, with both turbos feeding into a common inlet. This is a parallel arrangement, though it is the norm. Most refer to this as twin turbos.

Greg Huizenga took a lesser used but effective approach with his Cherokee build by going with compound turbos. They use two different sized turbos with the larger one feeding the smaller one. This makes boost nearly instantaneous and overcomes turbo lag if the turbos are sized properly. Ultimately, this setup may cost him some power in the higher RPM ranges, but it is very effective for getting his relatively heavy Cherokee moving fast on a short autocross course.

With turbos in Gen III Hemi applications, there are very few off-the-shelf solutions. One of the most versatile choices is from Stainless Headers Mfg. Inc. (stainless-headers.com). They have a modular turbo header that doesn't require any welding. It starts with 1/2-inch-thick flanges with two ports and includes purged TIG-welded primaries that feed into compound log manifolds with 2.5-inch V-band flanges. Modular bends in 22-, 45-, 90-, or 180-degree versions with V-band flanges allow lots of options for routing and terminate in T3 or T4 turbo flanges. Custom Y-pipe configurations and downpipe and wastegate dump tube setups are available for fender or hood exit, axle dumps, or full-length exhaust systems. Please note that Ram timing covers and accessory routing are recommended, as passenger-car styles may require some modifications.

Stainless Headers also offers a twin turbo kit with a choice of BorgWarner turbos, dual TiAL wastegates, and all the needed tubing, V-bands, and hardware. They also offer air-to-air intercoolers and just about everything needed for a turbo installation.

Motion Raceworks offers a turbo header kit in 304 stainless steel. It includes 3/8-inch flanges, a pair of 2.5-inch collectors, V-band assemblies, and eight bends. It has a video on its website that covers assembly of the headers.

Currently, there aren't any other turbo headers built for the Gen III Hemi, though I expect that to change in the near future, but there are plenty of other options. The simplest solution is to adapt a set of LSx turbo headers. While this sounds crazy, the port location between

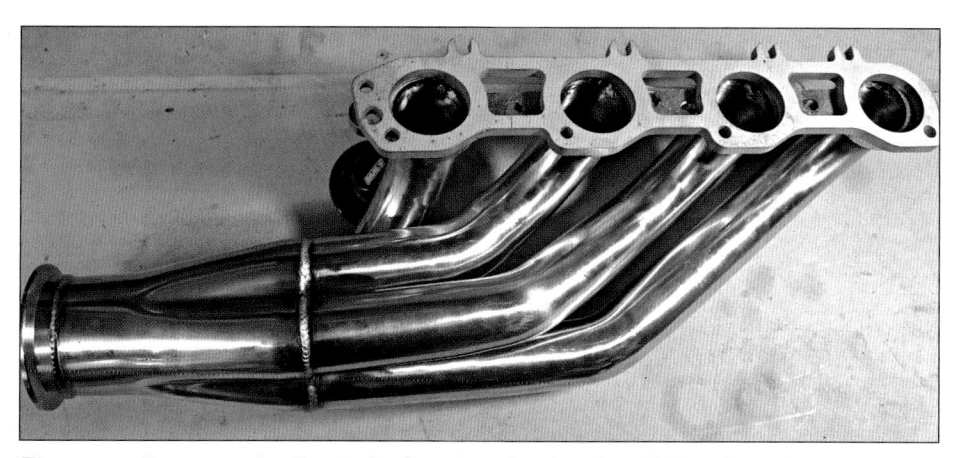

There aren't any production turbo headers for the Gen III Hemi as of yet. However, this Flowtech LSx header with 1⁷/₈-inch primaries has a port configuration close to the Gen III Hemi flange on top of it. It's easier and less expensive to cut away the original flange and weld on the new one than build a custom header.

The LSx flange is still in place, but I wanted to see how this header looked on the engine. I'm pleased.

the two engines is very similar and requires either an adapter to bolt up the headers (available from AEI Inc.) or cutting off your existing header flanges and welding on a set of Gen III Hemi flanges. The former should work well considering the thickness of the plates combined with the header flange, but space may be an issue on some vehicles. For this reason, I chose to modify a set of LSx turbo headers on my own Gremlin project.

Starting with Flowtech part number 11540FLT, a 304 stainless-steel polished header with an up-and-forward

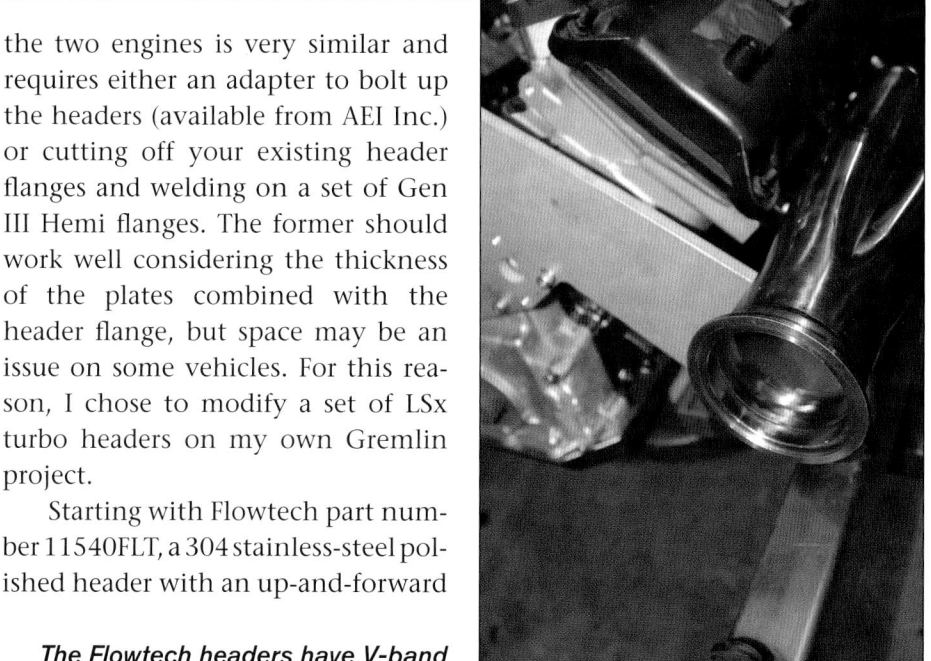

The Flowtech headers have V-band connections for easy plumbing. They are made of 304 stainless.

Mike Staveski's Combination

Gilbert Hass owns this RMR Dreamcars–built 1971 Barracuda. It is built on a modified 2001 ACR Viper chassis. Green pearl paint and the billboard stripe are perfect with the understated 6-lug Forgeline wheels.

Mike Staveski is no stranger to Mopars. He has built many fine examples over the years at RMR Dreamcars, and his old shop, Time Machines. He pioneered the Viper swaps of the 1990s and was one of the first to embrace the Gen III Hemi. He was the perfect man to transform a Viper ACR chassis and a 1971 Barracuda into what you see here, which is the perfect combination of both.

Installing later-model chassis into older vehicles doesn't often lead to good results, but Mike pulled this off with most not realizing what has been done. The 6-lug positive-offset wheels are the only discernable visible clue, but they look right on the vehicle.

For power, Mike dispensed with the idea of a V-10. They are heavy, difficult to package without lots of engine setback, and ruin the balance of the car. Plus, a Gen III Hemi with a supercharger makes more power with none of the drawbacks. The T56 6-speed manual was retained.

The Viper's suspension was more than up to the task. While this car wasn't built for the road course, it still is very capable. ∎

Fit and finish are perfect, as is everything I have seen come from RMR Dreamcars. The car was still under construction at the time these photos were taken.

The distinctive chrome gills identify this 'Cuda as a 1971 model.

The 392 Hemi with a Magnuson super-charger is from Arrington Performance, and it produces 650 hp through the Viper-spec T56. The intake tubing to con-nect to the air-filter housing in the radiator shroud is not yet in place.

Cold air is picked up through the hood and perfectly seals to the airbox.

design (which works best with our Gremlin's custom-built chassis, $1^7/_8$-inch primaries, and a 3-inch collector), cut off the LSx flanges. Then, TIG weld a pair of Hooker Blackheart flanges on. While these headers can be flipped to a down-and-forward position, the stock Hemi motor mounts will be in the way and necessitate a motor plate. This is an issue I encountered on the Gremlin back when it still had the stock unibody. It, along with changes in the project direction, resulted in the switch to a new chassis with none of the packaging issues I encountered before.

I will run the headers up and forward and above the motor plate to help with accessory drive clearance. To package the Hemi in our Gremlin and accommodate the huge tires that I am running front and back, the frame clip was ordered from Morrison with 28 inches between the rails, so the headers have to go over the top of the rails.

Another option is to run exhaust manifolds and flip them to the front. Unfortunately, with the Gen III Hemi engines, this is easier said than done. The bolt pattern for the exhaust isn't symmetrical like the LSx and most other engines. Because there is a right and left head casting, the cylinder heads aren't drilled for the different ways one might want to bolt up the manifolds. If you try to flip the factory manifold to the up-and-forward position, the existing bolt holes on the two center ports are fine, but the outer parts aren't.

There isn't enough meat there for the sealing surface the way they are cast, so to run the manifolds in this way, you need to build up the flange with a TIG welder, machine it flat, and add two bolt holes to each of the end ports. It's not a huge deal

This set of Gibson shorty headers for Ram applications is easy to use for turbo manifolds as long as the cylinder heads are drilled and tapped as per the text. They are very heavy and hold up to heat well.

if you already have the heads off and can do the work yourself, but otherwise it is going to add more cost and complexity.

If you switch the manifolds from side to side and run them in the down and forward position, things are a little easier. The end ports don't require any attention. The two center ports need to have two holes drilled and tapped each. I'd recommend doing this on an end mill or drill press, but some have done it with a hand drill and use the exhaust flange as a guide. Drill carefully and put a stop on the bit (a few wraps of tape will suffice) to avoid accidentally drilling into a coolant passage.

If you'd like to run cast exhaust manifolds but don't want to modify the heads, buy adapter plates from AEI and use LSx exhaust manifolds with them. These are cheap or free in some cases, and there is more variety available in LSx manifolds. You can even use new ones made for a turbo application that are available from Hooker Blackheart.

Either way, if you want to run turbos with an OEM exhaust manifold, most will cut off the stock flanges and use V-band connections to ensure a leak-free seal with the turbo plumbing.

Boost Control

The amount of boost produced by your engine is ultimately mechanical (either with springs in the case of the typical wastegates on a turbo setup) and by pulley drive ratio and a boost bypass valve (in the case of the typical roots, or with twin-screw-style supercharger, such as the Hellcat 6.2L). While the latter is typically controlled by the ECU's programming with no additional components required, a centrifugal supercharger system or turbo setup requires some extra components to go beyond the mechanical limits of the wastegate springs. This can be as simple as a manual boost controller in the wastegate pressure line, or a more elaborate system using carbon dioxide or compressed air from an onboard compressor.

Our example here is a turbo system, but this still applies to a centrifugal setup, though many lower output systems don't used wastegates. Our turbo system uses two STS (Turbosmart) 40-mm external wastegates (part number STS50). They are designed with an actuator housing that is 25 percent smaller than the norm for easier packaging and allows for easy spring changes. We'll also use an STS (Turbosmart) blow-off valve

In a world with too many LSx-powered Mustangs, it is nice to see one with a Gen III Hemi. This S550 drag car is competitive for far less money than a Coyote with a similar power level with the benefit of increased reliability. Matthew Kesatie is the owner, and he fitted it with a Demon-inspired 6.2L Hemi with Thitek heads.

This Mustang uses Boostlab 7675 twin turbos with dual 50-mm TiAL wastegates and a Plazmaman intake. Dome pressure is likely controlled by a carbon-dioxide system. Use braided AN hose for this application because the plastic line can get brittle and crack or blow out.

(BOV). Part number STS56 is 52 mm and flows over 330 cfm.

Since the springs in these wastegates are only rated to 5 psi, and I am planning to run much higher boost levels once our race engine is built, I am using a pair of Holley 3-port boost solenoid valves made by MAC and commonly known as MAC valves. A wastegate is merely a controlled air boost leak that gives unneeded air a path outward by diverting it from the turbine. The MAC valve's job is to put additional pressure on the wastegate spring and prevent it from opening at the spring's rating. This is called dome pressure, and the pressure itself usually comes from either an onboard carbon dioxide system or a small air compressor. The Gremlin will use carbon dioxide. Only a small bottle is required, and since it is a sealed system, no refills should be required unless there is a leak.

Speaking of leaks, it is standard practice to use plastic line and quick-disconnect fittings for plumbing the carbon dioxide. However, plastic line can be brittle, and most of us have experienced a quick-disconnect disconnecting at the worst possible time. I prefer to avoid that issue entirely and am using nothing but stainless hard line and steel-braided Teflon lines with AN fittings to plumb my system. Overkill? Maybe. But I prefer building things to fixing them. The valves will be controlled by the ECU through a PWM- output. Boost and dome pressure will be monitored. Tuning this is not something I recommend for a beginner, but there are plenty of tuning classes and helpful videos that can steer you in the right direction. There are multiple boost strategies that can be employed to suit your specific application and intended use.

Cooling the Intake Charge

Supercharging and turbocharging build something other than horse-power. They build heat, and lots of it, through compression of the intake charge. Some systems are more efficient than others, but to get the maximum advantage, your intake charge needs to be cooled significantly. The denser the air, the more of it can be packed into the cylinders. Given the right amount of fuel and proper timing, the more power will be made. You can run a low-boost setup without cooling of some sort, which works best in a blow-through carb or TBI system, but considering the cost of the supercharger or turbo, it may not be worth it from a dollars-spent to power-created standpoint.

There are many ways to cool the intake charge. One of the earliest methods that still has applications today is water/methanol injection. First used in the 1962–1963 Olds Turbo Jetfire 215 V-8s, the fluid was called Turbo-Rocket Fluid and consisted of distilled water and alcohol. This kept the intake charge cool and

This late-model Challenger has a serious single-turbo system to feed its Gen III Hemi. Turbo cars of this caliber aren't common in older bodystyles, but there is no reason that something similar couldn't be done with a classic muscle car.

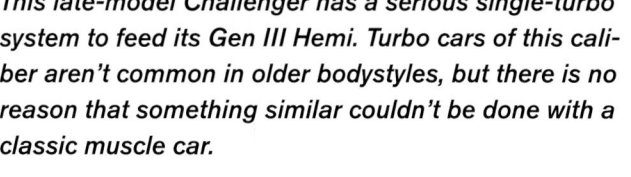

Custom down-and-forward stainless-steel headers feed into a V-banded Y-pipe to feed the turbo. The pump on the right is for the vacuum pump. Note that the AEI motor plate has no water pump. This one is run dry.

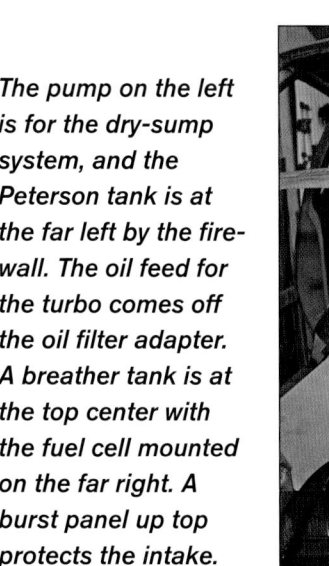

The pump on the left is for the dry-sump system, and the Peterson tank is at the far left by the firewall. The oil feed for the turbo comes off the oil filter adapter. A breather tank is at the top center with the fuel cell mounted on the far right. A burst panel up top protects the intake.

The Gremlin's engine is equipped with a Holley Hi-Ram intake and 105-mm LS-style throttle body. The top section of the intake will be replaced with the Shearer Fab intercooler. The intake spacers will be removed with the good engine that is planned. This is a 2007 5.7L engine with the early-style heads. The blocks tacked under the frame rails are temporary and for mockup only. They'll be replaced with 90-degree mandrel bends in 2x4.

curbed detonation. Buick experimented with the systems for the Buick GN in the 1980s. The instrument clusters in these cars have a "Power Injection" icon for the system, but it was never offered as a production item. Today, there are a few companies that offer water/meth injection as retrofits. Snow Performance and Holley are among them.

E85, a more recent fuel choice, consists of roughly 85 percent ethanol and 15 percent gasoline. It came

about as a supposedly environmentally conscious alternative to straight gasoline. While the main benefactor seemed to be the corn lobby, this fuel has been embraced by enthusiasts who want a cheaper alternative to race gas. Octane is typically in the 100 range, and E85 allows the use of higher compression or boost levels without detonation. Quality at the pump varies and should always be tested, and availability isn't good in some parts of the country.

The alcohol has less energy content than gasoline, so more will be required to produce the same amount of power. This can be 20 to 30 percent or more in extreme applications. Ethanol can be hard on rubber components, so high-quality fuel lines, preferably stainless hard lines and Teflon-lined AN hose, and filters are needed. Alcohol and the water attracted by it (alcohol is hygroscopic) can be corrosive, so plan on more maintenance to your fuel system. The benefit is enough of a cooling effect that lower-boost applications often don't run intercoolers with it. The addition of a flex fuel sensor, which is possible with most aftermarket EFI, allows easy transition from gasoline to E85 and vice versa. Otherwise, changing tunes and draining of the fuel is the best bet.

Methanol, or "alcohol," as it is known by many racers, has all the advantages and more of E85 in a racing application. It is less flammable than gasoline, which is a plus for safety reasons. Like E85, it has less energy content than gasoline but a higher octane rating. The BTU/pound rating of gasoline is around 18,400. Methanol is 9,500 BTU/pound, but if you are burning three times as much methanol, you are going to make more power.

Methanol also absorbs more heat; enough that often intercooling isn't necessary in forced induction applications. This isn't really a street-practical fuel for cost and availability reasons, but for a racer who is looking for a way to maximize power on their boosted engine, there is nothing better. Starting on methanol in a low-speed operation can be more difficult than with gasoline. For this reason, the use of multiple sets of injectors and dual fuel systems is becoming more popular. This way, you can back off the trailer or drive around the pits on smaller gasoline injectors and switch over to methanol for racing.

Air-to-Air Intercooling

For most applications, an air-to-air intercooler is the most practical and least complex way to cool the intake charge. For many years, it was the intercooling method of choice for most OEM applications. Simply speaking, an air-to-air intercooler is a heat exchanger that is fitted between the pressure side of the turbo or centrifugal supercharger and the throttle body. The heated air flows through the intercooler core, high-pressure air from the grille or ducting below the vehicle passes through it, and cools the intake charge significantly. Intercoolers are often rated by horsepower, and this is handy when available, but generally you want to run as large a core as possible.

The only real drawbacks to a larger intercooler are pressure drop, which can be compensated for with increased boost (wastegate settings or a change to a smaller pulley), and the physical size and weight of the unit. Air-to-air intercooling works well for most applications, but heat soak can be an issue in endurance and high-horsepower drag applications. In many cases, though, it is the best compromise.

Air-to-Water Intercooling

Air-to-water intercooling is similar, but instead of relying solely on air for cooling, the heated charge air is routed through a core, very similar to a standard air-to-air intercooler that is enclosed to allow water or coolant to circulate past it to remove heat. While air doesn't go through the core, the coolant lines

For a more street-oriented setup, a universal-type air-to-air intercooler, such as this Frostbite unit, is a bit easier to set up than an air-to-water system. It is generally better for vehicles that are really driven. (Photo Courtesy Holley)

go through a heat exchanger that removes some of the heat in the same way that the air-to-air core would. The intercooler itself can be placed where it will fit best. This could be in the passenger seat or back seat area of a drag car, in the dash, or in front of the engine if space allows.

The farther the intercooler is from the engine, the more plumbing there has to be and the greater the pressure drop. For this reason, a very popular location for air-to-water intercoolers is in the intake manifold. This is commonly seen in factory supercharged

Air-to-water intercooling makes sense in some applications. Shearer Fab makes this unit, which is rated for 2,000 hp. (Photo Courtesy Shearer Fab)

I chose a rear view of Greg Huizenga's Jeep for one reason. It is the view that most will see thanks to 880 hp of compound-turbo insanity.

Greg Huizenga's 1975 Jeep Cherokee is the epitome of a sleeper. It sounds a bit rowdy, has a low-slung stance and performance parts stickers all over the windows, but old sport utility vehicles aren't going anywhere in a hurry—or are they?

The traditional paint scheme with unassuming blue and white makes this look like something your grandfather might take camping, but a trip to Mexico might be more appropriate. The body looks stock, but the front end is a one-piece fiberglass unit that can be removed in four minutes.

Greg's Cherokee chassis is based on Chevy C10 dimensions with lots of modifications. The engine is a 2010 5.7L Hemi with a TR6060 6-speed, which motivates it well enough, but Greg built a compound turbo setup with an S480 feeding into an S366 with an air-to-air intercooler. It makes 880 hp on a mix of gasoline and ethanol (approximately E50). Boost comes up fast, and with anti-lag, it is an absolute monster on the autocross course. Engine management is by a Holley HP system.

This truck has run Drag Week and has turned as fast as 9.90s at 140 mph! For more information, check it out on Larry Chen's YouTube channel. ∎

At first glance, the casual observer sees that this truck has a large single turbo. What they don't see is the smaller one behind the grille.

The 2010 Hemi has a 6.1L intake, which is probably due to boost concerns with the plastic 5.7L intake as well as flow. The blow-off valve is a 50-mm JGS Precision unit.

The larger 96-mm turbo is blanketed to hold in heat and protect the hood. The hot-side plumbing is thermal wrapped.

Greg's cable-driven throttle body has the IAC function deleted with a block-off plate that doubles as a throttle cable bracket. The intake manifold is vented to a catch can on the firewall.

This is one of the Flowtech LSx headers with AEI adapter plates. Heat generated by turbo systems is substantial and appears to break down the header wrap.

Turbocharged vehicles, even trucks, can have issues with packaging. Note the location of the master cylinders for brakes and the clutch. The pedals are floor mounted.

A very thick air-to-air intercooler resides behind the grille.

The radiator is narrower than the intercooler for packaging reasons with the turbo piping.

The smaller S366 turbo spools up quickly and is fed exhaust by the larger turbo. Anti-lag doesn't hurt, either.

applications, and not just Hellcats. The GT500s, CTS-Vs, and all the other supercharged GM LS and LT applications use an air-to-water intercooler in the intake manifold), and also with most aftermarket roots or twin-screw superchargers. For racing applications, the Vortech Igloo Mondo Coolers were popular in the heyday of Pro 5.0 Racing and were probably the first truly successful application of this type of intercooling in a race application.

Guys with centrifugals or turbos aren't left out. The popular Holley Hi-Ram intake manifold, which features a removable lid, is the perfect solution for someone wanting to run an engine-mounted air-to-water intercooler. While Holley doesn't offer one, many companies have developed their own. Tick Performance, 417 Motorsports, and Shearer Fab all have their own intercoolers built for this intake bolt pattern that sandwich between the intake's upper and lower castings. This adds some height to an already-tall engine, so most can forget about keeping this setup under the hood.

With any of the air-to-water intercooler options, whether factory-based or aftermarket, a heat exchanger for the water/coolant, an electric pump to move the coolant, and a reservoir to contain the water, plus all of the necessary hose and fittings to move the water in between the components are still needed. Hellcat-based swaps do well to use as many of the OEM parts as possible and adapt them to the vehicle rather than try to assemble everything from aftermarket components. Typically, roots and twin-screw supercharger manufacturers will package everything needed in a kit. But keep in mind these kits are normally made for specific late-model applications. Some alterations or customiza-

tion may be needed to fit your vehicle.

When it comes to heat exchangers and water tanks, bigger is better within reason. Water weight is a definite consideration. A gallon weighs 8.3 pounds, and most street systems seem to do ok with one to two gallons. If you want to run ice (dry or regular) in the system, use at least a 5-gallon tank to give you some room for the ice and expansion.

Like the intercoolers themselves, there is a lot of latitude in where the water tank is placed. Most put it in the rear of the vehicle, like a fuel cell, or in the back seat area of a race car. Wherever you put it, be sure it is easily accessible so it can be filled and drained as needed without issue. Heat exchangers typically are on the smaller side, like a transmission cooler, for packaging reasons in a street system. For the most efficiency, go as large as you can without negatively affecting airflow to the radiator. They can be placed anywhere they get good airflow.

There are lots of opinions on intercooler plumbing; everything from clear nylon aquarium hose and heater hose to aluminum or stainless tubing and AN hose and fittings. A lot of this can be determined by where the components are located, their proximity to the driver and heat sources, and budget. For maximum driver protection, the lines should be routed through the subfloor as much as possible so if there ever was a failure, there is little chance the driver would come into contact with hot water.

The water or coolant needs to be pumped through the system with electric pumps. Do not use a pump designed for fuel; it will quickly fail. The majority use a marine-style bilge pump, such as those made by Rule; dedicated air-to-water/electric water pumps, like those from Davies

Craig, EMP/Stewart Components; or OEM-type units like the Bosch used in supercharged GM and Ford applications. Whichever you use, be sure to use an appropriate fuse and relay.

Hot-Side and Cold-Side Plumbing

With any forced induction engine, whether supercharged or turbocharged, the plumbing of the system is a major consideration. The intake air ahead of the compressor isn't too much of an issue other than the fact the tubing needs to be rigid enough to not deform under boost. Don't ever use dryer tubing or anything similar on a forced induction car. It can be sucked into the compressor.

Intake plumbing can vary from a conventional airbox and silicone coupler with heavy-duty clamps (sometimes dual clamps with a wire mesh in between) to a conical-style filter with a conventional aluminum tubing. In the case of some race vehicles, a screen/velocity stack assembly breathes unfiltered air or nothing at all. Tubing should be at the very least bead rolled on the edges to prevent the hoses from coming off easily. V-bands are popular for this. They require a little more fabrication with TIG welding the ends onto the tubing, but they are far more secure.

The hot side on a turbo application is far more critical considering the pressure of the exhaust pulses and the heat involved. V-band or flexible Wiggins clamps and their corresponding flanges are preferred to the traditional method of using gaskets, which can blow out, between exhaust components at a joint. Most turbo headers come with V-bands already installed, and they are often added to cast manifolds as well.

ENGINE MANAGEMENT SYSTEM INSTALLATION

Auto manufacturers go to great lengths to ensure all of the vehicle's electrical components work well together. When building a project car, follow the same school of thought and carefully consider each component and system to be sure the results are what you expect. Yes, this can add time and expense, but it's better done now while the car is apart than to have issues later. This is not an area where saving money should be the primary consideration.

Many builders skimp on electrical components and use cheap wire and connectors, which leads to problems later. You don't have to do a motorsports- or aircraft-quality wiring job, but high-quality TXL wire, good-quality non-insulated connectors, shrink tube to protect any crimped or soldered joints, and protective sleeving goes a long way to ensure that your wiring job performs reliably and looks good. The garbage sold at most auto parts stores isn't the right way to go.

The first step in preparing for your engine management installation is to read and reread the instructions and understand them completely before proceeding. This sounds obvious, but you'd be surprised how many

people just start mounting ECUs and running wires and then wonder why they have issues.

Your next step is an honest assessment of the vehicle's electrical system. If you are doing a swap into a later-model vehicle, electrical system upgrades and repairs may be minimal. An older vehicle, even a restored one, may have some issues to address. It surprises me how many muscle car–era vehicles, even those

that have been heavily modified, are still equipped with original or retro-style wiring harnesses and fuse blocks. Fully restored vehicles with OEM-style charging systems may not be up to the task.

The wiring system needs to accommodate all the new demands of the engine swap with particular attention paid to the amperage loading on the system. Electric fans, fuel pumps, ignition systems, and other

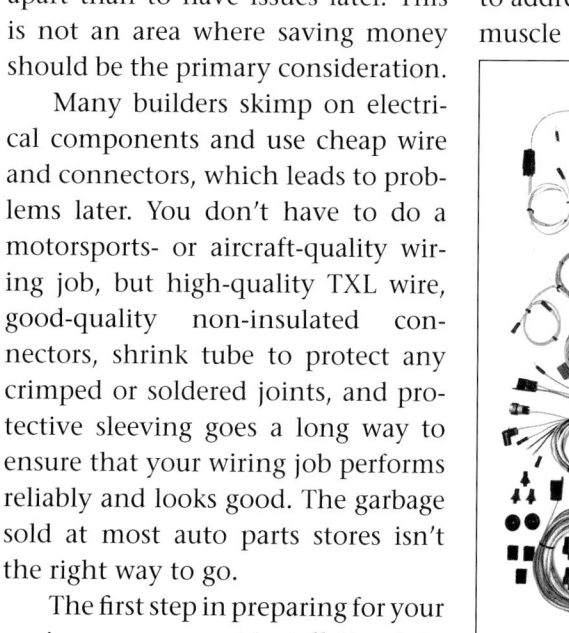

Wiring systems, such as American Autowire's Classic Update, include the fuse/relay panel, modern GXL wire, extra-long leads for custom routing, headlight and dimmer switches, and all the connectors and adapters that are needed. (Photo Courtesy American Autowire)

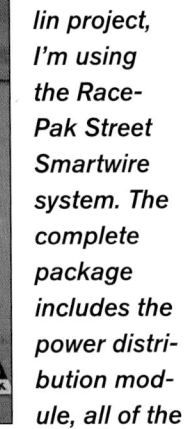

For the Gremlin project, I'm using the RacePak Street Smartwire system. The complete package includes the power distribution module, all of the necessary wiring and connectors, cables to connect to the ECU, and the switch panel.

necessary accessories to run your vehicle can add up quickly to overtax the system. Don't forget aftermarket lighting and stereo equipment when determining your overall electrical needs. If your vehicle requires rewiring, use an appropriate wiring kit from American Autowire or Painless Wiring. I have used both in the past with great success. For my current project, I am using the Racepak Street Smartwire Power Control Module for its greater versatility in a complex vehicle.

Alternator Options

In most cases with a swap application, the donor engine's existing alternator or a new aftermarket one is used, so it is a given that the original is going away. This isn't an issue with most factory alternators if you use an OEM-style PCM and harness, but there may be some questions to ask depending on your EFI system of choice.

For 2011-and-older Gen III Hemi alternators, you can use an external regulator with the heavy wire to the battery and the two smaller wires to the positive and negative termi-

nals on the regulator. It can be wired either way.

The later alternators require a 5V PWM signal, and this needs to be addressed. Some have converted the stock alternator to a one-wire operation, and most alternator shops can do this for you. But if you can keep it, there can be some advantages to the PWM alternators. The PWM operation is beneficial because the PCM can vary the voltage output and make corrections, such as idle adjustments to compensate for a weak battery.

This is all well and good if you have a stock PCM, but utilizing this feature can be a challenge to set up with an aftermarket ECU. I have seen some use a PWM generator to get around this issue in older GM PCM applications or use a 12V PWM+ output with a 5.1V Zener diode with aftermarket ECUs, such as the Holley. I haven't tried this myself, so I advise doing some research on your specific setup before going down this path.

For our Gremlin, I am using a Holley 197-302 alternator, which is part of the BBC mid-mount accessory drive I am adapting to my motor plate–equipped Hemi. The same alternator is used with Holley's Gen

III Hemi–specific mid-mount kits. I'm also using Holley's 197-400 pigtail. This alternator has a 150-amp output, which is sufficient for the considerable electrical demands. The Gremlin will be equipped with dual electric fuel pumps; a coolant pump for the air-to-water intercooler; electric oil pumps for the transmission and differentials (two 9-inch differentials and the Nissan center differential because it's going to be AWD); cooling fans for the radiator, oil, transmission, and differential coolers; active aero; and auxiliary lighting.

The alternator wiring is very simple. First, make sure the mounting surfaces between the timing cover/brackets and the alternator are clean and unpainted. This is the ground path for the alternator. An additional four-gauge ground cable that goes to the negative post of the battery ensures optimal performance. The L terminal on the alternator plug is wired to a good 12V switched source that is hot only when the key is in the Run position. This is accommodated by the 197-400 pigtail. I suggest

Holley has several alternators for Gen III Hemis. Some (like this one) are for stock accessory drives. There are also versions that come with the mid-mount accessory kits. (Photo Courtesy Holley)

2 gauge for the charge wire to the battery. Holley recommends at least 6 gauge from 0 to 4 feet, 4 gauge for 4 to 7 feet, and 2 gauge for 7 to 19 feet. My battery location will be very close to the engine, but I will still use at least 2 gauge. I diagnose strange EFI issues all day long, many due to poor grounding, so I always ensure that grounds are beyond question in my own projects.

For those using a truck accessory drive on 2003–2011 engines, Holley has alternator part number 197-305 that bolts up and wires up the same way as described above. I expect that other applications are to follow.

Battery Options

The battery should be up to the task of the increased load often encountered in a swap application. A typical lead-acid or wet-cell battery is fine as long as it is of adequate CCA rating for the application, is fully charged, and well vented if in a battery box inside the trunk or passenger compartment. Absorbed glass mat (AGM) batteries, such as Optima, Odyssey and Braille, have several advantages over the traditional batteries. One is that they can be mounted on their side and do not require venting since they do not discharge the corrosive and dangerous hydrogen/oxygen gas when operating and charging.

Lithium batteries, such as those from Braille and Antigravity, also work very well in more specialized, weight-conscious racing applications and high-end street cars. Whenever possible, I prefer to use a dual-terminal battery with top and side posts. This allows the dirty connections, like the starter, to be run to the top, with more sensitive and

clean connections, such as the ECU, made to the side.

In the case of most aftermarket ECUs, connection directly to the battery is highly recommended. While not required for OEM ECUs, it is still a good idea.

The existing battery cables may be reused if in good condition and are of adequate size. The farther your battery is mounted from the engine, the larger the cables need to be. Battery cable is available in bulk from a variety of sources such as Summit Racing, but I prefer to use welding cable. It is typically more flexible and easier to route, and it typically has smaller strands than a typical battery cable. Be sure to use a bulkhead or grommet whenever passing through sheet metal with battery cables. If you don't already have them, this is a great time to add some additional grounds.

For any EFI application, I like to ground both cylinder heads together at the rear and to the engine block. It seems redundant if you have a ground going to the engine block, since the heads rest on the block, but coated or composition head gaskets and thread sealant on the head bolts can prevent a good ground. Ever have any strange issues with coils not firing properly in an EFI swap? This will help avoid that issue. This is especially important with IGN1A Smart

Coils, as poor grounding causes resistance and heat, which will kill your coils. Run a ground from the engine block directly to the battery, another to the chassis, and an additional one to the body. The braided strap-style works well for this. Many EFI issues are traced to bad grounds, and doing all this ahead of time prevents that from being an issue.

ECU

Be aware of what supporting functions are covered through the ECU's harness, since some things such as alternators, fuel pumps, electric fans, and air conditioning may not be. Additional relays, inline fuses, connectors, and wiring may be needed, and it is best to discover this before you start the installation. It is also a good idea to ensure the harness connectors are all correct for your particular application, especially if you are deviating from stock components. Some companies, like Hotwire, request that you send them your original donor engine's harness to ensure that all connectors and wire lengths are correct for your application. This is a nice benefit, as having to lengthen a new harness or change connectors can be a hassle, especially if you don't have the proper tools to re-pin and modify the harness.

This harness is typical for factory-based harnesses, such as this one from Hotwires. Everything is properly sleeved for protection, and all connections are marked.

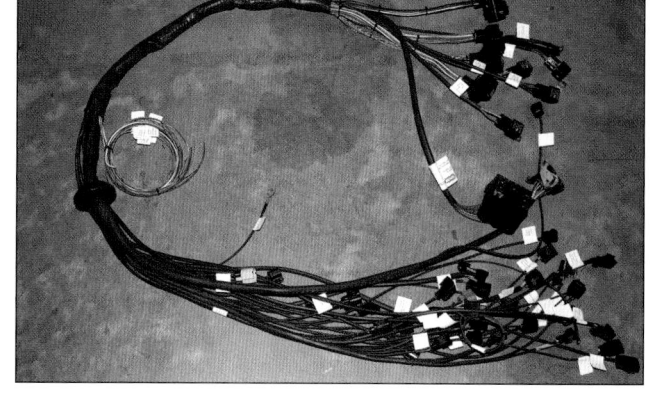

The harness is laid out over the Duster's 6.1L engine. A grommet protects it as it passes through the firewall. The ECU is mounted under the dash. The various connectors used for each sensor and the lengths of the wires themselves make it difficult to mess this up even without labels.

The Hotwire harness is clearly marked. All connectors fit as they should, and the wire lengths are perfect.

Mounting

Most OEM ECUs, and some aftermarket ones, can be mounted anywhere. They are sealed, or potted, to protect the internal components from water. Our Holley Dominator, which is being installed in the Gremlin X, fits into that category. While I can mount it in the engine compartment, it will be mounted to the subfloor on the passenger's side of the vehicle. This will allow for very short connections to the battery, which will also be mounted in the subfloor.

With the extreme amount of engine setback in the car, it will still be very close to the engine. I am

using preassembled Holley harnesses in this application, but they will be modified (mostly shortened) to better suit our requirements. I suggest mocking up the ECU and harness to be certain you have the length to put the ECU where you want it and properly route the harness itself.

The Dominator ECU comes with rubber-insulated nylon sleeves at all four mounting points to allow the ECU to be firmly secured and provide vibration resistance and protection. Stainless-steel hardware is also included. In my case, I am mounting the ECU securely with rivnuts (threaded inserts that are installed like a rivet), so there is no separate nut required. This will make for easier service.

Wiring and Ports

Our ECU has several ports along the top side for connection of the harnesses. It is the top in relation to the logo on the ECU. The ECU itself can be mounted any way you desire, but if it's in an area where moisture will be encountered, the connections should be on the bottom to allow the harnesses to act as a drip loop. From right to left, you have a blue

threaded plug that covers the Mini USB connector used for communication with the ECU. The J1A and J1B connectors are next.

If use a preassembled main engine harness like ours, it simply plugs in to these connectors. An unterminated harness with no connectors is available under part number 558-126. For our purposes, the premade harness made more sense. The J2A connector accommodates a second oxygen sensor as well as 23 user-programmable inputs. The J2B adds 4 additional injector driver outputs, 4 coil driver outputs, and 23 more inputs. The J3 is normally used for DBW throttle bodies, and the J4 is for transmission control.

If you aren't using these features, auxiliary harnesses are available for both connectors. The J3 includes a dedicated pin for the multi-map selector (part number 558-407). This allows the selection of one of four global folders (tunes) to accommodate fuel type, octane, track conditions, etc. The last connector is the main power connector. Holley's main power harness includes both the 12V constant and ground connections to the battery, is 13 feet long, and uses 10-gauge wire. A 40-amp fuse is installed inline.

With the ECU securely mounted, start with the installation of the power harness. Like all Holley harnesses, it plugs in and locks securely like an OEM unit. Attach the inline fuse holder to a convenient spot (it can be attached to the ECU mounting bolt if you wish) and route the pre-sleeved wires to your battery. Keep the harness as far away from the exhaust, moving parts, and other wiring. These are clean wires. You don't want dirty wiring (ignition coils, stereo equipment, cooling fans,

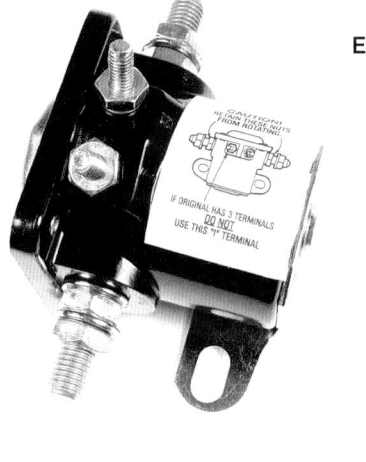

Ford-style starter solenoids are popular, but do not attach the ECU power supply wire to it. Go straight to the battery even if it isn't convenient. The battery acts as a filter to avoid ECU damage. (Photo Courtesy Holley)

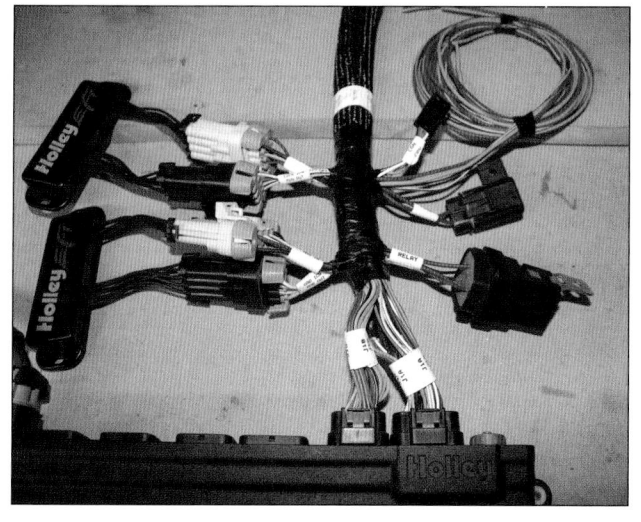

The J1A and J1B connectors make up the main harness. On the right (top to bottom) are the CAN connector, loose wires, the fuse, and the relay. On the left are the coil driver modules that are needed for dumb coils.

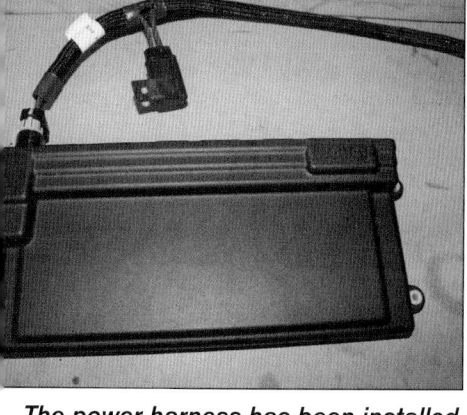

The power harness has been installed on the Dominator. There is plenty of wire here, but if you need to extend it, step up to a larger-gauge wire. This one will be cut down considerably.

etc.) near them if possible. Once you find a suitable route, cut the wires to length and terminate but don't connect the battery until the job is completed. Use grommets as required if the wiring will pass through a firewall.

Unless you are using DBW and transmission control, a typical Gen III Hemi street car will only use two more of the ECU connectors: the J1A and J1B. I use the Holley 558-115 main harness, which is for the early-style Hemi (ours is a 2007) and incorporates the separate TPS and IAC connections needed for a cable-driven throttle body. Plug in the J1A and J1B connectors to the ECU and work your way down the main trunk of the harness.

Two pairs of eight-pin connectors are on the right side of the harness. One of each pair is black, and the other is a light gray. These are for the coil drivers. Gen III Hemis use a dumb-style coil, and two four-channel coil drivers are required to drive the coils. The drivers have matching black and gray connectors, so plug them in and securely mount them. A relay and an inline fuse opposite these also need to be mounted.

The CAN connector will only be needed if you have a digital dash (Holley Pro Dash, Racepak, Dakota Digital, etc.), CAN-based gauges, or need to connect another external CAN device.

Next, locate the bundle of four loose wires. They are red, red with a white stripe, dark green, and dark blue with a white stripe. The red 14-gauge wire goes to the battery (this is the fused wire). The 18-gauge red wire with a white stripe is the switched 12V wire. Route this so it is only on when the ignition is on. If your ignition switch isn't capable of providing 12V in the start and run position, you need to wire a relay to be activated by the ignition switch to power this wire. This can be an issue on some older Mopars so beware. The dark blue with white stripe 20-gauge wire is for the tachometer. Depending on what type of tachometer you have, a tach adapter may be required for a proper signal. The tach output is a 12V square wave/4 pulse per revolution. The dark green 14-gauge wire supplies the fuel pump and powers the ignition and injectors. This wire is rated to 15 amps as-is. If your pump draws more than that, you need to use it to trigger a separate relay.

The next connection is the wideband oxygen sensor; choose either NTK or Bosch. This lead is set up as the left oxygen sensor in the software, so if you are going to run two, put the second one on the right side. To run a second sensor, you'll need a J2A adapter harness (part number 558-401). While the sensors are manufactured by Bosch and NTK, Holley calibrates them to work with its EFI systems. An off-the-shelf sensor of the same part number from another source will not deliver the same results. The Gremlin's sensors are NTK since they are better suited to the alcohol fuels (E85, eventually VP

Farther down on the right are the cylinder head grounds for the coils, injector harness connector, and I/O harness connection. Coils and the power tap feed from the left of the harness.

The coil harness plugs in and is marked for each side. The first connector on each side is the capacitor. Each one thereafter goes to an individual coil.

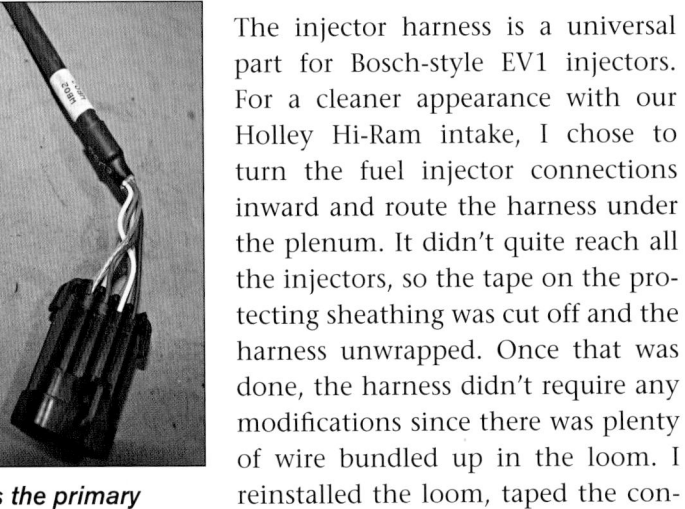

The black wire with the ring terminal goes to the back of the cylinder head. I will connect both heads for better grounding. The fuel wire goes to a fuel-pressure transducer that will screw into the fuel rail. The unmarked plug on the right is for one of the knock sensors. It is being removed from the harness.

This is the primary wideband oxygen sensor connector. The other one feeds off a J2A auxiliary harness.

The injector harness is a universal part for Bosch-style EV1 injectors. For a cleaner appearance with our Holley Hi-Ram intake, I chose to turn the fuel injector connections inward and route the harness under the plenum. It didn't quite reach all the injectors, so the tape on the protecting sheathing was cut off and the harness unwrapped. Once that was done, the harness didn't require any modifications since there was plenty of wire bundled up in the loom. I reinstalled the loom, taped the connections, and installed the harness to the injectors.

Press firmly on the connector to ensure the metal spring clip locks down on the injector. Beside the injector connection is a single black wire with a ring terminal preinstalled. Attach this to the cylinder head for grounding. This is in addition to the ground cables already installed.

Up next is the manifold absolute pressure (MAP) sensor connection. This connector is designed to work with most late Mopar MAPs. Since I'm using a Holley 3.5-bar MAP sensor (part number 554-134), I have to change the connector (the connector

M1 methanol) I will use for racing. Warning: Do not plug in the oxygen sensors until you have loaded a global file and installed the sensors. This can result in sensor damage if not followed.

Next, find the two large connectors that are plugged. The first is a power tap harness. Pin A is chassis ground, pin B is sensor ground, pin C is sensor 5V, and pin D is a 12V output from the fuel pump relay that provides 12V when the engine is running. The second connector is the input/output connector, which allows four of each (requires J1A/B harness, part number 558-400).

The next two connectors are labeled "coils" and "injector." I plugged in the coil harness (part number 558-311) and injector harness (part number 558-211), respectively.

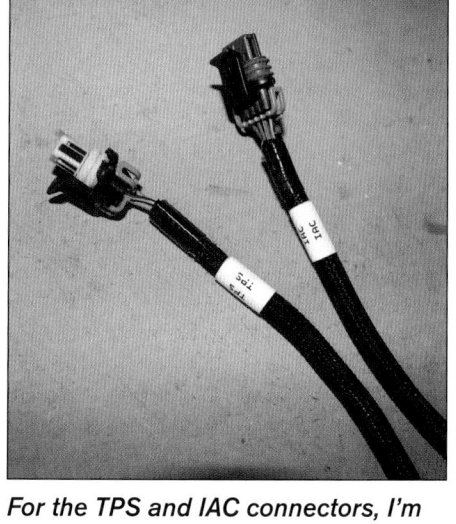

For the TPS and IAC connectors, I'm not using DBW, so these are needed. They have to be re-pinned to use with the LS-style 105-mm throttle body because they are set up for Holley 4-barrel-style throttle-body connections.

The MAP sensor connector is set up for the typical Chrysler MAP. In this case, it will be changed to a higher-bar GM unit.

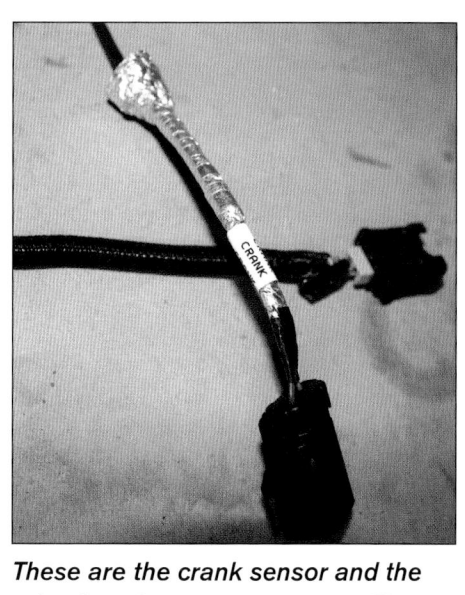

These are the crank sensor and the other knock sensor connector. The knock sensor wiring will be deleted.

comes with the sensor). The fuel sensor plug is identical to the one needed for the Holley transducer-style MAP, so do not mix these up. (They are beside each other in the harness). I have a Holley 100-psi transducer (part number 554-102) for this purpose.

The next plug, a larger gray three-wire, is for the cam sensor. It is located on the top right side of the timing cover. This will plug into the stock cam sensor.

Next on this branch of the harness are manifold air temperature (MAT), oil pressure, and coolant temperature (CTS). They all plug into the stock sensors. The MAT is in the intake manifold if you have a stock intake. I don't, so I'm using the recommended OEM sensor (part number 56028364). This will be installed in the intake air plumbing. The CTS (OEM sensor part number 05149077) is located in the water pump housing. Oil pressure (OEM part number 05149062) is on the front lower

passenger's side by the oil filter. I'm using another Holley 100-psi transducer (part number 554-102) for the oil pressure.

Idle air control (IAC) and throttle-position sensor (TPS) leads plug in to any LSx-style cable-driven throttle body. An additional harness (mentioned above) is needed if you are using the drive by wire (DBW).

Last on the main engine harness are two foil-wrapped strands. One has a single knock sensor (odd), and the other has a knock sensor (even) and the crank sensor. The knock sensor leads plug into the stock sensors located in the sides of the block, if desired. I am deleting these wires from the harness since I will not be using knock sensors in my application. The crank sensor lead plugs into the original crank sensor.

If you are using a DBW throttle body, you'll need a harness and the appropriate pedal. Holley offers three different harnesses for a single Mopar throttle body and one for a dual Mopar throttle body, which can be used if you have a custom-built

intake or one of the dual quad setups from Indy Cylinder Head/Modman or Edelbrock. OCP makes adapters to run these on a 4150-pattern intake. Alternatively, a GM DBW throttle body can be used with the correct harness. This may be a good way to go if you have an intake with a GM pattern, like a Hi-Ram. There are two versions of the single throttle body harness and one dual.

Installation of the DBW harness is simple and the same on all of the Holley DBW harnesses. Specific recommendations for throttle bodies and pedals are listed on Holley's website and in the instructions. Do not modify, shorten, lengthen, or otherwise alter the harness for safety reasons. There are three plugs. One goes to the throttle body, one to the pedal, and one to the ECU J3 port. The loose wire (red with a white stripe) is connected to the brake pedal switch. If you like to do foot-brake burnouts, you may want to consider putting a toggle switch on this connection so the throttle will open when the brake is applied.

If you're running an automatic overdrive, Holley makes harnesses for the 4L60E and 4L80E that are often used with the Gen III Hemi. No Mopar electronic overdrives (NAG1, 545RFE, 8HP70, 8HP90, etc.) are currently covered, though that may change in the future.

Dominator EFI uses the J4 connector for electronic overdrive transmission control, and has three connectors that plug into the transmission: turbine speed, VSS, and the main large round connector. There is a black 18-gauge loose lead from the included relay that goes to chassis ground. The red 18 gauge goes to 12V constant (battery power), and the red with a white stripe is the switched 12V.

A cool function to monitor through the Holley Dominator ECU is the G-force from acceleration, deceleration, and lateral movement. This is valuable for tuning purposes and may tie in to active aero.

High boost and lots of fuel means that more spark is needed. Gen III coils are good, but the new Holley Smart Coils (left) for this application ensure that ignition demands are met under any condition. They also allow the coil driver modules to be deleted.

The Gremlin is going to run on gasoline or E85 where possible, but when more power is needed and logistics allow, I want to be able to use M1 methanol. Huge injectors are needed in an application such as the one that has been planned, but those aren't great for idling or normal driving. This injector driver module allows you to run a second set of injectors for methanol.

Holley Software

While installing the harnesses and making all the electrical connections is very quick and easy, there is another step before firing up your Gen III-swapped project. Download the appropriate software (in our case, Holley V6.0.110) to your laptop and either load a global file (tune) or create one. Creating a basic global file isn't difficult, but take your time and make sure you understand what you are doing.

Open the software and click on "Open Global File." Click on "Custom Cals," then "Mopar," and then "Stock 57Hemi VE based Fueling.hefi." This will open a blank screen. Follow the steps below to enter the basic information needed to complete the global file:

1. Click on "File," then "Save As" to rename your global file and avoid overwriting a base map.
2. Click on the Holley EFI ECU icon. This will open up the "System Parameters" tab. Go to "Engine Parameters." This will display your basic engine info and may need some tweaking for your application. I adjusted the one shown to 345 ci (5.7L) and changed the "System Type" dropdown to "42LB Holley 522-428." Most popular high- and low-impedance injectors are loaded in the software. If yours aren't, you can input the correct injector data under "Custom." Select the correct type of oxygen sensor for your engine before you plug it in to avoid damage to the sensor. You can add a second sensor if you wish. Make sure your base fuel pressure is correct.
3. Click on "ECU Configuration" and be sure the proper ECU (Dominator in our case) is selected from the drop-down menu.
4. Go to "Ignition Parameters." I selected "Gen III HEMI 36-2+2, COP" since the engine is a 2007 5.7L Hemi with the late-style coils. Early Gen IIIs use the same reluctor with waste spark coils.
5. Set up the Sensor Scaling/ Warnings. This info will show up when you click on the gauge icon at the top when the engine is running with the laptop on.
6. Set up the Basic I/Os. Fans, a secondary fuel pump, and

AC kick and shutdown are preloaded as outputs. If you have an automatic transmission with a torque converter clutch, make the settings for this under TCC. The other categories are optional at this stage.

7. "Closed Loop/Learn" sets the parameters for if and when they are activated.
8. "Individual Cylinder" can be left alone for now.
9. "Inputs/Outputs" is grayed out. Click on "Toolbox," then "Add Individual Config" to open up the menu. Select "IO" and click "Open." Click "Base Config – Blank. io," then click the new I/O icon at the top. You can now name your I/Os, enable, and configure them for your engine and sensors. Transmission control and DBW are also configured through the same menu.
10. Click on "Pin Map" at the top. Any I/Os you created will populate under their respective tabs as "Unassigned Inputs" or "Unassigned Outputs." Drag and drop these at the appropriate pin. Be sure the pin offers the correct I/O type for what you are doing.

When you are satisfied with your settings, click on the save tab at the top of the screen. Send to the ECU by connecting the USB to the laptop. It may take a while the first time you do this. The communication status will change from offline to USB link. Turn the ignition on but do not start the car. Click the USB link. The system will ensure a match and upload the new global file to the ECU. The communications indicator will then show online. At this point, do a TPS autoset and perform final checks before starting the vehicle.

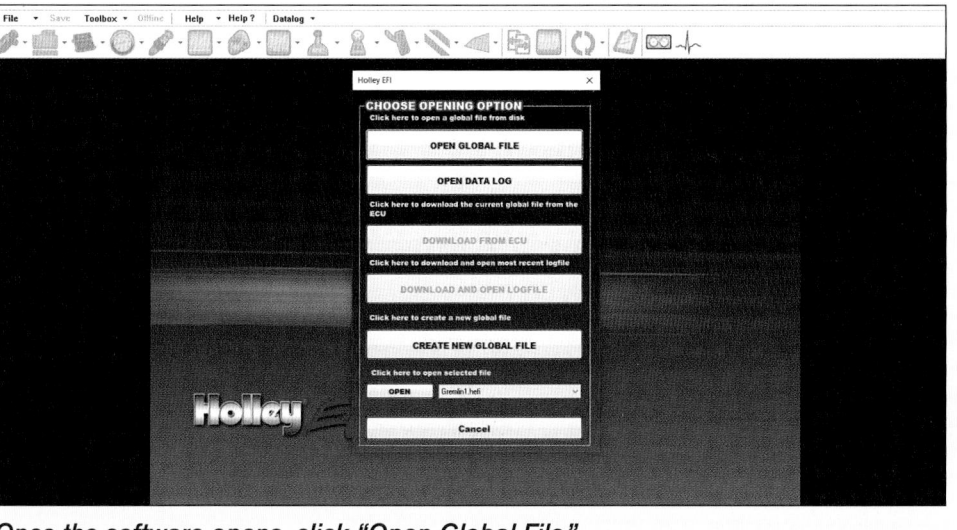

Once the software opens, click "Open Global File."

Holley Software *continued*

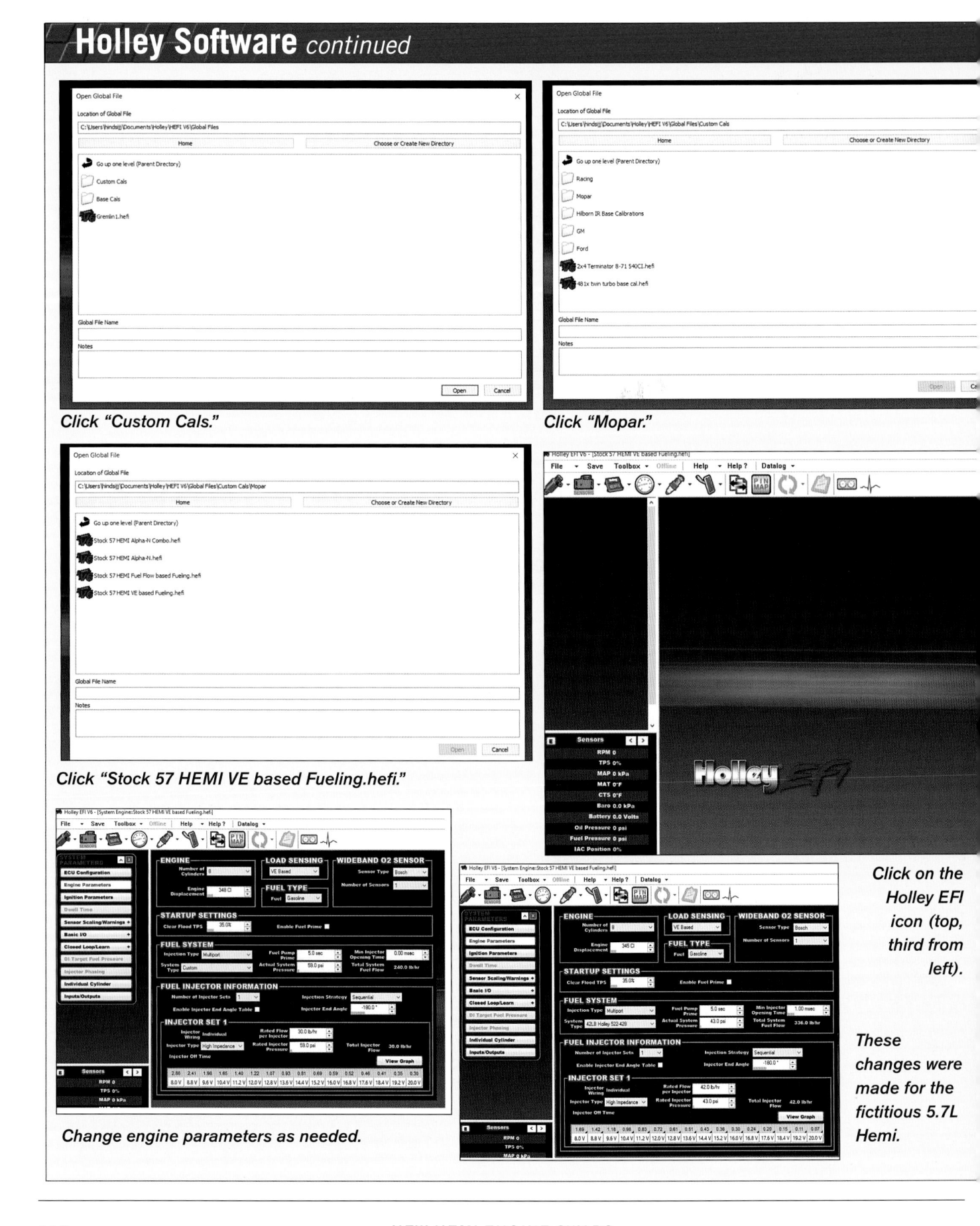

Click "Custom Cals."

Click "Mopar."

Click "Stock 57 HEMI VE based Fueling.hefi."

Change engine parameters as needed.

Click on the Holley EFI icon (top, third from left).

These changes were made for the fictitious 5.7L Hemi.

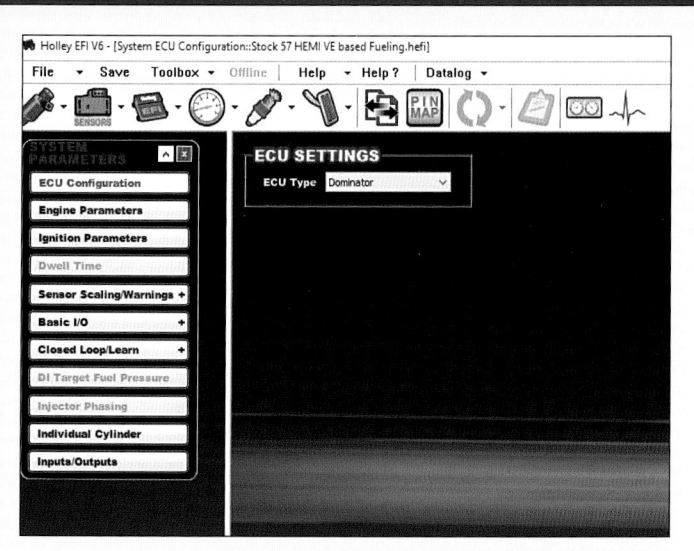

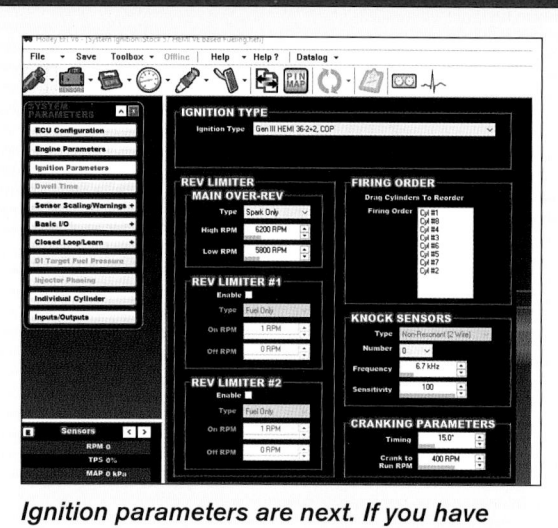

"ECU configuration." In our case, it is set on Dominator.

Ignition parameters are next. If you have late-style coils, you don't have to change anything here.

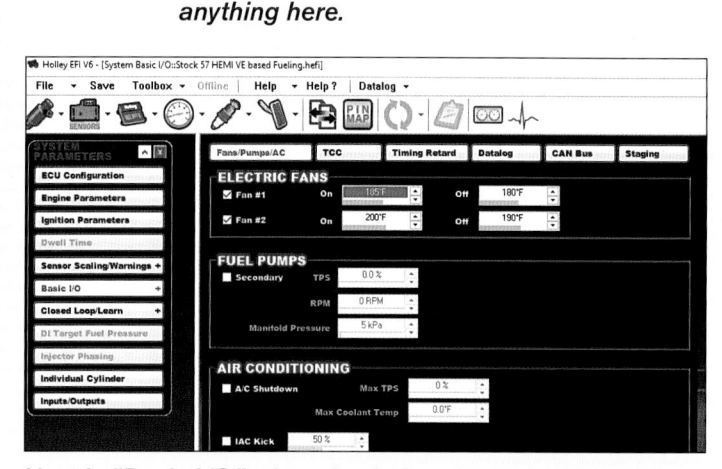

Any sensor scaling that must be changed or warnings that need to be set are done with the "Sensor Scaling/ Warnings" screen.

Next is "Basic I/O," where basic functions can be set. Some of these will not be needed for every application.

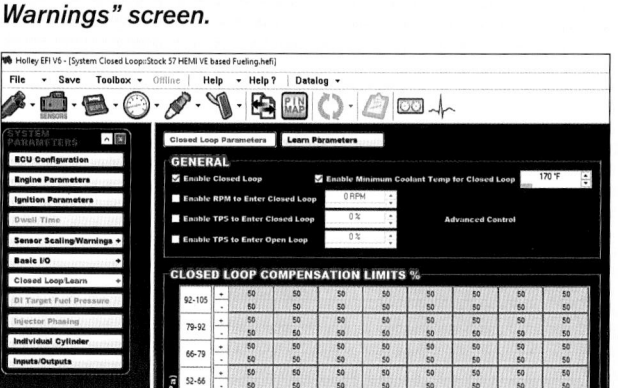

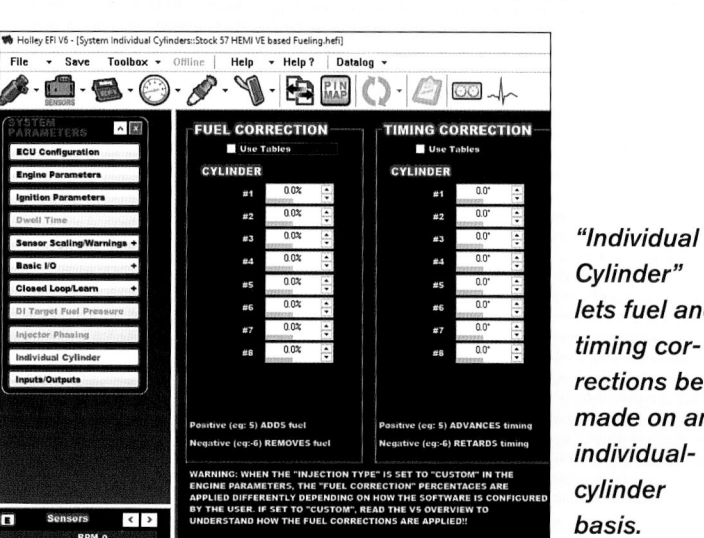

"Individual Cylinder" lets fuel and timing corrections be made on an individual-cylinder basis.

If you want to alter open/closed loop in any way, that is done through the "Closed Loop/Learn" tab.

Holley Software *continued*

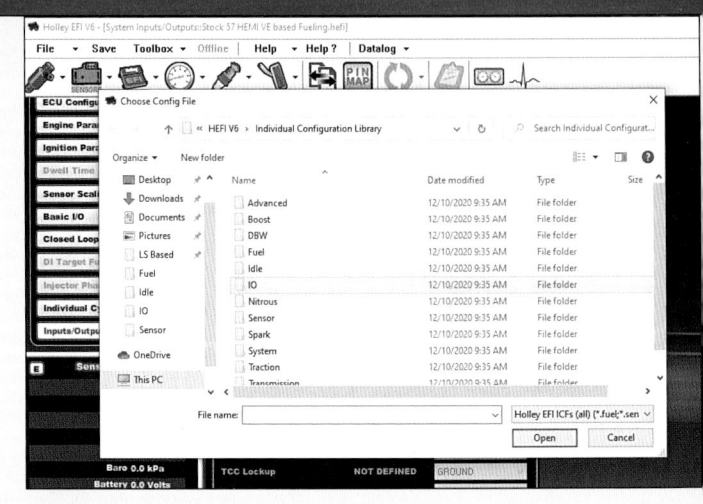

On the "Inputs/ Outputs" screen, the input and output types are grayed out.

Click "Toolbox," click "Add Individual Config," and select "IO," and "Open."

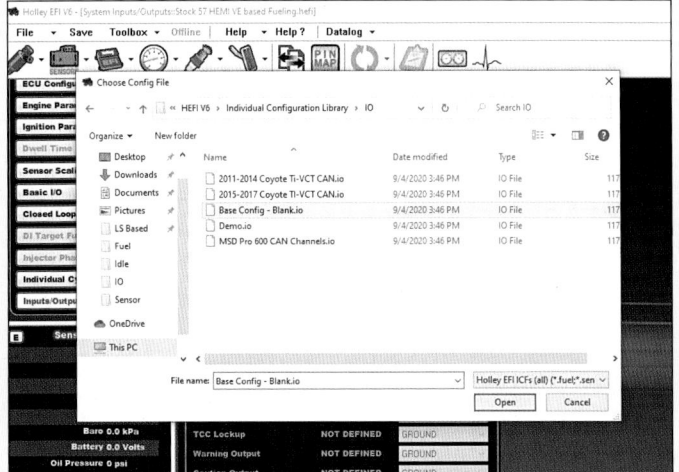

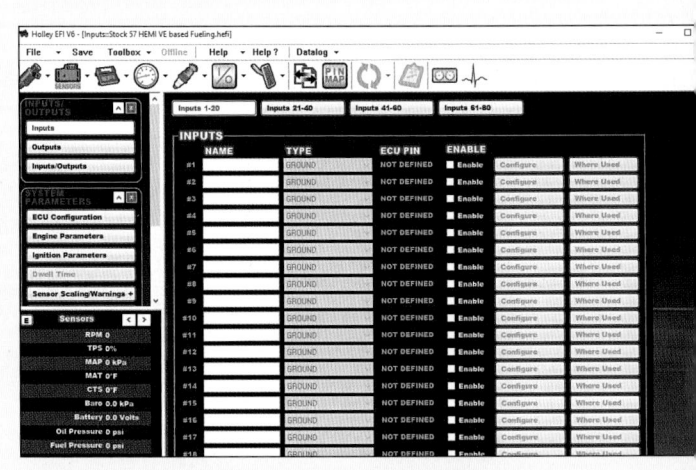

Click "Base Config - Blank.io."

Click the new "I/O" icon at the top of the screen. You can now name, enable, and configure new I/Os as needed.

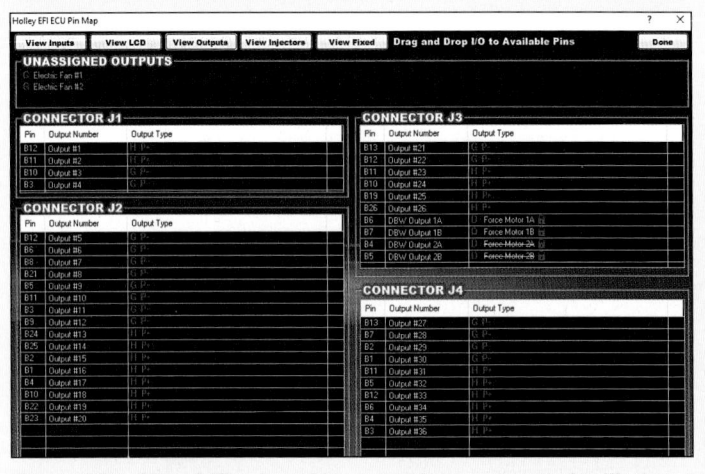

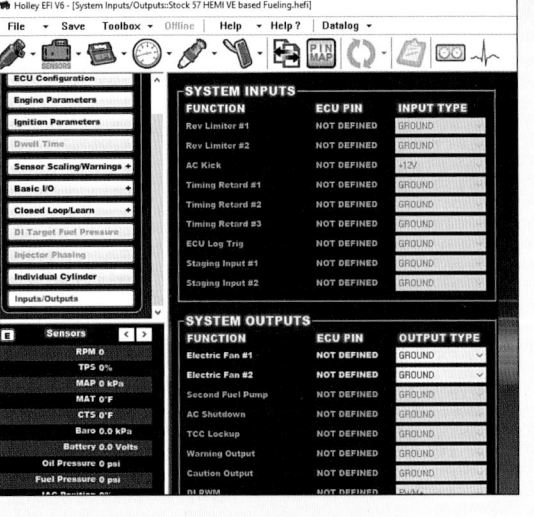

Go to "Pin Map." The two fan outputs we created will show up under "Unassigned Outputs." Drag and drop them to an available "G" (ground) pin. Inputs can be done the same way.

The fans are now assigned to B12 and B6, respectively.

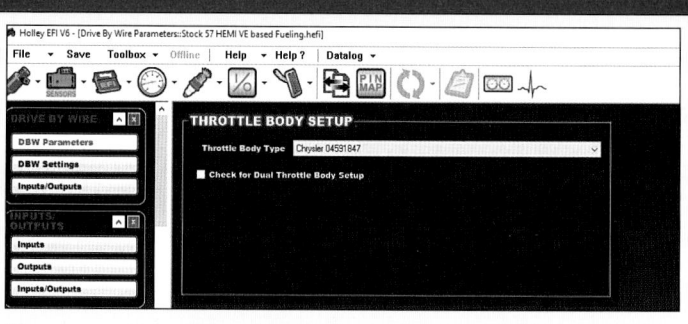

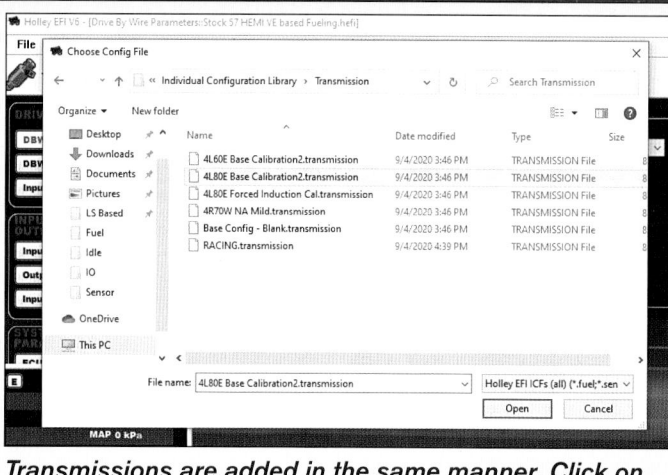

If you need to set up DBW, this is done through the Tool-box, just like with the "Basic IO." Use the new pedal icon to set it up.

Transmissions are added in the same manner. Click on the gear shift icon.

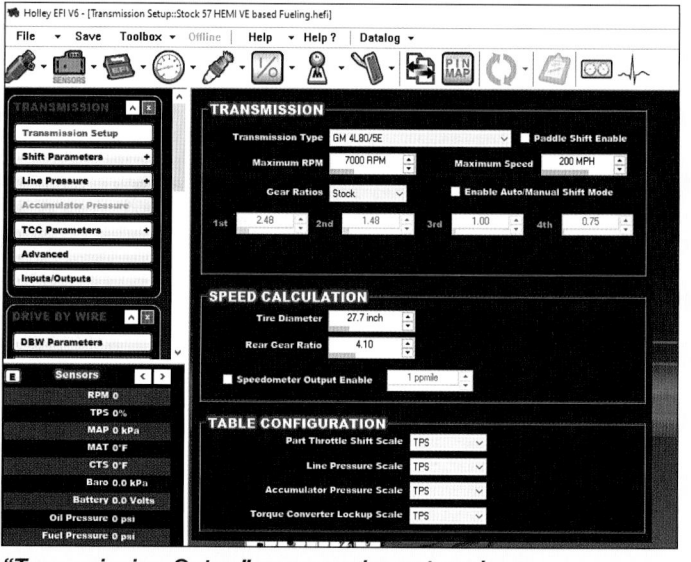

"Transmission Setup" can now be entered.

Author's note: The installation in this chapter serves as an example. The Hotwire, DIY Hemi, and Mopar plug-and-play options are all pre-terminated, plug-and-play-type installations, so installation doesn't vary much from manufacturer to manufacturer. ■

Arrington Performance
67 Motorsports Dr.
Martinsville, VA 24112
866-444-1245
shophemi.com
Details: Gen III Hemi Performance Parts
and Engines

Cherokee Speed Center
Canton, GA
678-767-7100
cherokeespeedcenter@yahoo.com
Details: Dealer for Holley Performance,
Silver Sport Transmission, and
others

Holley Performance Products
1801 Russellville Rd.
Bowling Green, KY
866-464-6553
Holley.com

Modern Muscle Performance
340 Colonel Lee Rd.
Martinsville, VA 24112
276-666-1934
modernmuscleextreme.com
Details: Gen III Hemi Performance Parts
and Engines

Pro Touring Store
Easley, SC
803-220-1634
protouringstore.com
sales@protouringstore.com
Details: Dealer for Over 50 Brands

Mancini Racing
33524 Kelley Rd.
Clinton Township, MI 48035
586-790-4100
manciniracing.com
Details: Mopar Specialist

Bouchillon Performance
937 Commerce Cir.
Hanahan, SC 29410
843-744-6559
bouchillonperformance.com
Details: Mopar Specialist

Tube Technologies Inc. (TTI)
1555 Consumer Cir.
Corona, CA 92878
951-371-4878
ttiexhaust.com
Details: Headers and Exhaust Systems
for Mopars

Summit Racing
1200 Southeast Ave.
Tallmadge, OH 44278
330-630-0250
summitracing.com
Details: Automotive Performance Parts
Retailer

Sound German Automotive
12700 Bell-Red Rd.
Bellevue, WA 98005
425-503-9233
soundgermanautomotive.com
Details: Mopar Transmission Controls

Hotwire Auto
256 Pole Rd. #43
Mena, AR
429-243-9115
hotwireauto.com
Details: Gen III Hemi Swap Wiring
Harnesses

OC Performance Parts
New Jersey
908-200-1039
ocperformanceparts.com
info@oc-performance.com

Schwartz Performance
455 Commanche Cir.
Harvard, IL 60033
815-770-0751
schwartzperformance.com
info@schwartzperformance.com
Details: Chassis Manufacturer, Car
Builder, Performance Parts

Silver Sport Transmission
2250 Stock Creek Blvd.
Rockford, TN 37853
865-609-8187
shiftsst.com
Details: Tremec Dealer

RMR Dreamcars
9134 Eden Ave.
Hudson, FL 34667
813-789-6179
restmodworld.com
Details: Car Builder

Speedtech Performance
4160 S River Rd.
St. George, UT 84790
435-628-4300
speedttechperformance.com
Details: Suspension and Chassis
Manufacturer

Shearer Fabrications, Inc.
2836 Creek Rd.
Elverson, PA 19520
216-242-2909
shearerfabrications.com
sales@shearerfabrications.com